First World War
and Army of Occupation
War Diary
France, Belgium and Germany

19 DIVISION
Divisional Troops
89 Brigade Royal Field Artillery,
Divisional Trench Mortar Batteries,
Divisional Ammunition Column
11 January 1915 - 31 October 1918

WO95/2068

The Naval & Military Press Ltd
www.nmarchive.com
Published in association with The National Archives

Published by

The Naval & Military Press Ltd

Unit 10 Ridgewood Industrial Park,

Uckfield, East Sussex,

TN22 5QE England

Tel: +44 (0) 1825 749494

www.naval-military-press.com

www.nmarchive.com

This diary has been reprinted in facsimile from the original. Any imperfections are inevitably reproduced and the quality may fall short of modern type and cartographic standards.

© Crown Copyright
Images reproduced by permission of The National Archives, London, England, 2015.

Contents

Document type	Place/Title	Date From	Date To
Heading	19th Division 19th Divl. Ammn Col. Jan 1915-Oct 1918		
Heading	19th Division 19th Divl. A.C. Vol I From 19 Jany to 31. Aug 15		
War Diary	Bulford	19/01/1915	12/07/1915
War Diary	Southampton	19/07/1915	19/07/1915
War Diary	France	20/07/1915	31/08/1915
Heading	19th Div 19th. Divl. A.C. Vol. 2 Sept & Oct 15		
War Diary	France	01/09/1915	01/11/1915
Heading	19th Division 19th D A.C. Vol 3. Nov 15		
War Diary	France	01/11/1915	30/11/1915
Heading	19th. D.A.C. Vol. 4 Dec 1915		
War Diary	France	01/12/1915	25/12/1915
Heading	19th. D.A.C. Vol. 5		
War Diary	In The Field	05/01/1916	31/01/1916
War Diary	Hanen-Kerqne	19/02/1916	19/02/1916
War Diary	Robermetz	23/02/1916	23/02/1916
War Diary	La Gorgue	29/02/1916	29/02/1916
Miscellaneous	19 D A C Vol 6		
Miscellaneous	In The Field	02/04/1916	02/04/1916
War Diary	L 28 D.C.	10/04/1916	10/04/1916
War Diary	L 25 b 8.8.	15/04/1916	15/04/1916
War Diary	J. 27. D.	20/04/1916	25/05/1916
War Diary	Norrent Fontes	09/05/1916	31/05/1916
War Diary	Belloy	09/06/1916	30/06/1916
Heading	19th Div. III. Corps. War Diary 19th Divisional Ammunition Column. July 1916		
War Diary	Lavieville	03/07/1916	22/07/1916
Heading	19th Divisional Artillery, 19th Divisional Ammunition Column August 1916		
War Diary	Albert	04/08/1916	06/08/1916
War Diary	Bavelincourt	07/08/1916	22/08/1916
War Diary	Westoutre	20/08/1916	20/08/1916
War Diary	Nieppe	02/10/1916	02/10/1916
War Diary	Schaexken	06/10/1916	31/10/1916
War Diary	Albert	19/11/1916	06/12/1916
War Diary	Authville	07/12/1916	24/12/1916
War Diary	Albert	06/12/1916	06/12/1916
War Diary	Authieule	07/12/1916	17/12/1916
War Diary	Hem	01/01/1917	15/01/1917
War Diary	Authu	17/01/1917	21/01/1917
War Diary	Bus	15/02/1917	11/03/1917
War Diary	Hem	12/03/1917	12/03/1917
War Diary	Monchel Conchy	13/03/1917	13/03/1917
War Diary	Anvin	15/03/1917	15/03/1917
War Diary	Fontes	17/03/1917	17/03/1917
War Diary	Steenbecque	18/03/1917	18/03/1917
War Diary	Verte Rue	20/03/1917	20/03/1917
War Diary	Godewaersvelde	05/04/1917	28/05/1917
War Diary	Westoutre	01/06/1917	30/06/1917

War Diary	Locre	01/07/1917	22/08/1917
War Diary	Outtersteine	01/09/1917	30/09/1917
War Diary	Locre	01/10/1917	30/12/1917
War Diary	Tally Ho Camp	01/12/1917	12/12/1917
War Diary	Schaexken	04/12/1917	13/12/1917
War Diary	Croix de Poperinghe	15/12/1917	01/01/1918
War Diary	Beaulencourt Meaulte	02/01/1918	11/01/1918
War Diary	Behencourt	16/01/1918	07/03/1918
War Diary	Buire	22/03/1918	23/03/1918
War Diary	Bazentin le P	24/03/1918	24/03/1918
War Diary	Buire	25/03/1918	25/03/1918
War Diary	Warloy	26/03/1918	26/03/1918
War Diary	Herrisart	27/03/1918	27/03/1918
War Diary	Sarton	28/03/1918	28/03/1918
War Diary	Halloy	31/03/1918	31/03/1918
Heading	19th Divisional Artillery. 19th Divisional Ammunition Column R.F.A. April 1918.		
War Diary	Aubremetz	01/04/1918	01/04/1918
War Diary	Outtersteine	03/04/1918	09/04/1918
War Diary	Bailleul-Armentiers Road	10/04/1918	10/04/1918
War Diary	Locre	11/04/1918	12/04/1918
War Diary	Mont Rouge	13/04/1918	15/04/1918
War Diary	Reninghelst	16/04/1918	16/04/1918
War Diary	Busseboom	19/04/1918	19/04/1918
War Diary	Hoograaf	20/04/1918	29/04/1918
War Diary		10/04/1918	28/04/1918
War Diary	Racquinghem	01/05/1918	20/05/1918
War Diary	Dampierre Tours	28/05/1918	29/05/1918
War Diary	Chaumuzy	30/05/1918	30/05/1918
War Diary	Vauciennes & Nanteuil	02/06/1918	19/06/1918
War Diary	Hautvillers Vaudancourt	20/06/1918	20/06/1918
War Diary	Vertus	21/06/1918	21/06/1918
War Diary	Bannes	30/06/1918	30/06/1918
War Diary	Sommesous	02/07/1918	02/07/1918
War Diary	Merck	13/07/1918	13/07/1918
War Diary	Febvin	20/07/1918	20/07/1918
War Diary		05/07/1918	30/07/1918
War Diary	Bomy	01/08/1918	06/08/1918
War Diary	Marles-Les-M	07/08/1918	30/08/1918
War Diary	La Beuvriere	31/08/1918	06/09/1918
War Diary	Bethune	10/09/1918	06/10/1918
War Diary	Loisne	17/10/1918	17/10/1918
War Diary	Cambrai	19/10/1918	19/10/1918
War Diary	Avesnes	24/10/1918	24/10/1918
War Diary	St Aubert	28/10/1918	30/10/1918
Heading	19th Division 89th Brigade R.F.A. Jly 1915-Sep 1916		
Heading	19th Division H.Q. 89th Brigade R.F.A. Vol. I. 14-31-7-15 Sep 16		
War Diary	Bulford	14/07/1915	19/07/1915
War Diary	Bonningues	15/07/1915	22/07/1915
War Diary	Wardrecques	23/07/1915	23/07/1915
War Diary	Bourecq	24/07/1915	31/07/1915
Heading	19th Division 89th. Bde. R.F.A. Vol. II August 15		
War Diary	Merville	01/08/1915	24/08/1915
War Diary	Rue des Chavattes	25/08/1915	31/08/1915
Heading	19th Division 89th. Brigade R.F.A. Vol. 3 Sept 15		

War Diary	Rue des Chavattes	01/09/1915	04/09/1915
War Diary	H.Q. and D/89. Rue des Chavattes	04/09/1915	04/09/1915
War Diary	A/89. Tuning Furk E of Gorre	05/09/1915	05/09/1915
War Diary	C/89 attd Lahore Div	05/09/1915	05/09/1915
War Diary	Croix Barbee	05/09/1915	05/09/1915
War Diary	H.Q. And D/89. Rue Des Chavattes	06/09/1915	06/09/1915
War Diary	A/89 Tuning Fork	06/09/1915	06/09/1915
War Diary	E of Gorre	07/09/1915	08/09/1915
War Diary	H.Q. and D/89	09/09/1915	09/09/1915
War Diary	Rue Des Chavattes	09/09/1915	09/09/1915
War Diary	A/89. Tuning Fork	09/09/1915	09/09/1915
War Diary	E of Gorre	10/09/1915	11/09/1915
War Diary	Hd qtrs & D/89	12/09/1915	12/09/1915
War Diary	Rue Des Chavattes	12/09/1918	12/09/1918
War Diary	A/89. Tuning Fork	13/09/1915	13/09/1915
War Diary	E of Gorre	14/09/1915	15/09/1915
War Diary	Hd qtrs & D/89 Rue Des Chavattes	16/09/1915	16/09/1915
War Diary	A/89 Tuning Fork	17/09/1915	17/09/1915
War Diary	E of Gorre	18/09/1915	19/09/1915
War Diary	Hd qtrs & D/89 at Rue Des Chavattes	20/09/1915	21/09/1915
War Diary	A/89. Tuning Fork	21/09/1918	21/09/1918
War Diary	E of Gorre	21/09/1915	21/09/1915
War Diary	Hd qtrs & D/89 Rue Des Chavattes	22/09/1915	22/09/1915
War Diary	A/89 Tuning Fork	22/09/1915	22/09/1915
War Diary	E of Gorre	22/09/1915	22/09/1915
War Diary	Hd qtrs & D/89 at Rue Des Chavattes	23/09/1915	23/09/1915
War Diary	A/89 at Tuning Fork	23/09/1915	23/09/1915
War Diary	E of Gorre	23/09/1915	23/09/1915
War Diary	Hd qtrs & D/89 at Rue Des Chavattes	24/09/1915	24/09/1915
War Diary	A/89 Tuning Fork	24/09/1915	24/09/1915
War Diary	E of Gorre	25/09/1915	25/09/1915
War Diary	Hd qtrs & D/89 Rue Des Chavattes	25/09/1915	25/09/1915
War Diary	A/89 Tuning Fork	25/09/1915	25/09/1915
War Diary	E of Gorre	25/09/1915	25/09/1915
War Diary	Hd qtrs & D/89 at Rue Des Chavattes	26/09/1915	26/09/1915
War Diary	A/89 Tuning Fork	27/09/1915	27/09/1915
War Diary	E of Gorre	28/09/1915	30/09/1915
Heading	19th Division 89th Bde. R.F.A. Vol. 4 Oct 15		
War Diary	A 89. F 5b.21	01/10/1915	02/10/1915
War Diary	D. 89 X 18a 3.2	02/10/1915	02/10/1915
War Diary	H.Q. X 17 b 0 2	02/10/1915	02/10/1915
War Diary	Bethune Combined Map 1/40,000	03/10/1915	03/10/1915
War Diary	A. 89 F.5b 2.1	04/10/1915	04/10/1915
War Diary	D.89 X18a 3.2	04/10/1915	04/10/1915
War Diary	H.Q. X17b 0.2	05/10/1915	05/10/1915
War Diary	Bethune Comb. Maps 1/40,000	06/10/1915	07/10/1915
War Diary	A/89 F.5 b 21	08/10/1915	08/10/1915
War Diary	D/89 X 18a 3.2	08/10/1915	08/10/1915
War Diary	HQ X17b 0.2	08/10/1915	08/10/1915
War Diary	Bethune Comb Map 1/40,000	09/10/1915	10/10/1915
War Diary	A/89 F 5 b 2.1	11/10/1915	11/10/1915
War Diary	D/89 X18 a 3 2	11/10/1915	11/10/1915
War Diary	H.Q. R 22a 8.4	11/10/1915	11/10/1915
War Diary	Bethune Com Map 1/40,000	12/10/1915	12/10/1915
War Diary	A/89 F 5 b 21	13/10/1915	13/10/1915
War Diary	D/89 X18 a 32	13/10/1915	13/10/1915

War Diary	HQ R 22a 84	13/10/1915	13/10/1915
War Diary	Bethune Comb Map 1/40,000	14/10/1915	16/10/1915
War Diary	A 89 F 5 b 21	17/10/1915	17/10/1915
War Diary	D. 89 X18a 32	18/10/1915	18/10/1915
War Diary	HQ. R22 A 84	18/10/1915	18/10/1915
War Diary	Bethune Comb Map 1/40,000	19/10/1915	20/10/1915
War Diary	A/89 F5 b 21	21/10/1915	21/10/1915
War Diary	D/89 X18 a32	22/10/1915	22/10/1915
War Diary	HQ X17 b 0 2	22/10/1915	22/10/1915
War Diary	Bethune Comb Map 1/40,000	23/10/1915	23/10/1915
War Diary	A 89 F.5.b.2.1	24/10/1915	24/10/1915
War Diary	D/89 X.18.a. 3.2	24/10/1915	24/10/1915
War Diary	H.2. X.17.b.0.2	25/10/1915	25/10/1915
War Diary	Bethune Combined Sheet 1/40,000	26/10/1915	27/10/1915
War Diary	A/89 F.5.b.2.1	28/10/1915	28/10/1915
War Diary	C/89 A.18.C.0.8	29/10/1915	29/10/1915
War Diary	D/89 X.18.a.3.2	29/10/1915	29/10/1915
War Diary	H.Q. X.17.b.0.2	30/10/1915	30/10/1915
War Diary	Bethune Combined Map 1/40,000	31/10/1915	31/10/1915
Heading	19th Division 89th. Bde. R.F.A. Vol. 5 Nov, 15		
Heading	War Diary Of 89th Bde. R.F.A. From 1st. Nov. 1915 to 30th. Nov. 1915.		
War Diary	A/89 F 5 b 2.1	01/11/1915	01/11/1915
War Diary	C/89 X 17D 9.7	02/11/1915	02/11/1915
War Diary	D/89 X 18A 3.2	03/11/1915	03/11/1915
War Diary	HQ. X17b.0.2 to X17 d 88	04/11/1915	04/11/1915
War Diary	Bethune Comb Map 1/40000	05/11/1915	06/11/1915
War Diary	A/89 F5b 21	07/12/1915	07/12/1915
War Diary	C/89 X17d 9.7	08/11/1915	08/11/1915
War Diary	D/89 X18a 32	08/11/1915	08/11/1915
War Diary	HQ X17d 8.8	09/11/1915	09/11/1915
War Diary	Bethune Comb Map 1/40000	09/11/1915	09/11/1915
War Diary	A/89 F 5 b 2.1	10/11/1915	10/11/1915
War Diary	D/89 X18a. 32	11/11/1915	11/11/1915
War Diary	H.Q. X17d 8.8.	11/11/1915	11/11/1915
War Diary	Bethune Comb Map 1/40000	12/11/1915	13/11/1915
War Diary	A/89 F 5 b 21	14/11/1915	14/11/1915
War Diary	D/89 X18a 32	15/11/1915	15/11/1915
War Diary	HQ X17d88	16/11/1915	16/11/1915
War Diary	Bethune Comb Map 1/40000	17/11/1915	18/11/1915
War Diary	A/89 F.5b 21	19/11/1915	19/11/1915
War Diary	D/89 X18a 32	20/11/1915	20/11/1915
War Diary	H.Q. X17d. 8.8.	20/11/1915	20/11/1915
War Diary	Bethune Comb Map 1/40000	21/11/1915	22/11/1915
War Diary	Hamet Billet	23/11/1915	24/11/1915
War Diary	Map 36A 1/40.000	25/11/1915	30/11/1915
Heading	19th Div. 89th Bde R.F.A. Vol. 6 Dec 1915		
Heading	War Diary Of 89th Brigade. R.F.A. From 1st. December 1915 to 31st. December 1915 (Volume. 6.)		
War Diary	Hamet Billet	01/12/1915	05/12/1915
War Diary	A/89 M 26 d 98	05/12/1915	05/12/1915
War Diary	C/89 M32b44	05/12/1915	05/12/1915
War Diary	D/89 X18a32	06/12/1915	06/12/1915
War Diary	H.Q. R35c98	07/12/1915	07/12/1915
War Diary	A/89 M26d 9.8	07/12/1915	07/12/1915
War Diary	C/89 M32b44	07/12/1915	07/12/1915

War Diary	D/89 X18a32	08/12/1915	08/12/1915
War Diary	HQ R 35.C.9.8	08/12/1915	08/12/1915
War Diary	A/89 M26d98	09/12/1915	09/12/1915
War Diary	C/89 M32b44	10/12/1915	10/12/1915
War Diary	D/89 X18a 32	10/12/1915	10/12/1915
War Diary	HQ R35c98	10/12/1915	10/12/1915
War Diary	A/89 M26 d 98	11/12/1915	11/12/1915
War Diary	C/89 M32b44	11/12/1915	11/12/1915
War Diary	D/89 X18c07	11/12/1915	11/12/1915
War Diary	HQ R35c98	12/12/1915	12/12/1915
War Diary	Bethune Map 1/40000	12/12/1915	12/12/1915
War Diary	A/89 M26d98	12/12/1915	13/12/1915
War Diary	C/89 M32b44	13/12/1915	13/12/1915
War Diary	D/89 X18cx07	13/12/1915	13/12/1915
War Diary	HQ R35c98	13/12/1915	13/12/1915
War Diary	Bethune Map 1/40.000	14/12/1915	14/12/1915
War Diary	A/89 M26d98	14/12/1915	14/12/1915
War Diary	C/89 M32b44	15/12/1915	15/12/1915
War Diary	D/89 X18C07	15/12/1915	15/12/1915
War Diary	HQ R35c98	15/12/1915	15/12/1915
War Diary	Bethune Map 1/40.000	16/12/1915	16/12/1915
War Diary	A/89 M26d98	16/12/1915	17/12/1915
War Diary	C/89 M32b44	17/12/1915	17/12/1915
War Diary	D/89 X18c07	18/12/1915	18/12/1915
War Diary	HQ R35c98	18/12/1915	18/12/1915
War Diary	Bethune Map 1/40.000	19/12/1915	19/12/1915
War Diary	A/89 M26d98	19/12/1915	19/12/1915
War Diary	C/89 M32b 44	19/12/1915	19/12/1915
War Diary	D/89 X18c 07	20/12/1915	20/12/1915
War Diary	H.Q R35c98	20/12/1915	20/12/1915
War Diary	Bethune Map 1/40.000	21/12/1915	21/12/1915
War Diary	A/89 M26d98	22/12/1915	22/12/1915
War Diary	C/89 M32b44	22/12/1915	22/12/1915
War Diary	D/89 X18c 07	22/12/1915	22/12/1915
War Diary	HQ R35c98	22/12/1915	22/12/1915
War Diary	Bethune Map 1/40.000	23/12/1915	23/12/1915
War Diary	A/89 M26 d98	23/12/1915	24/12/1915
War Diary	C/89 M32b 44	24/12/1915	24/12/1915
War Diary	D/89 X18c07	24/12/1915	24/12/1915
War Diary	HQ R35c98	25/12/1915	25/12/1915
War Diary	Bethune Map 1/40000	25/12/1915	25/12/1915
War Diary	A/89 M26 d98	26/12/1915	26/12/1915
War Diary	C/89 M32b44	26/12/1915	26/12/1915
War Diary	D/89 X18c07	27/12/1915	27/12/1915
War Diary	HQ R35c98	27/12/1915	27/12/1915
War Diary	Bethune Map 1/40.000	27/12/1915	27/12/1915
War Diary	A/89 M26 d98	27/12/1915	27/12/1915
War Diary	C/89 M32b44	28/12/1915	28/12/1915
War Diary	D/89 X18c07	28/12/1915	28/12/1915
War Diary	HQ R35c98	28/12/1915	28/12/1915
War Diary	Bethune Map 1/40.000	28/12/1915	28/12/1915
War Diary	A/89 M.26 d98	29/12/1915	29/12/1915
War Diary	C/89 M32b44	29/12/1915	29/12/1915
War Diary	D/89 X18c07	29/12/1915	29/12/1915
War Diary	HQ R35 C 98	30/12/1915	30/12/1915
War Diary	Bethune Map 1/400000	30/12/1915	30/12/1915

War Diary	A/89 M26d98	31/12/1915	31/12/1915
War Diary	C/89 M32b44	31/12/1915	31/12/1915
War Diary	D/89 M8c07	31/12/1915	31/12/1915
War Diary	HQ R35C98	31/12/1915	31/12/1915
War Diary	Bethune Map 1/40.000	31/12/1915	31/12/1915
Heading	19th Division. "A" Battery 89th Brigade R.F.A. Vol. I. 1-31-7-15		
War Diary	Bulford		
War Diary	Bulford	17/07/1915	17/07/1915
War Diary	Southampton	17/07/1915	17/07/1915
War Diary	Lehavre	18/07/1915	19/07/1915
War Diary	St Omer	20/07/1915	20/07/1915
War Diary	Bonningues	23/07/1915	23/07/1915
War Diary	Wardrecques	24/07/1915	24/07/1915
War Diary	Bourecq	31/07/1915	31/07/1915
Heading	19th. Division "A"/89 Battery R.F.A. Vol. II August 15		
War Diary	Merville	05/08/1915	05/08/1915
War Diary	R.5.6. 5'6.	07/08/1915	07/08/1915
War Diary	M10d 4'3	08/08/1915	23/08/1915
War Diary	Lesart	24/08/1915	24/08/1915
War Diary	Letouret	25/08/1915	31/08/1915
War Diary	19th. Division "B" Battery 89th Brigade R.F.A. Vol. I. July 22-31.7.15		
War Diary	Bonningues Lez-Ardres	22/07/1915	22/07/1915
War Diary	Bonningues Lez Ardres	21/07/1915	22/07/1915
War Diary	Wardrecques	23/07/1915	23/07/1915
War Diary	Bourecq	24/07/1915	30/07/1915
War Diary	Le Sart (Merville)	31/07/1915	31/07/1915
Heading	19th Division "B"/89 Battery R.F.A. Vol. II From 1-31.8.15		
Miscellaneous	A Form. Messages And Signals.	06/08/1915	06/08/1915
Miscellaneous	Appendix 1		
War Diary	Le Sart	01/08/1915	06/08/1915
War Diary	Dranoutre	07/08/1915	20/08/1915
War Diary	Landenhoek	21/08/1915	31/08/1915
Heading	19th Division "C"/89 Battery 89th. Brigade R.F.A. Vol I 16-31.7.15		
War Diary	Bulford	16/07/1915	16/07/1915
War Diary	En Route	17/07/1915	17/07/1915
War Diary	Havre No 1 Camp	18/07/1915	19/07/1915
War Diary	En Route	20/07/1915	20/07/1915
War Diary	Bonningues	21/07/1915	22/07/1915
War Diary	Wardrecques	23/07/1915	23/07/1915
War Diary	Bourecq	24/07/1915	30/07/1915
War Diary	Le Sart	31/07/1915	31/07/1915
Heading	19th Division "C"/89 Battery Vol. II August 15.		
War Diary	Richebourg St Vaast	08/08/1915	31/08/1915
War Diary		27/08/1915	27/08/1915
Heading	19th Division C/89 Battery Vol III Sept 15		
War Diary	Richebourg St Vaast	03/09/1915	27/09/1915
Heading	19th Division C/89 Battery Vol. 4 Oct 15.		
Heading	War Diary Of C/89th F.A. Bde. From 1/10/15 to 31/10/15 (Volume IV)		
War Diary	Richebourg St Vaast	06/10/1915	31/10/1915
Heading	19th Division C/89 Battery Vol. 5 Nov 15		

Heading	War Diary. Of. C/89th Bde R.F.A. From 1st Nov. 1915 to 30th Nov. 1915		
War Diary	Le Touret	01/11/1915	10/11/1915
War Diary	Richebourg St Vaast	11/11/1915	30/11/1915
Heading	19th. Division. "D" Battery 89th. Brigade R.F.A. Vol. I. 1-30-7-15		
War Diary	Bulford	17/07/1915	17/07/1915
War Diary	Ames way	17/07/1915	17/07/1915
War Diary	Southampton	17/07/1915	17/07/1915
War Diary	Havre	18/07/1915	19/07/1915
War Diary	Buchy	19/07/1915	19/07/1915
War Diary	Abbeyville	19/07/1915	19/07/1915
War Diary	Audriceq	19/07/1915	19/07/1915
War Diary	St Omer	19/07/1915	20/07/1915
War Diary	Bonninquis	20/07/1915	23/07/1915
War Diary	Norduches	23/07/1915	23/07/1915
War Diary	Wardrecques	24/07/1915	24/07/1915
War Diary	Bourecq	23/07/1915	30/07/1915
Heading	19th Division D/89 Battery Vol. II August 15		
War Diary	Bourecq	31/07/1915	31/07/1915
War Diary	Lillers	31/07/1915	31/07/1915
War Diary	Robecq	31/07/1915	31/07/1915
War Diary	Merville	31/07/1915	31/07/1915
War Diary	Le Sart	01/08/1915	01/08/1915
War Diary	La Sart nr Merville	01/08/1915	03/08/1915
War Diary	Le Sart	04/08/1915	11/08/1915
War Diary	Merville	12/08/1915	24/08/1915
War Diary	Le Sart	25/08/1915	31/08/1915
Heading	19th Division D/89 Battery R.F.A. Vol III Sep. 15.		
War Diary	Le Touret	01/09/1915	30/09/1915
Heading	19th Division D/89 Battery R.F.A. Vol 4 Oct 15		
War Diary		01/10/1915	31/10/1915
Heading	19th Div D/89 Battery Vol. 6		
War Diary		03/12/1915	31/12/1915
Heading	19th Divn. D/89 Battery Vol. 7		
War Diary		01/01/1916	30/01/1916
Heading	19th 89th Bde. R.F.A. Vol: 7		
Heading	War Diary Of 89th Brigade R.F.A. From 1st Jan. 1916 to 31st Jan. 1916 (Volume. 7)		
War Diary	A/89 M26d 9.8	01/01/1916	01/01/1916
War Diary	C/89 M32b44.	01/01/1916	01/01/1916
War Diary	D/89 X18c.0.7.	01/01/1916	01/01/1916
War Diary	H.Q. R.35c.98	02/01/1916	02/01/1916
War Diary	A/89 M26d.9.8	02/01/1916	02/01/1916
War Diary	C/89 M32b.4.4	03/02/1916	03/02/1916
War Diary	D/89 X18c 0.7.	03/02/1916	03/02/1916
War Diary	H.Q. R.35c.9.8.	03/02/1916	03/02/1916
War Diary	A/89 M26d.9.8	04/01/1916	04/01/1916
War Diary	C/89 M32b.4.4.	04/01/1916	04/01/1916
War Diary	D/89 X18c 0.7	04/01/1916	04/01/1916
War Diary	H.Q. R35c.9.8	05/01/1916	05/01/1916
War Diary	A/89 M26d.9.8	05/01/1916	05/01/1916
War Diary	C/89 M32b.44	05/01/1916	05/01/1916
War Diary	D/89 X18c 0.7.	05/01/1916	05/01/1916
War Diary	H.Q. R135c 9.8	06/01/1916	06/01/1916
War Diary	A/89 M26d.9.8	07/01/1916	07/01/1916

War Diary	C/89 M32b 44	07/01/1916	07/01/1916
War Diary	D/89 X18c 0.7	07/01/1916	07/01/1916
War Diary	H.Q. R 35c. 9.5	07/01/1916	07/01/1916
War Diary	A/89 M26d 9.8	08/01/1916	08/01/1916
War Diary	C/89 M32b 4.4	08/01/1916	08/01/1916
War Diary	D/89 M8c.0.7.	08/01/1916	08/01/1916
War Diary	H.Q. R35c.9.8	09/01/1916	09/01/1916
War Diary	A/89 M26d 9.8.	10/01/1916	10/01/1916
War Diary	C/89 M32b.4.4	10/01/1916	10/01/1916
War Diary	D/89 M8c 0.7.	10/01/1916	10/01/1916
War Diary	H.Q. R35c.9.8.	11/01/1915	11/01/1915
War Diary	A/89 M26d 9.8.	11/01/1916	11/01/1916
War Diary	C/89 M32b.4.4	11/01/1916	11/01/1916
War Diary	D/89 M8c 0.7.	12/01/1916	12/01/1916
War Diary	H.Q. R35c.9.8	13/01/1916	13/01/1916
War Diary	A/89 M26d.9.8.	14/01/1916	14/01/1916
War Diary	C/89 M32b.4.4.	15/01/1916	15/01/1916
War Diary	D/89 M8c 0.7.	15/01/1916	15/01/1916
War Diary	H.Q. R35c.9.8.	15/01/1916	15/01/1916
War Diary	A/89 M26d.9.8.	16/01/1916	16/01/1916
War Diary	C/89 M32b.4.4.	16/01/1916	16/01/1916
War Diary	D/89 M8c.0.7.	17/01/1916	17/01/1916
War Diary	H.Q. R35c.9.8	18/01/1916	18/01/1916
War Diary	A/89 M26 d 9.8.	19/01/1916	19/01/1916
War Diary	C/89. M32b.4.4.	19/01/1916	19/01/1916
War Diary	D/89 M8c.0.7.	19/01/1916	19/01/1916
War Diary	H.Q. R35c.9.8.	20/01/1916	20/01/1916
War Diary	A/89 M26 d.98.	21/01/1916	21/01/1916
War Diary	C/89 M32b.4.4	21/01/1916	21/01/1916
War Diary	D/89. M8c.0.7.	22/01/1916	22/01/1916
War Diary	H.Q. R35c. 9.8.	22/01/1916	22/01/1916
War Diary	A/89. M26d.9.8.	23/01/1916	23/01/1916
War Diary	C/89. M32b.4.4.	23/01/1916	23/01/1916
War Diary	D/89. M8c.0.7.	23/01/1916	23/01/1916
War Diary	H.Q. R35c.9.8.	24/01/1916	24/01/1916
Heading	A/89. M26 d.9.8.	25/01/1916	25/01/1916
War Diary	C/89. M32b.4.4.	25/01/1916	25/01/1916
War Diary	D/89. M8c.0.7.	25/01/1916	25/01/1916
War Diary	H.Q. R35c.9.8.	25/01/1916	25/01/1916
War Diary	A/89 M26d.9.8	26/01/1916	26/01/1916
War Diary	C/89 M32b.4.4	27/01/1916	27/01/1916
War Diary	D/89 M8c.0.7.	27/01/1916	27/01/1916
War Diary	H.Q. R35c.9.8.	27/01/1916	27/01/1916
War Diary	A/89. M26d 9.8	28/01/1916	28/01/1916
War Diary	C/89. M32b44	28/01/1916	28/01/1916
War Diary	D/89. M8c.0.4.	28/01/1916	28/01/1916
War Diary	HQ. R35c 9.8	29/01/1916	31/01/1916
Heading	War Diary. 89th. Bde. R.F.A. Commending 1st. Feb 1916 Ending 29th Feb. 1916 Volume-8		
War Diary		14/02/1916	15/02/1916
War Diary	A/89 M15d2	16/02/1916	16/02/1916
War Diary	C/89 M32 b.5.4	17/02/1916	17/02/1916
War Diary	D/89 M27d.0.0.	17/02/1916	17/02/1916
War Diary	H.Q. M9c.2.4	18/02/1916	18/02/1916
War Diary	A/89 M5d 2	19/02/1916	19/02/1916
War Diary	C/89 M32b54	20/02/1916	20/02/1916

War Diary	D/89 M27a. 0.0.	20/02/1916	20/02/1916
War Diary	H.Q. M 9c.2.4	20/02/1916	20/02/1916
War Diary	A/89 M15d 2	20/02/1916	21/02/1916
War Diary	C/89 M32b.5.4	21/02/1916	21/02/1916
War Diary	D/89 M27c.0.0.	21/02/1916	21/02/1916
War Diary	H.Q. M9c.2.4	21/02/1916	21/02/1916
War Diary	A/89 M15d 2	21/02/1916	22/02/1916
War Diary	C/89 M32b. 5.4	22/02/1916	22/02/1916
War Diary	D/89 M27a.0.0.	22/02/1916	22/02/1916
War Diary	H.Q. M9c 2.4.	23/02/1916	23/02/1916
War Diary	A/89 M15d 2	23/02/1916	23/02/1916
War Diary	C/89 M32b.5.4	24/02/1916	24/02/1916
War Diary	D/89 M27a.0.0	24/02/1916	24/02/1916
War Diary	H.Q. M9c.2.4	25/02/1916	25/02/1916
War Diary	A/89 M15d 2	25/02/1916	25/02/1916
War Diary	C/89 M32b.5.4	25/02/1916	25/02/1916
War Diary	D/89 M27a 0.0	25/02/1916	25/02/1916
War Diary	H.Q. M9c.2.4	26/02/1916	26/02/1916
Heading	A/89 M15d 2	27/02/1916	27/02/1916
War Diary	C/89 M32b.5.4	27/02/1916	27/02/1916
War Diary	D/89 M27a.0.0	27/02/1916	27/02/1916
War Diary	H.Q. M9c.2.4	28/02/1916	28/02/1916
War Diary	A/89 M15d 2 1/2 1/2	28/02/1916	28/02/1916
War Diary	C/89 M32b.5.4	28/02/1916	28/02/1916
War Diary	D/89 M27a.0.0.	28/02/1916	28/02/1916
War Diary	H.Q. M.9c.2.4	29/02/1916	29/02/1916
War Diary	A/89 M15d 2 1/2 1/2	29/02/1916	29/02/1916
War Diary	C/89 M32b.5.4	29/02/1916	29/02/1916
War Diary	D/89 M27a.0.0	29/02/1916	29/02/1916
War Diary	H.Q. M9c.2.4	29/02/1916	29/02/1916
Heading	War Diary Of 89th Brigade. R.F.A. From. 1st March to 31st March 1916 Volume 9		
War Diary	A/89 M 15.d. 2 1/2. 2.	01/03/1916	01/03/1916
War Diary	C/89 M.32b.5.4	01/03/1916	01/03/1916
War Diary	D/89 M.27.a.0.0	01/03/1916	01/03/1916
War Diary	H.Q. M.9.c.2.4	02/03/1916	02/03/1916
War Diary	A/89 M.15.d.2 1/2. 2.	02/03/1916	02/03/1916
War Diary	C/89 M.32.b.5.4.	03/03/1916	03/03/1916
War Diary	D/89.M.27.a.0.0.	03/03/1916	03/03/1916
War Diary	H.Q. M.9.c.2.4.	03/03/1916	03/03/1916
War Diary	A/89. M. 15.d.2 1/2. 2.	04/03/1916	04/03/1916
War Diary	C/89.M.32b. 5.4	04/03/1916	04/03/1916
War Diary	D/89.M.27.a.0.0	04/03/1916	04/03/1916
War Diary	H.Q.M.9.c.2.4.	05/03/1916	05/03/1916
War Diary	A/89.M.15.d.2 1/2. 2.	06/03/1916	06/03/1916
War Diary	C/89.M.32.b.5.4	06/03/1916	06/03/1916
War Diary	D/89. M.10.D.8.7	06/03/1916	06/03/1916
War Diary	H.Q. M.9.c.24	06/03/1916	06/03/1916
War Diary	A/89 M.15.d.2 1/2. 2.	07/03/1916	07/03/1916
War Diary	C/89. M.32.b.5.4.	07/03/1916	07/03/1916
War Diary	D/89. M.10.D.8.4.	08/03/1916	08/03/1916
War Diary	HQ M.9.c.24	08/03/1916	08/03/1916
War Diary	A/89.M.15.d.2 1/2. 2.	09/03/1916	09/03/1916
War Diary	C/89. M.32.b.5.4	09/03/1916	09/03/1916
War Diary	D/89. M.10.D.8.7.	09/03/1916	09/03/1916
War Diary	H.Q. M.9.c.2.4	09/03/1916	09/03/1916

War Diary	A/89. M.15.d.2 1/2. 2.	09/03/1916	09/03/1916
War Diary	C/89. M.32.b.5.4	09/03/1916	09/03/1916
War Diary	D/89. M.10.D.8.7.	10/03/1916	10/03/1916
War Diary	H.Q. M.9.c.2.4.	10/03/1916	10/03/1916
War Diary	A/89. M.15.d.2 1.2. 2.	11/03/1916	11/03/1916
War Diary	C/89. M.32.b.5.4	11/03/1916	11/03/1916
War Diary	D/89. M.10.D.8.7	12/03/1916	12/03/1916
War Diary	H.Q. M.9.c.2.4.	12/03/1916	12/03/1916
War Diary	A/89. M.15.d.2 1/2. 2.	13/03/1916	13/03/1916
War Diary	C/89. M.32.b.5.4.	13/03/1916	13/03/1916
Miscellaneous	D/89. M.10.d.8.7.	13/03/1916	13/03/1916
War Diary	H.Q. M.9.c.2.4.	14/03/1916	14/03/1916
War Diary	A/89. M.15.d. 2 1/2. 2.	14/03/1916	14/03/1916
War Diary	C/89. M.32.b.5.4.	14/03/1916	14/03/1916
War Diary	D/89. M.10d.8.7.	15/03/1916	15/03/1916
War Diary	H.Q. M.9.c.2.4.	15/03/1916	15/03/1916
War Diary	A/89. M.15.d.2 1/2. 2.	16/03/1916	16/03/1916
War Diary	C/89. M.32.b.5.4.	16/03/1916	16/03/1916
War Diary	D/89. M.10.D.8.7.	16/03/1916	16/03/1916
War Diary	H.Q. M.9.c.2.4	17/03/1916	17/03/1916
War Diary	A/89. M.15.d.2 1/2. 2.	18/03/1916	18/03/1916
War Diary	C/89. M.32.b.5.4.	18/03/1916	18/03/1916
War Diary	D/89. M.10.d.8.7.	19/03/1916	19/03/1916
War Diary	H.Q. M.9.c.2.4.	19/03/1916	20/03/1916
War Diary	A/89. M.15.d.2 1/2. 2.	21/03/1916	21/03/1916
War Diary	C/89. M.32.b.5.4.	21/03/1916	21/03/1916
War Diary	D/89. M.10.D.8.7	22/03/1916	22/03/1916
War Diary	H.Q. M.9.c.2.4.	23/03/1916	23/03/1916
War Diary	A/89. M.15.d.2 1/2. 2.	24/03/1916	24/03/1916
War Diary	C/89. M.32.b.5.4.	25/03/1916	25/03/1916
War Diary	D/89. M.10.D.8.7	25/03/1916	25/03/1916
War Diary	H.Q. M.9.C.2.4.	26/03/1916	26/03/1916
War Diary	A/89. M.15.d.2 1/2. 2.	26/03/1916	26/03/1916
War Diary	C/89. M.32.b.5.4.	27/03/1916	27/03/1916
War Diary	D/89. M.10.D.8.7.	27/03/1916	27/03/1916
War Diary	H.Q. M.9.c.2.4.	28/03/1916	28/03/1916
War Diary	A/89. M.15.d. 2 1/2. 2.	29/03/1916	29/03/1916
War Diary	C/89. M.32.b.5.4.	29/03/1916	29/03/1916
War Diary	D/89. M.10.D.8.7.	30/03/1916	30/03/1916
War Diary	H.Q. M.9.C.2.4.	30/03/1916	30/03/1916
War Diary	A/89. M.15.d.2 1/2. 2.	31/03/1916	31/03/1916
War Diary	C/89. M.32.b.5.4	31/03/1916	31/03/1916
War Diary	D/89. M.10.D.8.7.	31/03/1916	31/03/1916
War Diary	H.Q. M.9.C.2.4.	31/03/1916	31/03/1916
Heading	War Diary Of 89th Brigade R.F.A. April 1916. Volume 9		
Heading	A/89 M15 d2 1/2 1/2	01/04/1916	01/04/1916
War Diary	C/89 M31b54	01/04/1916	01/04/1916
War Diary	D/89 M10d8.7	01/04/1916	01/04/1916
War Diary	A/89 N. Line M2a 4.8	01/04/1916	01/04/1916
War Diary	C/89 N. Line R11a 1.1.	02/04/1916	02/04/1916
War Diary	D/89 W Line L36c5.4	02/04/1916	02/04/1916
War Diary	B.AC. R10b 2.5	02/04/1916	02/04/1916
War Diary	A/89. M15d 2 1/2 1/2	03/04/1916	03/04/1916
War Diary	C/89 M32b.5.4	03/04/1916	03/04/1916
War Diary	D/89 M10d 8.7	03/04/1916	03/04/1916

War Diary	A/89 W Line M2a 4.8	03/04/1916	03/04/1916
War Diary	C/89 W. Line R11a 1.1.	03/04/1916	03/04/1916
War Diary	A/89 W. Line L36.c.5.4	04/04/1916	04/04/1916
War Diary	B.A.C. R10.b.2.5	05/04/1916	05/04/1916
War Diary	A/89 M 15 D 2 1/2 1/2	06/04/1916	06/04/1916
War Diary	C/89 M 32 b 5.4	06/04/1916	06/04/1916
War Diary	D/89 M 10 d 8.7	06/04/1916	06/04/1916
War Diary	A/89 W. Line M 2a 4.8	06/04/1916	06/04/1916
War Diary	C/8 W. Line R 11a 1.1.	07/04/1916	07/04/1916
War Diary	D/89 W. Line L 36 C 5.4	07/04/1916	07/04/1916
War Diary	B.A.C. R 10.b 2.5	09/04/1916	10/04/1916
War Diary	A/89 M 15d 2 1/2 1/2	11/04/1916	11/04/1916
War Diary	C/89 M 32 b 5.4	11/04/1916	11/04/1916
War Diary	D/89 M 10 d 8.7	11/04/1916	11/04/1916
War Diary	A/89 W. Line M 2a 4.8	12/04/1916	12/04/1916
War Diary	C/89 W. Line R 11.a.1.1	12/04/1916	12/04/1916
War Diary	D/89 W. Line L 36.c 5.4	12/04/1916	12/04/1916
War Diary	B.A.C. R.10.b 2.5	13/04/1916	13/04/1916
War Diary	A/89 M15d 2 1/2 1/2	14/04/1916	14/04/1916
War Diary	C/89 M 32 b 5.4	14/04/1916	14/04/1916
War Diary	D/89 M 10d 8.7	14/04/1916	14/04/1916
War Diary	D/89 W. Line M 2a 4.8	14/04/1916	14/04/1916
War Diary	C/89 W Line R.11 a.1.1	14/04/1916	14/04/1916
War Diary	D/89 W Line L 36.25.4	14/04/1916	14/04/1916
War Diary	B.A.C. R 10 b 2.5	14/04/1916	14/04/1916
War Diary	Haverskerque	15/04/1916	15/04/1916
Miscellaneous	Memorandum		
Heading	War Diary Of 89th Brigade R.F.A. For Month of May 1916 (Volume II)		
War Diary	Clarques	01/05/1916	09/05/1916
War Diary	Yzeux	25/05/1916	25/05/1916
War Diary	Clarques	01/05/1916	09/05/1916
War Diary	Yzeux	25/05/1916	25/05/1916
Heading	War Diary Of 89th Brigade R.F.A. From 1st June 1916 to 30th June 1916 Volume 12.		
War Diary		01/06/1916	27/06/1916
Heading	19th Div. III. Corps. War Diary Headquarters. 89th Brigade R.F.A. July 1916		
War Diary	Denancourt	01/07/1916	05/07/1916
War Diary	A/89. X20 B 8 1/2. 1.	05/07/1916	06/07/1916
War Diary	B/89. X 20 B 7.2	06/07/1916	06/07/1916
War Diary	C/89 X 20 B 8 1/2.1.	07/07/1916	07/07/1916
War Diary	D/88.	07/07/1916	07/07/1916
War Diary	H.Q. X 20 B 8.1	07/07/1916	07/07/1916
War Diary	H.Q. X 20 B 8.1	08/07/1916	14/07/1916
War Diary	HQ. W. 23 D 3.6 1/2	15/07/1916	15/07/1916
War Diary	A/89 W.23 D 3.6.	15/07/1916	15/07/1916
War Diary	B/89 W. 23 D 3.5 1/2	15/07/1916	15/07/1916
War Diary	C/89 W 23 D 3.2 1/2	16/07/1916	18/07/1916
War Diary	Sheet. 57 D SE. 1/20000	18/07/1916	18/07/1916
War Diary	A/89. X 17 b.9.6	19/07/1916	20/07/1916
War Diary	B/89 X 17.b.7.7	21/07/1916	21/07/1916
War Diary	C/89. X 17.c.9.7	21/07/1916	21/07/1916
War Diary	Hd. Qtr. X 29 A.7.4.	21/07/1916	21/07/1916
War Diary	Lower Wood	21/07/1916	24/07/1916
War Diary	D/86. along Side C/89.	25/07/1916	31/07/1916

Heading	19th Divisional Artillery. 89th Brigade R.F.A. August 1916		
War Diary	Sheet 57D. SE 1/20,000	01/08/1916	01/08/1916
War Diary	A/89. X 17 b 9.6	01/08/1916	01/08/1916
War Diary	B/89 X 17 b 7.7	02/08/1916	02/08/1916
War Diary	C/89 X 17c 9.7	02/08/1916	02/08/1916
War Diary	HQ. X29 A 74.	03/08/1916	05/08/1916
War Diary	Becordel	05/08/1916	05/08/1916
War Diary	Frechencourt	06/08/1916	07/08/1916
War Diary	Eecques	07/08/1916	08/08/1916
War Diary	HQ. N 15 B 8.9	09/08/1916	09/08/1916
War Diary	A/89 M12a 8.0	09/08/1916	09/08/1916
War Diary	B/89 N27a 8	10/08/1916	10/08/1916
War Diary	C/89 N10a 3.8.	11/08/1916	21/08/1916
War Diary	A/89. H35c 1.4	21/08/1916	22/08/1916
War Diary	B/89 N4d 2 1/2.5	22/08/1916	22/08/1916
War Diary	B/154 N 15B19.	22/08/1916	22/08/1916
War Diary	C/154 N16a 4.8	22/08/1916	22/08/1916
War Diary	D/88 N14c 9.8	23/08/1916	24/08/1916
War Diary	HQ N7c 3.6	25/08/1916	31/08/1916
Heading	War Diary of 89th Brigade R.F.A. From Sept. 1st 16 to Sept 9th 16. Volume 15		
War Diary		01/09/1916	09/09/1916
Heading	19th Division Trench Mortar Batts Jun 1916-Oct. 1918		
War Diary	Map Sheet 5.2 M.4.	01/06/1916	29/06/1916
War Diary	?	30/06/1916	30/06/1916
War Diary	Beaurains	30/06/1916	30/06/1916
War Diary	Locre	01/07/1917	04/07/1917
War Diary	Vierstraat	05/07/1917	31/07/1917
War Diary	Locre	04/07/1917	04/07/1917
War Diary	Vierstraat	05/07/1917	31/07/1917
War Diary	Locre	04/07/1917	09/07/1917
War Diary	Vierstraat	10/07/1917	31/07/1917
War Diary	Meterin	27/08/1917	31/08/1917
War Diary	Vierstraat	01/08/1917	10/08/1917
War Diary	Caudescure	11/08/1917	16/08/1917
War Diary	Locre	04/07/1917	04/07/1917
War Diary	Vierstraat	05/07/1917	31/07/1917
War Diary	Vierstraat (Parrot Farm)	01/08/1917	09/08/1917
War Diary	Caudescure	10/08/1917	21/08/1917
War Diary	Meteren	22/08/1917	31/08/1917
War Diary	Vierstraat	01/08/1917	10/08/1917
War Diary	Caudescure	11/08/1917	21/08/1917
War Diary	Meteren	22/08/1917	31/08/1917
War Diary	Vierstraat	01/08/1917	10/08/1917
War Diary	Caudescure	11/08/1917	21/08/1917
War Diary	Meterin	22/08/1917	26/08/1917
War Diary	Caudescure	17/08/1917	21/08/1917
War Diary	Meteren	22/08/1917	31/08/1917
War Diary	Meteren	01/09/1917	01/09/1917
War Diary	Strazeele	02/09/1917	06/09/1917
War Diary	Vierstraat	07/09/1917	30/09/1917
War Diary	Strazeele	01/09/1917	06/09/1917
War Diary	Vierstraat	07/09/1917	30/09/1917
War Diary	Meterin	01/09/1917	01/09/1917
War Diary	Strazeele	02/09/1917	06/09/1917

War Diary	Vierstraat	07/09/1917	30/09/1917
War Diary	Strazeele	01/09/1917	06/09/1917
War Diary	Vierstraat	07/09/1917	06/11/1917
War Diary	La Clyte	07/11/1917	11/11/1917
War Diary	Berthen	12/11/1917	13/11/1917
War Diary	Croix De Poperinghe	14/11/1917	30/11/1917
War Diary	Vierstraat	01/11/1917	06/11/1917
War Diary	Pompier Camp	07/11/1917	12/11/1917
War Diary	Berthen	13/11/1917	13/11/1917
War Diary	Croix De Poperinghe	14/11/1917	30/11/1917
War Diary	Vierstraat	01/11/1917	05/11/1917
War Diary	La Clyte	06/11/1917	11/11/1917
War Diary	Berthen	12/11/1917	13/11/1917
War Diary	Croix De Poperinghe	14/11/1917	30/11/1917
War Diary	Vierstraat	01/11/1917	06/11/1917
War Diary	La Clyte	07/11/1917	11/11/1917
War Diary	Berthen	12/11/1917	13/11/1917
War Diary	Croix De Poperinghe	14/11/1917	30/12/1917
War Diary	Claire Camp	31/12/1917	31/12/1917
War Diary	Croix De Poperinghe	01/12/1917	12/12/1917
War Diary	St Jans Cappel	13/12/1917	31/12/1917
War Diary	Ridge Observatry	01/12/1917	04/12/1917
War Diary	Croix De Pope	05/12/1917	14/12/1917
War Diary	Tally Ho Camp	15/12/1917	16/12/1917
War Diary	St Jans Capel	17/12/1917	31/12/1917
War Diary	Croix De Poperinghe	01/12/1917	12/12/1917
War Diary	St Jans Cappel	13/12/1917	31/12/1917
War Diary	Roquiny Camp	01/01/1918	03/01/1918
War Diary	Havrincourt Wood	04/01/1918	31/01/1918
War Diary	Pt Jans Cabel	31/12/1917	01/01/1918
War Diary	Rocquigny	01/01/1918	03/01/1918
War Diary	Havrincourt Wood	04/01/1918	31/01/1918
War Diary	St Jans Capel	31/12/1917	01/01/1918
War Diary	Rocquigny	01/01/1918	03/01/1918
War Diary	Havrincourt	04/01/1918	31/01/1918
War Diary	St Jans Capel	31/12/1917	01/01/1918
War Diary	Rocquigny	01/01/1918	03/01/1918
War Diary	Havrincourt Wood	04/01/1918	30/01/1918
War Diary	Havrincourt Wood	01/02/1918	15/02/1918
War Diary	Montigny	16/02/1918	28/02/1918
War Diary	Havrincourt Wood	01/02/1918	16/02/1918
War Diary	Montigny	17/02/1918	18/02/1918
War Diary	Havrincourt Wood	01/02/1918	16/02/1918
War Diary	Montigny	17/02/1918	28/02/1918
War Diary	Havrincourt Wood	01/02/1918	16/02/1918
War Diary	Montigny	17/02/1918	03/03/1918
War Diary	Salamanca Camp	04/03/1918	05/03/1918
War Diary	Havrincourt Wood	06/03/1918	31/03/1918
Heading	19th Divisional Artillery. X/19 Trench Mortar Battery April 1918.		
War Diary	Petit Houvin	01/04/1918	01/04/1918
War Diary	Grand Sec Bois	02/04/1918	02/04/1918
War Diary	Wulverghem	03/04/1918	11/04/1918
War Diary	Buller Camp	12/04/1918	13/04/1918
War Diary	Locre	14/04/1918	16/04/1918
War Diary	La Clyte	17/04/1918	17/04/1918

War Diary	Ouderdom	18/04/1918	20/04/1918
War Diary	Heksken	21/04/1918	26/04/1918
War Diary	Hilhoek	27/04/1918	29/04/1918
War Diary	Racquinghem	30/04/1918	30/04/1918
Heading	19th Divisional Artillery. Y/19 Trench Mortar Battery April 1918.		
War Diary	Frevent	01/04/1918	01/04/1918
War Diary	Grand Sec Bois	02/04/1918	04/04/1918
War Diary	Wulverghem	05/04/1918	08/04/1918
War Diary	Grand Bois	09/04/1918	10/04/1918
War Diary	Buller Camp	11/04/1918	13/04/1918
War Diary	Locre	14/04/1918	15/04/1918
War Diary	La Clyte	16/04/1918	17/04/1918
War Diary	Ouderdom	18/04/1918	20/04/1918
War Diary	Heksken	21/04/1918	26/04/1918
War Diary	Hilhoek	27/04/1918	30/04/1918
War Diary	Montigny	01/05/1918	03/05/1918
War Diary	Salamanca Camp	04/05/1918	05/05/1918
War Diary	Havrincourt Wood	06/05/1918	23/05/1918
War Diary	Neuville	23/05/1918	23/05/1918
War Diary	Barastre	24/05/1918	24/05/1918
War Diary	Miraumont	25/05/1918	25/05/1918
War Diary	Lealvillers	26/05/1918	27/05/1918
War Diary	Halloy	28/05/1918	30/05/1918
War Diary	Aubrometz	31/05/1918	31/05/1918
War Diary	Racquinghem	01/05/1918	17/05/1918
War Diary	Arques	18/05/1918	18/05/1918
War Diary	Dampierre	19/05/1918	27/05/1918
War Diary	Bissuel	28/05/1918	28/05/1918
War Diary	Nanteuil	29/05/1918	29/05/1918
War Diary	Damery	30/05/1918	31/05/1918
War Diary	Racquinghem	01/05/1918	17/05/1918
War Diary	Arques	18/05/1918	18/05/1918
War Diary	Dampierre	19/05/1918	27/05/1918
War Diary	Bissuel	28/05/1918	28/05/1918
War Diary	Nanteuil	29/05/1918	29/05/1918
War Diary	Damery	30/05/1918	31/05/1918
War Diary		27/05/1918	27/05/1918
War Diary	Vaucienen	01/06/1918	04/06/1918
War Diary	Vaudancourt	05/06/1918	20/06/1918
War Diary	Vertus	21/06/1918	21/06/1918
War Diary	Bannes	22/06/1918	30/06/1918
War Diary	Damery	01/06/1918	04/06/1918
War Diary	Vaudancourt	05/06/1918	20/06/1918
War Diary	Vertus	21/06/1918	21/06/1918
War Diary	Bannes	22/06/1918	01/07/1918
War Diary	Anvin	02/07/1918	02/07/1918
War Diary	Forestel	03/07/1918	12/07/1918
War Diary	Febvin	13/07/1918	13/07/1918
War Diary	Palfart	14/07/1918	15/07/1918
War Diary	Febvin	16/07/1918	16/07/1918
War Diary	Palfart	17/07/1918	21/07/1918
War Diary	Groeuppe	22/07/1918	31/07/1918
War Diary	Mailly-Le-Camp	01/07/1918	01/07/1918
War Diary	Hesdin	02/07/1918	02/07/1918
War Diary	Grand-Manillet	03/07/1918	12/07/1918

War Diary	Febvin-Palfart	13/07/1918	21/07/1918
War Diary	Groeuppe	22/07/1918	06/08/1918
War Diary	Chocques	07/08/1918	31/08/1918
War Diary	Groeuppe	01/08/1918	06/08/1918
War Diary	Chocques	06/08/1918	12/09/1918
War Diary	Bethune	13/09/1918	30/09/1918
War Diary	Chocques	01/09/1918	12/09/1918
War Diary	Bethune	13/09/1918	05/10/1918
War Diary	Loisne	06/10/1918	17/10/1918
War Diary	Cambrai	18/10/1918	21/10/1918
War Diary	Avesnes-Les-Aubert	22/10/1918	31/10/1918
War Diary	Bethune	01/10/1918	05/10/1918
War Diary	Loisne	06/10/1918	17/10/1918
War Diary	Bapaume	18/10/1918	18/10/1918
War Diary	Cambrai	19/10/1918	21/10/1918
War Diary	Avesnes	22/10/1918	31/10/1918

19TH DIVISION

19TH DIVL AMMN COL.
JAN 1915 – OCT 1918

121/6609

19th Division

19th Divl. A.C.
Vol I

From 19 Jany to 31 Aug 15

Oct .15

Army Form C. 2118

WAR DIARY
or
INTELLIGENCE SUMMARY

(Erase heading not required.)

Instructions regarding War Diaries and Intelligence Summaries are contained in F. S. Regs., Part II. and the Staff Manual respectively. Title Pages will be prepared in manuscript.

Place	Date	Hour	Summary of Events and Information	Remarks and references to Appendices
BULFORD	19.1.15		Formation of Unit. Major J.C. HANNA, R.G.A. in command. R.F.L.¿	
"	19.4.15		Colonel R.F. McCREA, R.F.A. appointed to command. R.F.L.¿	
"	19.6.15		Column engaged in 3 sections R.F.L.¿	
"	5.7.15		Orders to Mobilize. R.F.L.¿	
"	11.7.15		Bulk of Mobilization equipment drawn. R.F.L.¿	
"	12.7.15		S.A.A. Ammunition drawn. R.F.L.¿	
SOUTHAMPTON	19.7.15	3.45 A.M	Proceeded in 8 trains to SOUTHAMPTON and entrained for Service in FRANCE. R.F.L.¿	
FRANCE	20.7.15	7.30 A.M.	Disembarked at HAVRE and marched thence that day. R.F.L.¿	
"	21.7.15		Entrained at HAVRE in 5 trains. R.F.L.¿	
"	22.7.15		Detrained at AUDRUICQ and ST OMER and marched to ZOUAFQUES. R.F.L.¿	
"	23.7.15	2 P.M.	Marched to TILQUES. R.F.L.¿	
"	24.7.15	7 A.M.	Marched to AIRE. R.F.L.¿	
"	27.7.15	4 P.M.	Gun and Howitzer Ammunition drawn. Joined Indian Corps, consisting of MEERUT, LAHORE & 19th Divisions. R.F.L.¿	
"	28.7.15		Issue of Lyddite to Howitzer Brigade. R.F.L.¿	
"	31.7.15	11.30 A.M	Lyddite drawn from Park to replace rounds, and 18 pr Shrapnel emptied. R.F.L.¿	
"	1.8.15	9.30 A.M	Marched to ST FLORIS. R.F.L.¿ 19th Division in Reserve. R.F.L.¿	
"	2.8.15	11 A.M.	Howitzers drawn from Park. 10 pr & Howitzer H.E. shells exchanged for Shrapnel in Brigades. R.F.L.¿	
"	3.8.15			
"	4.8.15		Remained billeted at ST FLORIS. R.F.L.¿	
"	5.8.15		Do.	
"	27.8.15		2 Sections moved billets from East to West of ST FLORIS. R.F.L.¿ Head Quarters and No.1 Section marched to PARADIS. 19th Div. relieved 7th Div. and 19th D.A.C. took over	
"	28.8.15		for 7th D.A.C. supply of Ammunition in area. R.F.L.¿	
"	29.8.15		Ammunition park established in field North of LOCON. R.F.L.¿	
"	30.8.15		Do. Head Quarters and No.1 Section at PARADIS, Nos 2 & 3 Sections at ST FLORIS. R.F.L.¿	R.F.L.¿ 7 & 2 teams 15.6.15 R.F.L.¿ 15 D.A.C
"	31.8.15		Do.	Bomb R.F.L.¿
"			Do.	

12/7593

19th Distrih: ll.
Vol. 2

Sep 14 Oct 15

Army Form C. 2118.

WAR DIARY
or
INTELLIGENCE SUMMARY
(Erase heading not required.)

Instructions regarding War Diaries and Intelligence Summaries are contained in F. S. Regs., Part II. and the Staff Manual respectively. Title Pages will be prepared in manuscript.

Place	Date	Hour	Summary of Events and Information	Remarks and references to Appendices
FRANCE	1.9.15		Head-Quarters & No 1. Section still at PARADIS. No 2 & 3 Sections at ST FLORIS.	
"	7.9.15		No 2 & 3 Sections moved to PARADIS.	
"	19.9.15		Advanced H.Q. Park fixed at Refilling Point, North of LOCON. 2nd Hd. of Section in charge.	
"	21.9.15		Commenced 4 days heavy bombardment of German trenches.	
"	24.9.15		Head Quarters Road to LOCON.	
"	25.9.15		First day of Battle along whole front.	
"	30.9.15		Nov 7. Found a spirit level of the day running 1st phase of operation telegram from H.M. the King.	
"	3.10.15		Head Quarters returned from LOCON to PARADIS.	
"	4.10.15		Front of Supper unchanged. New Refilling Point established at LES LOBES.	
"	18.10.15		Advanced Fd. Park disbanded.	
"	20.10.15		Head Quarters, No 1, 2 & 3 Sections moved from PARADIS to ROBECQ - CALONNE Road.	
"	23.10.15		Refilling Point moved from LES LOBES to old Refilling Point North of LOCON.	
"	30.10.15		Head Quarters, No 1 & 2 Sections moved from ROBECQ to TOMBE WILLOT.	
"	1.11.15		No 3 Section moved to TOMBE WILLOT.	

R.H. Price, Lt Col.
Comdg. 1st D.A.C.

19th S.A.C.
Vol. 3.

12/7656

19th Hussars

Nov 15

WAR DIARY
or
INTELLIGENCE SUMMARY

(Erase heading not required.)

Army Form C. 2118

Instructions regarding War Diaries and Intelligence Summaries are contained in F.S. Regs., Part II. and the Staff Manual respectively. Title Pages will be prepared in manuscript.

Place	Date	Hour	Summary of Events and Information	Remarks and references to Appendices
FRANCE	1.11.15		Head Quarters No 1 & 2 Sections at TOMBE W. of No 3 Section moved from ROBECQ.	
"	4.11.15		No 3 Section moved to PARADIS.	
"	6.11.15 to 8.11.15		(Exchange of Mules for Heavy and Light Draught Horses with MEERUT Division	
"			Received 194 H.D. and 88 L.D. for 454 Mules.	
"	9.11.15		Construction of Horse standings commenced.	
"	11.11.15		Formed XI Corps consisting of GUARDS, 19th and 46th Divisions.	
"	22.11.15		Refilling Point landed over to 48th Division.	
"	24.11.15		Section moved to 1st Army Reserve (Head Quarters & No 3 Section moved to CROIX MARRAISE No 1 & 2 Sections to LE FORET. (CROIX MARRAISE N. and LE FOREST N.W. of HAVERSKERQUE	
"	26.11.15		Section Training commenced under Demand orders	
"	30.11.15		Construction of Horse standings commenced	

R.F.K. Greenhalgh
Comdg. 19th D.A.C.

19th S.A.
Vol. 4

121/7936

Dec 1915

Army Form C. 2118

19th Divisional Ammunition Column

WAR DIARY
or
INTELLIGENCE SUMMARY
(Erase heading not required.)

Instructions regarding War Diaries and Intelligence Summaries are contained in F.S. Regs., Part II. and the Staff Manual respectively. Title Pages will be prepared in manuscript.

Place	Date	Hour	Summary of Events and Information	Remarks and references to Appendices
FRANCE	1.12.15		Head Quarters & No 3 Section at CROIX MARRAISE, Nos 1 & 2 Sections at LE FORET near HAVERSKERQUE. RFZM	
"	3.12.15		Head Quarters, Nos 1, 2 & 3 Sections moved to QUENTIN. {Sections moved for 1st Army Reserve into lines relieving 46th Division. Sections No 2 & 4 OSTREM, R.A. Head FOSSE. RFZM	
"	6.12.15		Commenced supply of ammunition to Brigade Ammunition Columns in our Wagons. RFZM	
"	7.12.15		Running miles exchanged for H.D. Horses with 46th Division. RFZM	
"	13.12.15		Major-General G.T.M. BRIDGES, C.M.G., D.S.O. assumed command of 19th Division in succession to Major-General C. FASKEN C.B. RFZM	
"	20.12.15		No 1 Section moved to PACAUT. RFZM	
"	25.12.15		Brig-General R. FITZMAURICE assumed command of 19th Divisional Artillery in succession to Brig Gen C.E. LAURIE, C.B., D.S.O. RFZM	
			R.F.F. O'Grady, A.S.C. Comdg. 19th D.A.C.	

19ᵗʰ ʙ.ᴀ.ᴄ.
Vol: 5

WAR DIARY
or
INTELLIGENCE SUMMARY
(Erase heading not required.)

Army Form C. 2118

Instructions regarding War Diaries and Intelligence Summaries are contained in F.S. Regs., Part II. and the Staff Manual respectively. Title Pages will be prepared in manuscript.

Place	Date	Hour	Summary of Events and Information	Remarks and references to Appendices
In the Field	Jan 5.		Capt. J. Kirkpatrick took over temporary command & the column from Lt. Col. R.F. McEwen.	Ell
"	6.		Lt. Col. R.F. McEwen proceeded on leave to England —	Ell
"	31.		The Unit were at Lew Abbele at Rest.	Ell

J A Kirkpatrick Capt. RFA
Commanding 15 C.S.T.C.

Army Form C. 2118

WAR DIARY
or
INTELLIGENCE SUMMARY
(Erase heading not required.)

Feby/16   19 DAC   Vols. 6.

Place	Date	Hour	Summary of Events and Information	Remarks and references to Appendices
Hinin-Kerque	1944		Column moved into billets at Robermetz and La Gorgue.	
Robermetz	23rd		Headquarters moved into billets at La Gorgue	
La Gorgue	29		Lieut Robert Johnstone R.F.A. appointed Adjutant as from 1st Feb /16.	

J. S. Kelly
Lt Col R.F.A.
Commanding
19 DAC

19 D a e
vol 7~~7~~6

WAR DIARY
or
INTELLIGENCE SUMMARY

Army Form C. 2118

Place	Date	Hour	Summary of Events and Information	Remarks and references to Appendices
In the Field.	2"		Hd Qts moved from L.25.c to L.28.d.	EW

J. A. Ridge Major RFA
O.C. 19TH (WESTERN) DIVL AMMN COLN

WAR DIARY or **INTELLIGENCE SUMMARY**
(Erase heading not required.)

Army Form C. 2118

14 D.A.C. Vol 8

Place	Date	Hour	Summary of Events and Information	Remarks and references to Appendices
L.28.D.c.	1916 10/4.		Hd. Qrs. moved to L.25.B.8.8. (36.A N E 1/4) 1/20000	Ell
L.25.6.8.8.	15/4.		Column moved to J.27.D. " (36.A. combined) 1/100,000	Ell
J.27.D.	20/4.		" N.24.A. "	Ell
	24/4.		The M.O. died of cerebro spinal Meningitis.	Ell
	25/5.		M.O. appointed to the Column.	Ell

1st May 1916

J. Rudolph Lybrechts
Commanding 19th D.A.C.

Army Form C. 2118

WAR DIARY
or
INTELLIGENCE SUMMARY

MAY 1916

Place	Date	Hour	Summary of Events and Information	Remarks and references to Appendices
Nieuport Bains	9		Left for Engineers by tram from Lillers, Rue d'Aerquette arrived Engineers 15th & Wellies at Belloy & the 4th Army Area.	GM
	18		Ammunition Column reorganized -	
	31		Lieut G. G. Thorne appointed Adjutant	

Nordelyn Myers
Maj. 19 D.A.C.

Army Form C. 2118.

19th D.A.C.
19th Division

WAR DIARY
or
INTELLIGENCE SUMMARY
(Erase heading not required.)

VOL 10

June 1916

Place	Date 1916	Hour	Summary of Events and Information	Remarks and references to Appendices
BELLOY	JUNE 9		Column moved to LAVIEVILLE in advance of Divisional Artillery.	
	10) 16) 18)		Drawing ammunition through 8th and 31st D.A.C's, and of 1000 rds. also to fire two forms for 86th and 87th Inf Bdes. Dumps completed night of 18th inst.	
	30		No 3 Section moved to advance position E.3.d. on the outskirts of ALBERT. to supply the Mobile Brigade attached 34th and 9th Divisions	

J.F. Phore Lieut RFA.
ADJUTANT, 19TH D.A.C.

19th Div.
III.Corps.

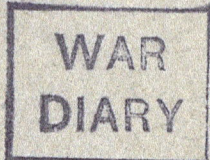
WAR DIARY

19th DIVISIONAL AMMUNITION COLUMN

J U L Y

1 9 1 6

Army Form C. 2118

19th Div Amm. Col.
19th DIVISION - Vol 11

WAR DIARY
or
INTELLIGENCE SUMMARY
(Erase heading not required.)

Instructions regarding War Diaries and Intelligence Summaries are contained in F.S. Regs., Part II. and the Staff Manual respectively. Title Pages will be prepared in manuscript.

Place	Date	Hour	Summary of Events and Information	Remarks and references to Appendices
LAVIEVILLE	1916 July 3		No 3 Section moved from LAVIEVILLE to forward position at E.3.d.5.5. hea ALBERT to supply mobile batteries of 88th and 89th FA Bde.	
	4		A forward refilling point was put under construction at E.3.d. J.3.	
	7		Nos 1, 2 & 4 Sections moved from LAVIEVILLE to ALBERT.	
	19		The whole Column moved from ALBERT to Camp at F.1.A. near BECOURT WOOD. Established forward dump at E.12.b. Billets in ALBERT	
	20		Column returned to former billets in ALBERT	
	22		Nos 1, 2 and 4 Sections moved to LAVIEVILLE and No 3 to E.6.d. hear forward dump	

[signature]
LIEUT. R.F.A.
ADJUTANT 19TH D.A.C.

19th Divisional Artillery,

19th DIVISIONAL AMMUNITION COLUMN

AUGUST 1 9 1 6 :::::

WAR DIARY or INTELLIGENCE SUMMARY

Army Form C. 2118

Vol 12

19th Divn Col

Place	Date	Hour	Summary of Events and Information	Remarks and references to Appendices
Albert	Aug 4		The whole Column moved Artillery at Bavelincourt.	
Bavelincourt	6		Column entrained at Lozeau and Selence and detrained at Candas, Gorenneroides and Staubreche, remaining in billets in Wostrate area.	
	22		No 1 Section moved into billets at R.26 c 3.3. Sheet 20 S6.	
Wostrate		20:00	No 3 Section moved into billets at R.34 b 1.9. Letts	
	20		Nos 2 & 4 Sections moved into billets at R.33 c 3.3 & S.3 c 4.7 respectively. Sheet 20 S6. 1/20000	

R. Barrington Post 2/Lt LIEUT. R.F.A.
ADJUTANT 19TH D.A.C.

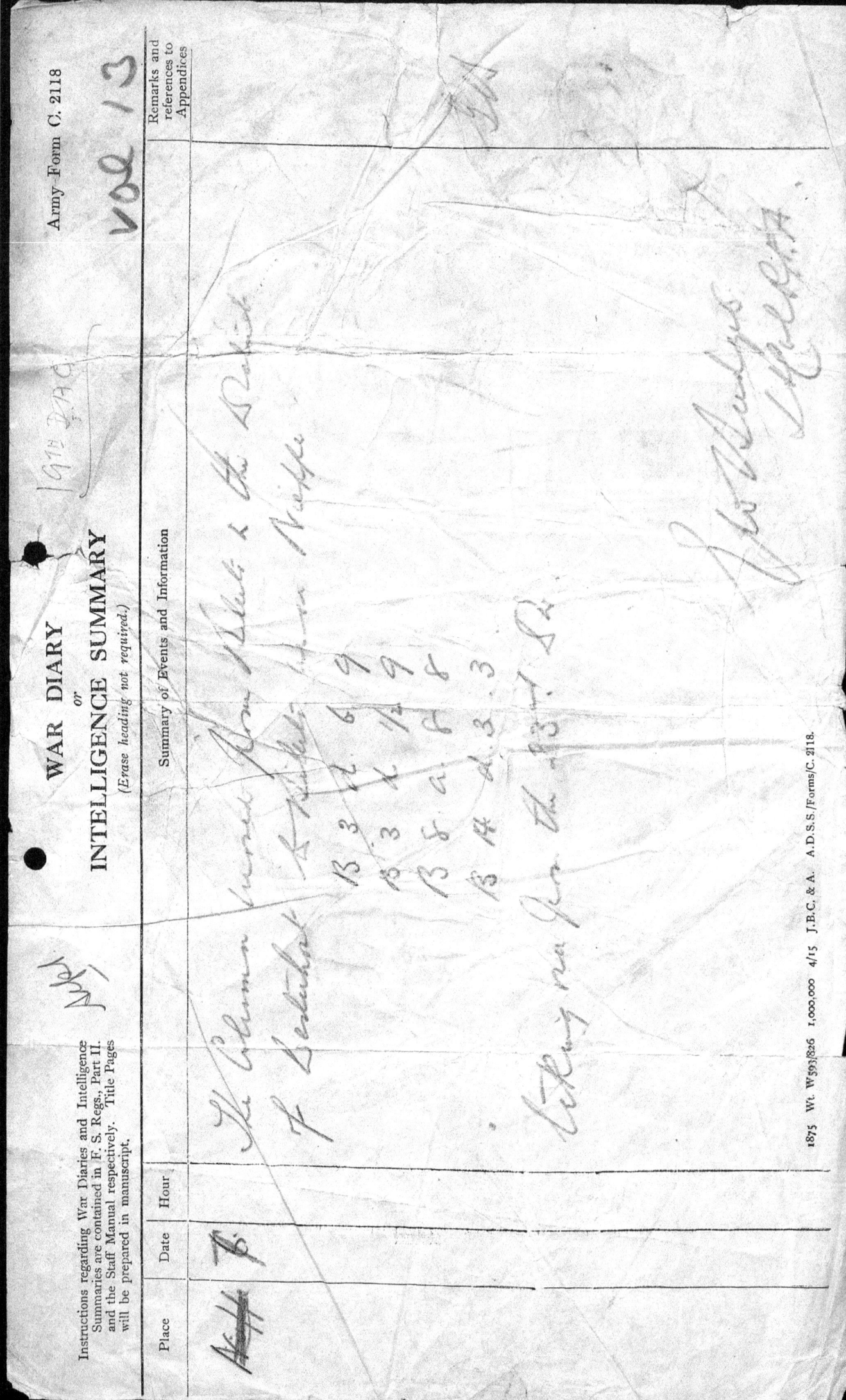

Army Form C. 2118

Vol 14

19th DAC

WAR DIARY
or
INTELLIGENCE SUMMARY
(Erase heading not required.)

Instructions regarding War Diaries and Intelligence Summaries are contained in F.S. Regs, Part II. and the Staff Manual respectively. Title Pages will be prepared in manuscript.

Place	Date	Hour	Summary of Events and Information	Remarks and references to Appendices
Nispe	2/10/16		Column moved to Tilleuls at Schaerken.	
Schaerken	6/10/16		Column entrained at Bailleul and grassemeld proceeded to Somme area detraining at Doullens & Candas.	
	7/10/16		Marched to Tilleuls at Coigneux.	
	17/10/16		Column marched to Acheux.	
	18/10/16 to 31/10/16		Ammunition drawn from various Parks to replenish dumps of 6.50 rds per gun & 4.50 for Howitzers today. twenty tons. Total amount of ammunition issued between dates 77,000 rds.	

R C Bannington Foot
2/W.
ADJUTANT, 19TH D.A.C.

WAR DIARY
or
INTELLIGENCE SUMMARY

Army Form C. 2118

Place	Date	Hour	Summary of Events and Information	Remarks and references to Appendices
Alost	19th		Capt Stone & party attempted to recover small Belgian field gun from trench under our infantry. Had taken gun was enfiladed & retired.	
			Left 4 horse work at 11 in [?] of my horse & drove into road, a matter of 1000x.	
	20/15		Saw party drews up with cases & charges 3 guns about 100 yds in with a team of horses. Our fire was very heavy shelly the road to our left from [?] to [?]	
			Shelling Pierremont	

WAR DIARY
or
INTELLIGENCE SUMMARY
(Erase heading not required.)

Army Form C. 2118

Place	Date	Hour	Summary of Events and Information	Remarks and references to Appendices
	23rd		The fire was off for two nights. The adjutant of our went up with a party from Coys shores section but nothing could be done. Capt Shore was in Hospital from two wounds.	
	24th		Capt Scott & a party from two our B. section (No 2) & drew the gun out & delivered it to H.Q. at 5.30 am the weather 7 m 25.h.	

A E Baughton Root
2/W

WAR DIARY
or
INTELLIGENCE SUMMARY

(Erase heading not required.)

19th Division
Ammunition Column

2-1-17

Vol 16

Place	Date	Hour	Summary of Events and Information	Remarks and references to Appendices
Albert	6.12.16		Column moved back to Heu via Authuile	
Authuile	7.12.16		Stopped at Authuile overnight. Moved at 10 a.m. to Heu to rest billets. Column rested for 7 days.	
	17		Commenced route march horse & vehicle.	

A. Bruno
To foot
Lt.

WAR DIARY
or
INTELLIGENCE SUMMARY

(Erase heading not required.)

Army Form C. 2118

Place	Date	Hour	Summary of Events and Information	Remarks and references to Appendices
	23rd		The gun was up of two nights. The argument of am went up with a party from Capt Shores section but nothing could be done.	
	24th		There was no Hospitale from the trenches Capt Scott & a party from two men Echelon (No 2) & drew the gun out & delivered it to H.A.L. at 6.30 am the morning of May 25.15.	A Bamford Scott 2/W

WAR DIARY
or
INTELLIGENCE SUMMARY
(Erase heading not required.)

19th Divisional
Ammn Column

Vol/6

Place	Date	Hour	Summary of Events and Information	Remarks and references to Appendices
Albert	6.12.16		Column moved back to Heun via Authuille	
			Stopped at Authuille overnight.	
Authuille	7.12.16		Moved at 10 a.m. to Heun to rest billets.	
			Column rested for 7 days.	
	17		Commenced to make brick horse standing.	

To Spot
Lunn Jr.

A Bunn Jr.

Army Form C. 2118

WAR DIARY
or
INTELLIGENCE SUMMARY
(Erase heading not required.)

Instructions regarding War Diaries and Intelligence Summaries are contained in F.S. Regs., Part II. and the Staff Manual respectively. Title Pages will be prepared in manuscript.

15th DIVISIONAL AMMUNITION COLUMN, R.F.A.
Date 1-3-17

JULY 17

Place	Date	Hour	Summary of Events and Information	Remarks and references to Appendices.
HEM	1st–15th		Physical training & construction of Permanent Horse Standings.	
	15th		Column marched into training area.	
Aultie	17th		Arriving in Billets at Aultie & Lamesson. Commenced construction of Ammunition Dumps at Arqueves & Aultie.	
	21st		Construction & improvement of Horse standings. No 1 Section returned to Column from of army	
	23rd		Reorganization of personnel knocked down to Army	
			B.A.C.	

A Bunny Lt Col
Adjt 15 D.A.C.

WAR DIARY
or
INTELLIGENCE SUMMARY

(Erase heading not required.)

Army Form C. 2118

19 D Am Col

N of 18

Place	Date	Hour	Summary of Events and Information	Remarks and references to Appendices
On the	21st		Column moved to new area & went into billets at BUS	
BUS	15th		Took over ARP at BUS from 32nd Div. Traverses constructed at all Ammunition Dumps.	
	28th		No.1 Section advanced & new area & formed a camp at K.31.a.1.4. Sheet 57 D. Handed over ARP Authuile - 96th BAC Handed over ARP Cognevue to 31st DAC	

R C Barnes ToStock
Lt
Adj 19 DAC

Army Form C. 2118.

Oct 19

WAR DIARY
or
INTELLIGENCE SUMMARY
(Erase heading not required.)

19th D.A.

Place	Date	Hour	Summary of Events and Information	Remarks and references to Appendices
BUS	11		Commenced march in to the 2nd Army area. Billeted at HEM on the night of 11th.	
HEM	12		Resumed march arriving at Monchel-Conchy at 3pm. Billeted at this place for the night.	
MONCHEL CONCHY	13		Continued march arriving at Anvin 2pm. Remained till morning of 15th.	
ANVIN	15		Marched to FONTES. Arrived at this village at noon. Column remained in fields here the evening of 17th.	
FONTES	17		Marched entered Anvin at STEENBECQUE at 3pm. Remained thru the night.	
STEENBECQUE	18		Marched to VERTE RUE. Remained in this billets the morning of 20th.	
VERTE RUE	20		Marched to area between Eecke & Godewaersvelde. Between Hennes reparé etc. Reconnecy line.	NCBampty Capt Adjt 19 D.A.C

WAR DIARY
or
INTELLIGENCE SUMMARY

Army Form C. 2118

19th Divnl
Ammn Column

Place	Date	Hour	Summary of Events and Information	Remarks and references to Appendices
Gonnehem	April 5. 20.		Am Dump at H.H. 41.7. Shut 25 taken over from 16 DAC. No 2. Section here lits bw Rtls. sy. B. 4.3.9. " " " " " G.35.C.5.6. No 3. Sector " " "	

JM 20

Army Form C. 2118

WAR DIARY
or
INTELLIGENCE SUMMARY 19
(Erase heading not required.)

Instructions regarding War Diaries and Intelligence Summaries are contained in F.S. Regs., Part II. and the Staff Manual respectively. Title Pages will be prepared in manuscript.

Place	Date	Hour	Summary of Events and Information	Remarks and references to Appendices
Godwansdorp. May	2		Column moved – H.Q. to Piperough.	
	6		H.Q. moved to Buxatone.	
	8-10		RE Medical convoys forward. 35 G.S. Wagons returned to this purpose. Barges started at 9am & took all night.	
	11		Column moved to Wedworth area. M.D. M7 & 84 Sheet 28. Nos 1 & 2 Section N76. No 3 Section N11 C.	
	13-25		Commenced delivery of ammunition from forward group stations at which ammunition arrived by rail. The ammunition was released to M/S. Wagons & taken up to R. O. battery positions. Amount to the dumps: 1st April 1300.18hr & 4.5 Howe 1100 rnds. Following amounts were transhed each night at Hackebeest Cross: was the main railhead.
13th 6400 18hr 14th 6400 18hr 15th 6400 18hr 16th 6400 18hr 17th 8000 10hr
18th 1600 18hr 2700 10hr 19th 16.00 Howe 20th 4500 18hr 21st 500 Howe
22nd 3200 18hr 500 Howe 23rd 1730 10hr 24th 5000 10hr 1350 Howe 25th 360 10hr
2500 7Ht
(200 18hr)	

WAR DIARY or INTELLIGENCE SUMMARY

Place	Date	Hour	Summary of Events and Information	Remarks and references to Appendices
	13-2-5t		Grand Total delivered at T.S. bays from Hallibast
S4710 I0/m
13,150 Hour (A.S)
2.40 TMF

Ottn/rrojt station. 158A, RSB, KSC hrs hrs a great deal further forward than Hallebast then rum by an officer from the column. Embassing & carrying parties were supplying T batteries which each station fed. 60 em railway was right up to each station & trains were sent up nightly. Ammunition was then distributed by these officers to batteries as required. The batteries took the ammunition up in their lorries & the above total does not include any ammunition which was met handed by the column.
3 Officers & 80 OR hrs at Hallibast. Somebody finds were used. The work has carried on very satisfactorily, ammunition nightly & about H.Q.S. wagons | |

WAR DIARY
or
INTELLIGENCE SUMMARY

(Erase heading not required.)

Army Form C. 2118

Place	Date	Hour	Summary of Events and Information	Remarks and references to Appendices
	28th		In addition to the ammunition work we were supply'g any to troops nightly for RE material delivery. The work was as far as possible usually apportioned to sections of 2 in each section o/c & subalterns officer who g'even separate work. The Bdes sent up coverers in two nights by supply trams & drivers with the view of relieving column men horses. A B.A.C. attached to the Division sent 50 coverers up to supply a party for unloading 1 each night. 80 men in all. Ammunition taken up by tramway from batty dumps to advanced M.A. bolting positions. One party working within 900 yds of German front line. Work carried out able under great difficulties. Working parties were found by	

… D.A.C. & all B.A.C's attached to their Division, also the 2 wagon-
80 supply from 18th Bde were also attached to wagons were
to recuperate the fatigue. Casualties were [illegible] on
the whole. Two men from this Column & 5 from B.A.C's wagons.
Infantry lost 2 men killed.

A. Bonney for Forte.

LIEUT. R.F.A.
ADJUTANT [illegible] D.A.C.

Army Form C. 2118

WAR DIARY
or
INTELLIGENCE SUMMARY

19th Divisional—Ammunition Column.

(Erase heading not required.)

Instructions regarding War Diaries and Intelligence Summaries are contained in F.S. Regs., Part II. and the Staff Manual respectively. Title Pages will be prepared in manuscript.

Place	Date	Hour	Summary of Events and Information	Remarks and references to Appendices
WESTOUTRE.	JUNE. 1.-5.		Delivery of ammunition by 60 cm. track continued to M.G. positions continued. Working parties found by D.A.C., Infantry and attached B.A.Cs. Considerable difficulty experienced owing to enemy's constant shell fire.	
	3.		Lieut. Col. Geo. Bridges D.S.O. awarded C.M.G. (London Gazette dated 3.6.17).	
	9-19		Removal of empty shell cases from forward area. Total removed 322,000, average of 29,274 per day. Employed on this fatigue daily were 3 officers, 103 O.R. 21 trucks; 35 G.S. wagons.	
	10.		H.Q. Nos 1 & 2 Sections moved to area around SCHERPENBERG. H.Q. at M 11 & 2 7 Sheet 28.	
	13½.		H.Q. and all Sections moved into camps on LOCRE - KEMMEL road, H.Q. at M.23.d.8.9. Sheet 28.	
	21.		Column moved to rest area at N 26 d. Sheet 28. Party consisting of 3 officers, 13 G.S. wagons and 18 teams with drivers, detached at PARRET FARM - Corps fatigue rebuilding VIERSTRAAT - WYTSCHAETE road. Several mules killed and wounded on this fatigue.	
	28. 30.		Column returned to camps on LOCRE - KEMMEL road. officers sent out to reconnoitre forward area for live ammunition and empties.	

[signature]
2/Lieut. R.F.A.
a/Adjutant 19th D.A. COLUMN.

WAR DIARY
or
INTELLIGENCE SUMMARY
(Erase heading not required.)

Army Form C. 2118

Place	Date	Hour	Summary of Events and Information	Remarks and references to Appendices
LOCRE	1st July	9.15	Removal of live ammunition from various positions in forward area & old gun positions to the Divisional A.R.P. at YORK HOUSE. Total amount removed 3946 rds A 2332 A×X 2609 BX. Six teams & wagons (necessary proportion of T.R.&V.Q.S.) also 20 men were used daily for this fatigue.	
	7th		Road Screening fatigue. In conjunction with R.E.'s for the purpose of screening plank etc. Transport & fatigue party were supplied by this Column. The material was carried & handed over to R.E.'s at various points according to their instruction. A great deal was returned to PHEASANT DUMP & PRESTON DUMP. A certain amount of the material was collected from dumps not previously erected. Was collected from wagons & tractor column. 10 G.S. wagons & 25 men were used for this fatigue.	
	16th			

WAR DIARY
or
INTELLIGENCE SUMMARY

(Erase heading not required.)

Army Form C. 2118

Instructions regarding War Diaries and Intelligence Summaries are contained in F.S. Regs., Part II. and the Staff Manual respectively. Title Pages will be prepared in manuscript.

Place	Date	Hour	Summary of Events and Information	Remarks and references to Appendices
	7th–16th		Gun pits etc Salvaged. Dump formed at Brigtire Farm from issue of material to Bdes. This supplied fatigue party of 40 men daily. Six – 10 q.s. wagons were sent daily to work in conjunction with ThM. Dump found was most useful to Bdes who could get supplies etc without any unnecessary delay. Ammunition delivery. The Sections gave great assistance to affiliated Bdes. On many days as many as 30 teams complete were out on this work. To issue 21st – 28th averaged 1 man & 2 animals wounded per casualties f night. Ammunition was also drawn in G.S. wagons from BB – York House, 15 wagon dump 2 trips. Having the 2 places of ammunition dumps greatly reduced congestion of traffic on road alongside the Div. A.R.D. 3b, No 2 Section of	
	14th		4 German Field guns were brought in from rearward area. This work casualties during this work was 1 sgt & 2 men. was carried out most effectually under very difficult conditions. The officers & N.C.O.'s in charge were an excellent example to their men.	

R. P. Bening Lt/Col.?
O. C. 1st D.A.C.

Army Form C. 2118.

19 D Ammo Coy
Vol 24

WAR DIARY
or
INTELLIGENCE SUMMARY.
(Erase heading not required.)

Instructions regarding War Diaries and Intelligence Summaries are contained in F. S. Regs., Part II. and the Staff Manual respectively. Title pages will be prepared in manuscript.

Place	Date	Hour	Summary of Events and Information	Remarks and references to Appendices
LOCRE	10th August		Column went to join troops at Verte Rue in Merville area, with the exception of No1 Section which on arrival is able for a further 10 days work the 87th FA Bde.	
	13.		O.C. RA inspected the Column which has had 5 days its previous 2 days in clearing up. Inspection was quite satisfactory.	
	22nd		The Column moved to billets in + around Outtersteene. No 1 Section being stabled near Croix Rouge.	

R C Pannington Poste
Capt R.F.A.
Capt 19 D.A.C.

19th Divisional Ammunition Column.

Army Form C. 2118.

Instructions regarding War Diaries and Intelligence
Summaries are contained in F.S. Regs., Part II.
and the Staff Manual respectively. Title pages
will be prepared in manuscript.

WAR DIARY
or
INTELLIGENCE SUMMARY.

(Erase heading not required.)

September 1917.

Vol 25

Place	Date	Hour	Summary of Events and Information	Remarks and references to Appendices
OUTTERSTEINE.	1-7.		Resting in OUTTERSTEINE area.	
	7.		No.3 Section moved complete to M 9 c (Sheet 28) becoming part of 19th D.A. Reserve Camp, formed for the purpose of centralizing the delivery of ammunition to the forward positions.	
	10.		Headquarters, Nos.1 & 2 Sections moved into billets in LOCRE area, H.Q. at M 23 d 6 9. No.1 Section at M 17 d 7 7, and No.2 Section at M 23 b 7 0. (Sheet 28)	
		10-30	Owing to the detachment of No.3 Section with the whole of their G.S. wagons fatigues have been fairly light. Small fatigues, such as delivery of R.E. material to forward dumps and empties from YORK HOUSE A.R.P., to KENNEBAC railhead carried out. Parties of 30 men were also employed to supplement personnel at Reserve Camp in the delivery of ammunition forward. In addition 50 men from 1 & 2 Sections were permanently attached to Reserve Camp for ammunition work.	

Lieut. Colonel R.F.A.
Commanding 19th D.A.COLUMN.

WAR DIARY
INTELLIGENCE SUMMARY

19 D Coy Army Troops Coy
October 1917

Oct 26

Place	Date	Hour	Summary of Events and Information	Remarks and references to Appendices
LOCRE	1-31		No 3 Section have worked direct from area of O/C 19th Reserve Camp in the delivery of ammunition, erection of cupolas & general camp fatigues. Nos 1 & 2 Section when on R E fatigues, have been also supplied personnel & transport to assist with the erection of permanent horse standings, such supervision of work.	

W Bonnin Lt
Capt & actg OC 19 DAC

Army Form C. 2118.

WAR DIARY
or
INTELLIGENCE SUMMARY.
(Erase heading not required.)

November 1917

Place	Date	Hour	Summary of Events and Information	Remarks and references to Appendices
LOCRE	1-12		Usual Carps & RE fatigues -	
	12		"B" Echelon moved to Corps Reserve area nits camp at X5a35. (sheet 27)	
	13		HQ & No1 Section moved to Corps Reserve area nits camp at X5a55 (TALLY HO CAMPS). No 2 section to RUDDIGORE camp M28d45 (sheet 26).	
		13.30	General cleaning up of camps. All horses clipped. Recreational training carried out.	

N.P.Bunney? Potts
CAPTAIN. R.F.A.,
ADJUTANT 19TH D.A. COLUMN.

19 D Arm Col
Army Form C. 2118.

WAR DIARY
or
INTELLIGENCE SUMMARY.

December 1917

(Erase heading not required.)

Place	Date	Hour	Summary of Events and Information	Remarks and references to Appendices
TALLY HO CAMP	1-12		Recreational training.	
SCHAEXKEN	4		Column Inspected by Divisional Commander.	
	13		Column moved to camp at CROIX de POPERINGHE.	
CROIX de POPERINGHE	15		No 2 Section moved to forward own AMS camp at N.E.	
	24		No 2 Section moved to camp at HALLEBAST CORNER	
	29		Column commenced rehearsing with batteries (Ugs wagon & HRA wagons for battery) 13 THIRD ARMY attacking at BAPAUME.	
Jan 1918	1		Column billeted in ROCQUINY CAMP for 2 days. Then marched to camp at NURLU entrail (Shelters) Ammunition (gun) dump at ARP at P12 d 40 (Nu ARP being taken over by 192 B.A. on Jan 24th.)	

A V Barring Roberts
Capt & Bay A.D.A.C

19th Divisional Ammunition Column.

WAR DIARY
or
INTELLIGENCE SUMMARY.
(Erase heading not required.)

Army Form C. 2118.

January 18

Place	Date	Hour	Summary of Events and Information	Remarks and references to Appendices
BEAULEN-COURT	Jan 2		General clearing up of vehicles, equipment to conform to D.A.C. concentration and new V Corps R.A.	
MEAULTE		11	Column marched via COMBLES, SUZICOURT to MEAULTE.	
			Owing to straw column remained in trucks till 16.	
BEHENCOURT	16th		Column marched to trucks at BEHENCOURT.	
		16-30	Clearing up of trucks, inclusion of stragglers + recreational training.	
		30	First relief of 200 men & horses sent for attachment with the DSOS 14 days battery training personnel.	

A.C. Barry
Capt RFA
Adjutant 19th D.A.C.

CAPTAIN, R.F.A.
ADJUTANT 19TH D.A.C.

Army Form C. 2118.

WAR DIARY
or
INTELLIGENCE SUMMARY.

(Erase heading not required.)

1st Divisional Ammunition Column

February 1918

Place	Date	Hour	Summary of Events and Information	Remarks and references to Appendices
BETHEN-COURT	Feb 2		Battery personnel returned to men from Column arrived all doing routine and not doing instruction & gaining interior economy.	30
	26		Recruitoid drawn and taken by having men. Preparation made to arrival of Italian personnel.	

W.C. Brown Lt. Ret.
Captain & OC
1st DAC

Army Form C. 2118.

19th Divisional Ammunition Column **WAR DIARY**
or
INTELLIGENCE SUMMARY.
(Erase heading not required.)

MARCH. 1918.

Place	Date	Hour	Summary of Events and Information	Remarks and references to Appendices
BEHENCOURT.	Mar. 7.		Column moved to BUIRE area to be within one days march of batteries. C.O. in command of Vth Corps Ammunition Columns (4 D.A.Cs and three B.A.Cs) Great difficulty was experienced in maintaining communication with these units and the various D.As owing to constant moves.	
BUIRE.	22 & 23.		Column moved to BAZENTIN le PETIT. H.Q. remaining at MEAULTE in order to be near Corps. S.A.A.Section sent forward to YTRES to work under direct orders of "Q" and to assist Infantry. This section did splendid work - officers, men and animals working day and night - apart from hurried moves which had to be made owing to the withdrawal of our troops. 9 extra teams sent to assist No.3 Sec. from 'A' Echelon. 24 teams sent forward to assist 88 Bde. owing to casualties in latter. 12 Guns (8 - 18 pdr. and 4 - 4.5 Hows. delivered to Column for despatch to 47th and 63rd D.As. 2nd D.A.C. 19th D.A.C. and 34th B.A.C. all camped at BAZENTIN le PETIT. 47th and 63rd D.A.Cs remained in rear billets at DERNANCOURT and were called upon to supply teams to assist with work. H.Q. removed to BAZENTIN le PETIT.	
BAZENTIN le P.	24.	(6.30 p.m.)	Column moved at short notice to BECORDEL,- heavy and field guns having come into action at BAZENTIN. Owing to teams sent to assist Brigades it was necessary for horses from No.1 Section to return together with teams from 63rd D.A.C. to BAZENTIN to withdraw 15 R.A. waggons which would otherwise have been left. This was accomplished without any casualties, only two R.A. limbers being left, these were destroyed by shell fire. Roads were being machined gunned by Enemy aeroplanes. Column rested in BECORDEL for 4 hours then moved to BUIRE owing to batteries having come into action in rear. BUIRE siding heavily bombed all night. Still great difficulty experienced in keeping in touch with various units. Orderlies of this H.Q. did good work during this time, being up day and night maintaining communication with Corps H.Q. and various D.As.	
BUIRE.	25.		Ammunition Columns marched to their own Divisions. Column moved to WARLOY. Drew from ROSEL gun park 12 guns for and delivered, to 58th Bde. No.2 Section split up and attached to 88th Bde. re-equipping latter. No.1 Section in direct touch with 87th Bde. R.F.A. Owing to Brigades being transferred from one Division to another, difficulty was experienced in obtaining rations. For two days rations for 87th Bde. and D.A.C. were	

Army Form C. 2118.

19th Divisional Ammunition Column. WAR DIARY or INTELLIGENCE SUMMARY.

March 1918.

(Erase heading not required.)

Place	Date	Hour	Summary of Events and Information	Remarks and references to Appendices
	Contd.		were drawn from nearest R.S.O. Teams attached to 88th Brigade rejoined Column.	
WARLOY.	26.		Column moved with 88th Bde. to HERISSART.	
HERISSART.	27.		Column moved to SARTON.	
SARTON.	28.		Column moved to HALLOY into Corps area - Corps area having moved southwards - remaining there 36 hours. Personnel and animals had first rest for 8 days. No.2 Section rejoined Column from 88th Brigade. No.3 Section joined from IVth Corps.	
HALLOY.	31.		Column marched to AUBREMETZ.	
			Casualties during period 21st to 31st March very slight. No.3 Sec. had 7 men missing, 34 animals and 5 S.A.A. carts lost.	
			Officers and men did all they were called upon to do, without faltering, in a most trying and difficult operation.	

[signature]

Lieut. Colonel R.F.A.
Commanding 19th D.A. COLUMN.

19th Divisional Artillery.

———————

19th DIVISIONAL AMMUNITION COLUMN R.F.A.

APRIL 1918.

19th Divisional Ammunition Column.

Army Form C. 2118.

WAR DIARY or INTELLIGENCE SUMMARY

(Erase heading not required.)

APRIL 1918.

Instructions regarding War Diaries and Intelligence Summaries are contained in F.S. Regs., Part II. and the Staff Manual respectively. Title pages will be prepared in manuscript.

Place	Date	Hour	Summary of Events and Information	Remarks and references to Appendices
AUBREMETZ.	1.		Column entrained at Petit Houvin and Frevent for Second Army area, detraining at Caestre and Godewaersvelde, and marched to camps around Outtersteine.	
OUTTERSTEINE.	3. to 9.		Column moved to lines on Bailleul Armentieres road. As far as possible the Column was refitted and deficiencies in personnel, animals and equipment made good after the operations on the Somme in which the 19th Division took part in March 1918.	
BAILLEUL-ARMENTIERS road.	10.		Column took over A.R.P. at Le Romarin. A.R.P. at La Polka taken over on 8th. SAA Section put under the direct orders of "Q" to work with the Infantry and attached to 58th Infantry Brigade.	
	11.		Column moved to LOCRE.	
LOCRE.	12.		A.R.P. formed at Bruloose Siding.	
MONT ROUGE.	13.		H.Q. D.A.C. moved to Mt. Rouge. T.M. Batteries attached to D.A.C. for work on A.R.Ps. H.Q. and No.1 Section moved to Reninghelst-Caméla Corner road. No.2 Section moved to Westoutre, moving on the 15th to the north western slopes of Mt. Rouge. A.R.P. transferred to Locre Avoiding Road.	
RENINGHELST.	15.		A.R.P. formed at La Clytte.	
BUSSEBOOM.	16.		Column moved to Busseboom area and A.R.P. commenced at Ouderdom.	
	19.		Column moved to Westoutre-Poperinghe road near Hoograaf Cabaret.	
HOOGRAAF.	20.		A.R.P. started at G.33.o.0.1. sheet 27. near Heksken.	
	21.		H.Q. D.A.C. moved to ———————————————— Abeele – Poperinghe road.	
	25.		Column moved to area around L.13. Sheet 27. near Abeele – Watou road.	
	26.		A.R.P. commenced on bye road off Poperinghe – Abeele road.	
	29.		Column came out of action and marched to Racquingham area where they encamped on Common.	
			During the period 10th – 28th April. the Divisional Artillery were heavily engaged continuously in the operations which commenced at Messines and Wulverghem and developed into the fight for Mt. Kemmel. Battery wagon lines were affiliated to Sections according to grouping of Batteries in the line and were located in the vicinity of the Section to which they were attached. Each time it was necessary to withdraw the wagon lines Section Commanders reconnoitred positions for the battery wagon lines as well as for their own Section.	

Army Form C. 2118.

WAR DIARY
or
INTELLIGENCE SUMMARY.
(Erase heading not required.)

Place	Date	Hour	Summary of Events and Information	Remarks and references to Appendices
	10-28th.		The teams of Sections and batteries were pooled and under the supervision of the Section Commanders the work of ammunition delivery to the guns was evenly distributed amongst all teams. The work was exceptionally heavy and this system proved the most satisfactory in dealing with the large amount of ammunition to be taken forward. The approximate amount of ammunition handled during this period was 120,000 rounds. Between the 10th and 19th the daily average was 11,000 rounds and between the 20th and 27th 8100 rounds. Taking into consideration the thorough method in which the enemy bombarded the back areas and roads leading to battery positions the casualties suffered by the D.A.C. were slight. Throughout this difficult and trying period all ranks performed their duty in a most exemplary manner, displaying wonderful cheerfulness, courage and scorn of fatigue in the face of all hardships and dangers and in no case was any shortage of ammunition at the guns reported.	

[signature]

Lieut. Colonel R.F.A.
Commanding 19th D.A. COLUMN.

Army Form C. 2118.

19th Divisional Ammunition Column.

WAR DIARY
or
INTELLIGENCE SUMMARY.

(Erase heading not required.)

MAY 1918.

Instructions regarding War Diaries and Intelligence Summaries are contained in F. S. Regs., Part II. and the Staff Manual respectively. Title pages will be prepared in manuscript.

Place	Date	Hour	Summary of Events and Information	Remarks and references to Appendices
Recquinghem.	May 1918. 1-18.		Column remained in Second Army rest area. Recreational and other training being carried out.	
-do-	18.) 19.)		Column entrained at ST.OMER and ARQUES and WIZERNES and proceeded on train journey duration of which was 36 hours.	
	19) 20.)		(4th French Army) Column arrived in CHAMPAGNE area/detraining at CHALONS sur MARNE and VITRY la VILLE,/marching to DAMPIERRE sur MOIVRE where they took over French Reserve Barracks, remaining there for eight days, during which time training was proceeded with.	
Dampierre. Tours.	28. 29.		Column marched at short notice to TOURS sur MARNE, where they were billetted for one night continuing the march to forward area and encamping around CHAUMUZEY, remaining there for one night, coming under orders of the 5th French Army.	
Chaumuzy.	30.		Column marched to NANTEUIL la FOSSE. The G.S. wagon echelons were ordered to march as a detached unit to the southern banks of the MARNE encamping at VAUCIENNES, the Ammunition wagons remaining at NANTEUIL for the supply of ammunition to the Batteries.	

(Sgd) Metcalfe.
Captain R.F.A.
Adjutant 19th D.A.Column.

Army Form C. 2118.

WAR DIARY
or
INTELLIGENCE SUMMARY.
(Erase heading not required.)

19th Divisional Ammunition Column.

June 1918.

Place	Date	Hour	Summary of Events and Information	Remarks and references to Appendices
Vauciennes & Nanteuil.	2.		G.S. wagon echelons moved to Vaudancourt.	
	3. to 19.		Headquarters and R.A. wagons of Nos.1 and 2 Sections moved to a position in the Bois de Reims 1 mile north of Hautvillers, remaining there until 20th June. During this period the Divisional Artillery were engaged in the operations around Bligny hill, the defence and recapture of which was carried out by the Division. The D.A.C. were occupied continuously throughout the operations in supplying ammunition to the 87th and 88th F.A.Brigades. For the purpose of the operations No.2 Sec of the 8th D.A.C. was attached to 19th D.A.C. until 4th June when they were relieved by No.2 Section 25th D.A.C. These Sections supplied ammunition to the 112th F.A.Brigade which was working under 19th D.A. under the title of BALLARDS GROUP. The daily average of ammunition handeled from 30th May to 9th June was 5200 rounds. The largest amount on any one day was 11000 rounds. As during previous operations, No.3 Section (SAA) were detached and attached to the Infantry, working under direct orders of "Q" Office. During the latter part of the operations good work was performed by officers and men in salving ammunition and empties from positions in close proximity to the front line in the Bois d'Eclisse and Champlat.	
Hautvillers.	20.		Column moved as a whole to Vertus, remaining there for one night. S.A.A. Section.rejoined on line of march.	
Vaudancourt.			Column moved to Bannes, remaining there in rest until 29th May during which period training and recreation were carried out. D.A.C. sports held on 28th May. on ground 3 K. south of Bannes. followed on 29th May by Divisional Artillery Sports.	
Vertus.	21.			
Bannes.	30.		Column commenced entraining from Sommesous, Fere Champenoise and Mailly le Camp.	

[signature]
Captain R.F.A.
Adjutant 19th D.A.Column.

Army Form C. 2118.

WAR DIARY
or
INTELLIGENCE SUMMARY.

19th Divisional Ammunition Column.

July 1918.

(Erase heading not required.)

Place	Date	Hour	Summary of Events and Information	Remarks and references to Appendices
SOMMESOUS.	2nd.		Detrained at ANVIN, marching to billets at MERCK St. LIEVEN.	
MERCK.	13th.		Column moved to FEBVIN PALFART.	
FEBVIN.	20th		Column moved to BOMY area.	
	5th to 30th.		Column remained in the reserve area undergoing training.	

Lieut. Colonel R.F.A.
Commanding 19th D.A.Column.

Army Form C. 2118.

WAR DIARY
or
~~INTELLIGENCE SUMMARY.~~
(Erase heading not required.)

Instructions regarding War Diaries and Intelligence Summaries are contained in F. S. Regs., Part II. and the Staff Manual respectively. Title pages will be prepared in manuscript.

19th D.A.C.

August 1918

Place	Date	Hour	Summary of Events and Information	Remarks and references to Appendices
Bouy	August 1918		Column undergoing training in this area	M36
	August 11th		Major R.A. Dyatt O.R.I.R. attached for duty as adjutant from D/87 S.G.Y	
	Aug 12th		Column Marched from Bouy to Marles-les-Mines	
	August 13th		Lt Col. R. Marques Bailie joined and assumed command of 19th D.A.C.	
Marles-les-M.	August 7th		Capt. M. Caliph attached to G.H.Q. for temporary staff duty	
	" "		Lt. M.B. Simpson M.R.C. U.S.A relieved by Lt H.S. Duckot M.R.C. U.S.A and posted to 55, 57 + 4.A.	
	August 14th		Inspection of Column by Lieut. Sir W.K. Birkwood KCB etc Commanding 5th Army	
	Aug 17th		Lt. J. Mundella R.H.A. finally relinquishes duties as adjutant & returns to Major Dyatt	
	August 18th		Column inspected by C.R.A. 61 Brigadier Genl W.F. Mulchone C.M.G. M.V.O.	
	" "		Major R.A. Dyatt posts to 6 th Army. Ret: Re: in general Conf.	
	Aug 23rd		No 2 Section D.A.C. march 5 cur arriving positions in closefire	
	Aug 26th		Hqrs D.A.C. and also No 1 and 3 Sections moved to Rue Bethame: Lt Duckel M.R.C U.S.A 32nd C.C.S. B.E.F	
Robecourse	Aug 30th		No 1 Section moved Annequin and relieved by Lt De Jones M.R.C. U.S.A.	
	Aug 31st			

Exley Lt Col.
CMDG. 19th DAC column

Army Form C. 2118.

WAR DIARY
INTELLIGENCE SUMMARY.
(Erase heading not required.)

Instructions regarding War Diaries and Intelligence Summaries are contained in F. S. Regs., Part II. and the Staff Manual respectively. Title pages will be prepared in manuscript.

Sept 1918

Place	Date	Hour	Summary of Events and Information	Remarks and references to Appendices
La Bouverie	Sept 1st 1918		A.R.P. & La Bouverie moved to Crucifix Hall Annequin	
	Sept 2nd	—	No details D.A.C. moved to Gonnehem	
	Sept 3rd	—	A.R.P.s opened at Long Cornet & Cornet Malo	
	Sept 5th	—	N.R.P.s opened at Colde d'Ecors & Ecors	
	Sept 11th	—	DAC moved to Canal Bank Bethune. ARP Long Cornet moved to Essars Zelobes Dump &	
	Sept 13th	—	Ezelles Dump opened at Locon. Cruxifix Dump Nulosses over by XIII Corps. Cornet Malo closed & to Zelobes.	
Bethune	Sept 14th	—	E.T.R.s Lieut. J.M. Parkhouse C.M.G. (?) M.O. for A.S.C. to be Capt.	
	Sept 16th	=	Lt. E D Jarrett U.S.A. posted to division. Relieved by Lt Keller U.S.A.	
	Sept 23rd	—	Invalides by CRA Major E.T.R. Peel CMG DSO) Zelobes Dump closed.	

Peel Lt Col R.A.
Cmdg. 14th D.A.C.

Army Form C. 2118.

19th Divisional Ammunition Column.   WAR DIARY or INTELLIGENCE SUMMARY.   October 1918.

Place	Date	Hour	Summary of Events and Information	Remarks and references to Appendices
Bethune.	6th.		Headquarters moved to Loisne Chateau.	
Loisne.	17th.		Column marched to Bethune and Chocques entraining for Bapeume and Fremicourt. Detrained and marched to Cambrai.	
Cambrai.	19th.		Column marched to Avesnes lez Aubert.	
Avesnes.	24.		Nos. 1 and 2 Sections moved to St.Aubert area, and placed under orders of 87th and 88th F.A. Brigades respectively.	
St.Aubert.	28.		No.2 Section moved to Montrecourt.	
-do-	30.		No.1 Section moved to Saulzoir.	

Lieut. Col. R?A.
Commanding 19th D.A.C.

19TH DIVISION

89TH BRIGADE R.F.A.
JLY 1915 - SEP 1916

BROKEN UP

19th Division.

H.Q. 89th Brigade R.F.A.

Vol. I.

14-31-7-15

Sept 16

131/1496

Army Form C. 2118

WAR DIARY
or
INTELLIGENCE SUMMARY

(Erase heading not required.)

89th Brigade. R.F.A.

Place	Date	Hour	Summary of Events and Information	Remarks and references to Appendices
BULFORD	14.7.15	4.30	Orders were received to embark on the 17th July. Units were busily engaged in drawing equipment.	MAP BELGIUM HAZEBROUCK 1/100,000
	15.7	4.30	Message with time table of entraining received	
	16.7	1 pm	Orders were received to commence drawing at 3 p.m. at half hour intervals. She units went to commence drawing at 3 p.m. but had been fine turned to a gale with heavy rain - great weather which had been fine turned to a gale with heavy rain - great delay was caused in the issue of the ammunition A & B batteries did not return to BULFORD until 10 p.m. and the ammunition column did not get back till after 4 a.m.	
	17.7		At 2.45 a.m. B battery left BULFORD followed by C. Bde. D. A. and HQ last train left at 12.15. The men had not slept or were changed the wet clothes, but they were all in the best of spirits at the prospect of getting to the front. On reaching SOUTHAMPTON the batteries embarked their wet clothes, but they were all in the best of spirits at the prospect on the S.S. COURTFIELD, the B. A. column on the KEPHERNES one the horses of the batteries on LA MARGERITE. The storm had passed over and it was a fine passage, the brigade arrived at HAVRE at 4 a.m. and were all disembarked by mid-day. The brigade (less B. battery) marched to no.1 Camp N. of the town. B entrained the same evening.	
	18.7		The units from No.1 Camp entrained during the afternoon in the following order. H.Q. and A. C. D. Bae. the first train left at 8.15 p.m.	
	19.7			

WAR DIARY
or
INTELLIGENCE SUMMARY 84 Brigade R.F.A

(Erase heading not required.)

Army Form C. 2118

Place	Date	Hour	Summary of Events and Information	Remarks and references to Appendices
BONNINGUES	20.7		H.Q. and A batteries arrived at ST OMER at 4.30 p.m. and marched to BONNINGUES (distance 13 miles) the other batteries and B.A.C. came in the course of the night.	MAP BELGIUM, HAZEBROUCK 1/100.000
"	21.7		General Coude R.A. 19th Division visited the billets in the course of the morning. Batteries were issued with smoke helmets. General FASKEN Comdg 19th Division, visited the billets of B. battery and H.Q. about midday.	
"	22.7		Since leaving BULFORD Casualties HAVRE. H.Q. 1 horse exchanged 1 man sick A.Batty 1 horse " B. " exchanged 5 horses SOUTHAMPTON 2 " " HAVRE 1 " " ST OMER 1 died MOULLE 1 Sick BONNINGUES C.Batty exchanged 5 horses HAVRE 1 sergeant sick HAVRE D " 1 " " HAVRE 1 man " BONNINGUES B.A.C " 16 " HAVRE	

Army Form C. 2118

89 Brigade R.F.A. (3)

WAR DIARY
or
INTELLIGENCE SUMMARY
(Erase heading not required.)

Instructions regarding War Diaries and Intelligence Summaries are contained in F. S. Regs., Part II. and the Staff Manual respectively. Title Pages will be prepared in manuscript.

Place	Date	Hour	Summary of Events and Information	Remarks and references to Appendices
WARDRECQUES	23.7.15		The Brigade took its place in the column at 10.20 at NORDASQUES, & marching with the 58th Brigade. There was a halt from 11.30 till 2, after which the march was continued via TILQUES. – ST MARTIN AU LAERT – ARQUES to WARDRECQUES where the brigade found billets for the night	REF MAP BELGIUM HAZEBROUCK 1/100,000
BOURECQ	24.7		The march was continued, the brigade reached the starting point at 9.0. There was a halt from 10.30 till noon, when the march was continued via AIRE and ST HILAIRE to BOURECQ, where the brigade was billeted.	
"	25.7		Halt	
"	26.7		Halt	
"	27.7		Halt	
"	28.7		Halt	
"	29.7		Halt. The billets were visited by the Commdr of the First Army Corps in the afternoon	
"	30.7		Halt	
"	31.7		The brigade marched at 9 a.m. via LILLERS – ROBECQ – CALONNE and arrived at MERVILLE at 2 p.m. after a halt for 1½ hours at CALONNE, the brigade moved into billets in the area LE SART. Signed SteD Rae Cmdg 89 Bgde RFA	

121/6787

19th Division

Sig/19/Bde: R.F.A.
Vol: II
August 15

Army Form C. 2118

WAR DIARY
or
INTELLIGENCE SUMMARY

89 Brigade. R.F.A. August 15 (1)

(Erase heading not required.)

Instructions regarding War Diaries and Intelligence Summaries are contained in F. S. Regs., Part II. and the Staff Manual respectively. Title Pages will be prepared in manuscript.

Place	Date	Hour	Summary of Events and Information	Remarks and references to Appendices
MERVILLE	1		HALT	Sheets 36 & 36A $\frac{1}{40,000}$
"	2		HALT	
"	3		HALT. Orders were received that 2 batteries were to be attached to LAHORE and MEERUT divisions respectively. Brig Cmdr went to see batt: Cmdrs of 60 and 61 batteries with a view to selecting positions and making arrangements	
"	4		HALT. Inspection of the Brigade by Sir J. Wilcox at 11.0. a. m. at 11 p.m. orders were received to select a battery for transfer to the 2nd Army. State of personnel and horses required.	
"	5		Capt~~ain~~ MILFORD and LIEUT WHITE went up for a course of instruction to b. batt: A Battery moved out at 1/5 p.e. to wagon line and detachments moved to batt: position accompanied the battery M10d 1 officer and section B.A.C. accompanied the battery in square M10d 1 officer and detachments moved to batt: position	
"	6		C battery moved at noon to wagon line A batty. orders received for Battery to march to in M.32.b. Brig Cmdr visited A batty. (a section of the B.A.C. accompanied C. battery.)	
"	※		the 28th Division	

WAR DIARY
or
INTELLIGENCE SUMMARY

Army Form C. 2118

89. Brigade R.F.A

August 15

Place	Date	Hour	Summary of Events and Information	Remarks and references to Appendices
MERVILLE	7		B Battery - strength 4 officers 128 other ranks (BARR attached) 122 horses 6 H.D. attached with B.A.C. section strength 1 officer 21 other ranks 27 horses and 3 G.S. wagons from D.A.C. moved out at 9.15 pm 28th Division at LUGRE. Brig Comdr visited C. Battery.	SHEET 36 8 36 D. $\frac{1}{40.000}$
"	8.		H.Q of Brigade with D/89 billeted at MERVILLE A/89 attached with MEERUT DIV. C/89 detached with LAHORE DIV. B/89 detached with 28th DIV.	
	9		"	
	10		"	
	11		"	
	12		"	
	13		"	
	14		"	
	15		"	
	16		"	
	17		"	
	18		"	

Army Form C. 2118

WAR DIARY
or
INTELLIGENCE SUMMARY
(Erase heading not required.)

89 Brigade R.F.A.

August 15

Place	Date	Hour	Summary of Events and Information	Remarks and references to Appendices
MERVILLE	19		Orders were received that the 19th Division would relieve the LAHORE Division and Brig Cmdr was instructed to arrange for D/89 relieving 61st Battery and to select position for H.Q.	Ref Maps Corpl Sheet BETHUNE 1/40,000
	20.		Arrangements were made to carry out the above orders	
	21.		Orders cancelled.	
	22.		Orders received to proceed to X 16 17 b. and reconnoitre positions for A/89 B/89 and C/89 in relief of the 37th Brigade.	
	23.		Above carried out. A/89 was relieved the night 23/24 by a battery of the 29th Division and returned to billets at LE SART. Information was received in the afternoon that C/89 would not be relieved for the present.	
	24.		Bde Cmdr with Battery Cmdrs and H.Q. left MERVILLE at 1.0 p.m. A/89 occupied position vacated by 35th Battery at X 17 d 9.8 and D/89 relieved the 31st battery at X 18 a.8.1. Batteries were relieved by one section at a time. One section from each battery moving into position at 9 p.m. on the night 24/25	

WAR DIARY or INTELLIGENCE SUMMARY

Army Form C. 2118

89th Brigade R.F.A. (4)

August 1915

Place	Date	Hour	Summary of Events and Information	Remarks and references to Appendices
RUE des CHAYATTES	25		Batteries engaged in registration. Second sections relieved sections of B/ and 35th batteries at 9 p.m. on the night 25/6 August	Ref Maps Corps Sheet BETHUNE 1/40,000
"	26		Forward Ammn Column relieved B.A.C. 3rd Brigade at 9 p.m. Batteries engaged in registration of fronts & allotted form FERME du BOIS. S.16.c.5 German trench in A.3.d.1.0 sub divided at S.27.b.9.3. D/89 allotted left and A/89 the right zone.	
"	27.		registration continued	
"	28		" registration continued	
"	29.	11.30	2 machine guns located at S.22.c.1.7. S.22.c.4.5. S.28.a.3.3. found registered batty A/89. The others by D/89.	
"	30.		Batts A/89 and D/89 fired a few rounds in retaliation. Left batteries engaged in proving communications and gun emplacements.	
"	31.		Ordns from B.G. R.A. 15 Gns. 30 rounds of Lyddite into enemy parapet at S.22.c.4.0. opposite the ORCHARD Salient. Same was carried out successfully by D/89. Only 50 yards between the trenches necessitated F.O.O. in the French considerable difficulty experienced in getting the line through. Same opened at 5/15 p.m. A/89 retaliated on a machine gun emplacement across roads S.28.d.3.3. at 3 p.m.	JMMcLinie Lt Col Comdg 89th Bde RFA

121/7051

19th Division

89th Brigade R.F.A.
Vol: 3
Sept. 15

Army Form C. 2118

89 Brigade R.F.A.
September 15

WAR DIARY
or
INTELLIGENCE SUMMARY
(Erase heading not required.)

Place	Date	Hour	Summary of Events and Information	Remarks and references to Appendices
RUE des CHAVATTES	1st		A wet day and little observing. Received communication about rear positions. Batteries engaged in "informing positions". Fired a few rounds in retaliation.	TRENCH MAPS. 36. S.W. SHEET 3 — 36. c. N.W.
	2nd		Another wet day. Very little doing. Battery commanders reconnoitred rear positions. Batteries strengthening emplacements and digging comm? trenches.	
	3rd	12 noon	Orders were received from G.O.C. R.A. 19th Div? to reconnoitre a new position for A/89 in square F5B 2.1. BETHUNE & Lille map 1/40,000. It was a very wet day. A/89 fired a few rounds in retaliation. D/89 was ordered to fire H.E.	
		2 pm	at a machine the arms of what resembled a crane appearing over the enemy parapet at S.22.A.60.55. The battery fired from 2 pm to 2.50. She gun appeared to be effective, a quantity of material was seen in the air. At the conclusion however the arm was still there.	
	4th		Brigade H.Q. telephone connected up with new position A/89. The gunners of A/89. Right Section moved off in the morning and worked all day clearing gun emplacements and cleaning up. B/89 retaliated at the request of the infantry on the German trenches in S.28.c.0.6 from 2.30 till 3.30	

1875 Wt. W593/826 1,000,000 4/15 J.B.C. & A. A.D.S.S./Forms/C. 2118.

WAR DIARY
or
INTELLIGENCE SUMMARY 89th Brigade R.F.A.

(Erase heading not required.) Sept. 15

Army Form C. 2118

(2)

Place	Date	Hour	Summary of Events and Information	Remarks and references to Appendices
H.Q and D/89.	4	5/Bde 5/20	D/89 at the request of the infantry retaliated on German trenches in S28 A.2.3. Time 17.20 to 17.40.	TRENCH maps 36 S.W. Sheet 3
RUE des CHAVATTES A/89.		10:15 22:45	Right section of A/89 moved from its position to new position abt. 20 on the 5th. A very wet day, heavy showers fell all through the night –	
Turning Fork E of GORRE C/89. alta LATTRE DIV.	5		Requests from R.A. Group Commanders I and II on howitzer fire in retaliation the former to demolish a minnen werfer at S 28 A.2.2. The latter to destroy some wires which appeared to be the opening of a mine shaft at S.22 c 5.3 H.E shell were asked for on German trenches opposite the CANAD(IAN) orchard.	36. e NW
		13	A/89 fired 10 rounds of Lyddite on the spot indicated in S28 A.2.2	
CROIX BARBEE.		15.25 to 17.10	D/89 fired on the trenches from S.22.e.5.3. to S.22 c 84. this fire appeared to be very effective. Registration of the junction of the Emma? trench at S.22 c.84. was carried on with the assistance of the balloon. Hostile air craft were more active German artillery shelled points near the RUE du BOIS some shell fell near D/89 in the afternoon most of them were duds.	
		22.45	The L/section A/89 moved into the new position.	

WAR DIARY
or
INTELLIGENCE SUMMARY

(Erase heading not required.)

Army Form C. 2118

Sept 15
30 Brigade R.F.A.

Place	Date	Hour	Summary of Events and Information	Remarks and references to Appendices
H.Q. and D/89.	6		Weather improving. G.O.C. R.A. 19 Division held a meeting of Brigade Comdrs at the Distillery of Co R.A. Group IND. 1. at 10.a.m.	TRENCH MAPS. 36.S.W Sheet 3
RUE DES CHAVATTES			A/89. registered targets from its new position, men were entrenching most of the day and night improving the position and making communications	36 c N.W.1
A/89.			D/89. Hostile Artillery more active. Some 15" Shell fell near the Battery. Registration was carried out with the assistance of an aeroplane, it was hoped to get some points near the ORCHARD but owing to engine trouble little result was obtained. Forward position for A/89 near FESTUBERT and for D/89 near the BREWERY near FESTUBERT were reconnoitred.	
TUNING FORK E of GORRE.	7.		Fine clear weather. Registering points. A/69 RUE D'OUVERT. D/89 LATURE AREA. Built batteries engaged in strengthening emplacements and digging communications. Enemy Artillery again fired a few shells on RUE DU BOIS while fell near D/89. Enemy aeroplanes more active.	
	8		Fine clear weather. D/89. emplacements required strengthening, overhead cover made, mines in details for and work begun. Batt Batteries fired a few rounds registration.	

WAR DIARY
or
INTELLIGENCE SUMMARY

(Erase heading not required.)

89th Brigade de R.F.A.
September 15

Army Form C. 2118

(4)

Place	Date	Hour	Summary of Events and Information	Remarks and references to Appendices
H.Q. and D/189. RUE DES CHAVATTES	9		Fine clear weather. A battery registered a target in the morning and was to have worked with an aeroplane in the afternoon but wireless communication failed. Strengthened rows of gun emplacements O.C. In o 2 asked for H.E. shell in German trenches opposite ORCHARD. Fired 5 rounds at 18 o'clock into German Support trenches –	TRENCH MAPS 36 & SW Sheet 3 36c NW 1
A/89 TUNING FORK E of GORRE	10		Fine clear weather A/89. Took numbers of O.C. Group IND I D/89 " " " " IND II Batt batteries busy laying and burying cables, A hostile aeroplane was brought down in front of C/89 at about 16. o.c.	
	11		Fine clear weather strong East wind. A/89. busy with communications. D/89. fired 13 rounds at the parapet of GERMAN S 22 C0 4 opposite CANADIAN orchard. The Germans had been firing H.E. shell into the front trench at the ORCHARD causing casualties. D/89's fire was very effective –	

WAR DIARY
or
INTELLIGENCE SUMMARY   89th Bde RFA
Sept 1915

Army Form C. 2118

Place	Date	Hour	Summary of Events and Information	Remarks and references to Appendices
Hdqrs + D/89 RUE DES CHAVATTES	12		Fine clear weather + very hot. A/89 making magazine recess & improving communications. Tried to work with aeroplane but machine did not arrive. D/89 Nothing to record.	Brussel Map
A/89 TUNING FORK E. of GORRE	13		Fine very hot. Very little doing. D/89 fired 6 rounds at night into German trenches opposite Salient.	36. S.W Sheet 3
	14		Cloud & misty morning, cleared later but rain in the evening. Quiet day. The enemy fired a few shell on the roads in the evening. Enemy in the Salient opposite CANADIAN ORCHARD gave trouble at night. D/89 fired 3 rounds lyddite.	36 e NW1
	15		Cloudy but fine weather. A quiet day. D/89 fired a few rounds testing various sorts of ammn. A/89 registered and line trenches at RUE D'OUVERT and tried to register with the 5·410m cg but it failed again.	

Army Form C. 2118

(6)

WAR DIARY
or
INTELLIGENCE SUMMARY

89th Bde. R.F.A.
Sept. 1915

(Erase heading not required.)

Instructions regarding War Diaries and Intelligence Summaries are contained in F.S. Regs., Part II. and the Staff Manual respectively. Title Pages will be prepared in manuscript.

Place	Date	Hour	Summary of Events and Information	Remarks and references to Appendices
Hdqtrs & D/89. RUE DES CHAVATTES.	16.		Dull & cloudy. quiet day until the evening when infantry were finished with bombs in CANADIAN ORCHARD, causing casualties. D/89 fired a few rounds in reply. A/89. registered lines & again attempted to register with aeroplane but it did not arrive. trying to get bridging material	
A/89.	17.		D/89 registered a point in RUE du PETILLON Bay and fired some AMATOL ammunition which was not satisfactory. A/89. spent the morning trying to register with an aeroplane but unless failed. In the afternoon however they brought off their registration & got 3 targets with 5 rounds. G.O.C. held a conference in 89th Bde. Hdqtrs at 5 P.M. Orders to have a	Send Sniper 36. S.W. Sheet 3 36 c. NW.1
TUNING FORK E. of GORRE:	18.		gun ready for ORCHARD SALIENT at all times. Fine day with East wind. 250 rounds of ammn. issued surplus to establishE + arrangements made for bridge for both batteries	
	19.		Fine clear day with East wind. Orders to fire a series of 30 rounds of AMATOL ammn. with 100 fuze. These were fired by D/89 into the German trenches at S27 c 4.8. Results not very satisfactory.	

Army Form C. 2118

WAR DIARY
or
INTELLIGENCE SUMMARY

39th Div. Arty.
Sept. 1916

(Erase heading not required.)

Place	Date	Hour	Summary of Events and Information	Remarks and references to Appendices
Hd Qrs at Dsa at RUE DES CHAVATTES. A/89. TUNING FORK. E. of GORRE	20. 21.		Fine weather, east wind, clear, not much during. Fine weather, east wind, clear. Bombardment of enemy trenches commenced at 8am. A/89 fired 94 rounds at 2nd line trenches in front of Rue D'OUVERT between 8.0 and 9.30 and were in action from 12.15 to 5 P.M. on the enemy second line trenches A3 d.3.4. to A3 b 4.5 and communication trenches A3 b 6.5½ to A 4. c 9.9 firing 16 rounds. D/89 commenced a bombardment of the enemy trenches opposite the ORCHARD salient, this was very effective, no. of rounds 104. The battery fired again at 2.30 P.M. at the support trenches behind the BOAR'S HEAD. S16 A5.4. number of rounds 94. at 2.45 the enemy way S10 d 6.3 to S11 c 3.5 was attacked along its entire length 16 rounds were expended and at 5 P.M. the battery fired on the tramway where it joins the communication trench S2 Ba 1.4 (13 rounds were fired). During the night the battery fired on the following points at the time stated. 10 P.M. S22 e 5.3 (two rounds) 11 P.M. DISTILLERY S 17 (eighteen rounds)	 Trench Maps. 36. S.W. SHEET 3 36 c NW 1

Army Form C. 2118

WAR DIARY
or
INTELLIGENCE SUMMARY 89th Bde. R.F.A.
(Erase heading not required.) Sept 1915

Place	Date	Hour	Summary of Events and Information	Remarks and references to Appendices

Ndgrs & D/89 RUE DES CHAVATTES. A/89. TUNING FORK E. of GORRE.	22.		A nice clear day – no wind and hot/fine
			At 0-30 D/89 fired 2 rounds at S.22.c.3.0
			    2-0 " " 4 " S.22.c.8.4
			    4-10 " " 2 " S.28.a.2.5
			
			A/89 from 11.10 until 12.35 bombarded the enemy front line trench from A.3.d.0.4 to A.3.a.9.2 fired 116 rounds with erasable effect. Fire from 12-40 to 13-10 15 rounds were expended in registering the following points A.3.d.0.2, A.3.d.2.4, A.3.d.7.4, A.3.d.9.5. From 13.15 to 14.30, 96 rounds were expended in bombarding ROTHESAY BAY. 27.c.6.1 to 27.a.1.6. The effect was reported excellent.
			D/89. 10-10 to 11-45 bombarded S.22.c.1.4 and S.22.a.3.1 (MOULIN D'EAU), (16-14) 30 rounds were expended with most satisfactory results support trenches were also well shelled and the H.E. shell were reported bursting in the trenches from 12.5, 13.20 S.22.a.2.8 and S.22.a.3.4 were attacked 50 rounds (16.34) were fired with similar results at 14.0. D/89 took part in a joint attack on the BOAR'S HEAD. S16A67 15 rounds were fired at the support trenches for the first five minutes after which fire was raised for 5 minutes when 6 rounds were fired on the junction of support and communicating trench. At 14-10, 30 rounds were fired on the BOAR'S HEAD with excellent results. The ground was covered with impenetrable smoke & dust no not dumps of air ents, clothing, material and furniture could be distinguished. At 22.30, 18 rounds were fired from the DISTILLERY S.17.A.7.7 and at 24.0. 12 rounds were fired in the trenches from S.22.a.3.4 to S.22.c.1.7.
				Trench maps
				
				36.S.W.
				SHEET 3
				
				36.c.N.W!

WAR DIARY or INTELLIGENCE SUMMARY

Army Form C. 2118

89th Bde. R.F.A.

Sept. 1915.

Place	Date	Hour	Summary of Events and Information	Remarks and references to Appendices
HdQtrs + D/89 at RUE DES CHAVATTES	23.		Bright with light clouds, still and hotter. D/89 fired at 2 o'clock on the trench from S.22 a 3.4 to S.22 c 1.9 with 12 rounds and at 11 o'clock fired another 18 rounds into the DISTILLERY. D/89 bombarded the COUR D'AVOUÉ and the ground in the vicinity from 11.40 to 12.45, 80 rounds were expended and the result appeared to be very effective. B/89 bombarded the	Travel maps 36 S.W.
A/89 at TUNING FORK			BOAR'S HEAD at 13.0 and expended 10 rounds afterwards they turned on to the French across to the LA BASSÉE road and expended 20 rounds, the battery then fired 10 rounds on to the covered way and 10 rounds on to a house at the Eastern end of the covered way. The effect on the BOAR'S HEAD appeared	Sheet 3 36 C.N.W.I
E. of GORRE			to be good. The support trench was difficult to observe, the enemy were very considerably knocked about. Several shelters were obtained but on its own little horse. At 15.0 o'clock B/89 fired 3.4 and re-enforced 5.3 were shelled in conjunction with a feint attack. The support trenches were also engaged 12 rounds were fired at the former and 10 at the latter. At 21 o'clock 11 rounds were fired at the DISTILLERIE and at 22 o'clock the head of the communication trench was again fired on (8 rounds) At 23 o'clock 4 rounds were fired into the COUR D'AVOUÉ. A/89 fired 192 rounds at 11 o'clock on the enemy's front trench from A.3.d.11 to A.3.a.8.2 and at 13.15 10 rounds were fired in the communication trench at A.3.d.6.7. At 14 o'clock 6 rounds were fired at a French billet at RUE D'OUVERT to assist D/89 in driving its position. Rain about 18 o'clock	

Army Form C. 2118

WAR DIARY
or
INTELLIGENCE SUMMARY

89th Bde RFA
Sept 1915

(Erase heading not required.)

Instructions regarding War Diaries and Intelligence Summaries are contained in F. S. Regs., Part II. and the Staff Manual respectively. Title Pages will be prepared in manuscript.

Place	Date	Hour	Summary of Events and Information	Remarks and references to Appendices
Hdqtrs + D/89 at RUE DES CHAVATTES	24		Wet and muggy weather. At 9 a.m. D/89 fired 6 rounds into the COUR D'AVOUÉ. At 7.45 to 8.20. 6 rounds were fired to enfilade the line on Reference at the N. end of the RUE D'OUVERT, at 9.0.5. 9.20, 9 more rounds were fired. 13 more rounds do were fired between 9-30 and 9.40. At 11.40. 29 rounds were fired into the FERME de TOULETTE very good effect through AMATOL was seen and there were 4 blind shells + 5 very poor bursts. At 15.45 28 rounds were fired at S22.b37 - S22.b85 and 20 rounds at S23.a04. Afterwards the horses	Special fuzes 36 S.W. Sheet 3
A/89. TUNING FORK			at LA TOURELLE and the LA BASSEÉ Rd were engaged 68 rounds were fired. the effect was very good. several horses were seen at a gallop. A/89 fired 192 rounds into the trenches on the RUE D'OUVERT from A4.c.04 to A.6.d.6.5. At 16.40 the battery fired 40 rounds into the french E. of the RUE D'OUVERT A3 d 95.4 and ten rounds to shorten into communication trench S.27.d.5.4	36 c.N.W.1
E. of GORRE	25		Weather still wet and misty. Operations commenced at 5.50. Reports of batteries given separately. A/89 reports at 5.60 accessory and smoke starting from the right rolled everything the front. only about a dozen of our infantry ever it seen the battery opened fire from 5.55 to 6.5 on points A3.d.2.2. A3.d.2.4. A3.d.7.4. A3.d.9.5 fired 40 rounds.	

Army Form C. 2118

WAR DIARY
or
INTELLIGENCE SUMMARY 89 Bde R.F.A.
(Erase heading not required.)   Sept. 1915

Instructions regarding War Diaries and Intelligence Summaries are contained in F. S. Regs., Part II. and the Staff Manual respectively. Title Pages will be prepared in manuscript.

Place	Date	Hour	Summary of Events and Information	Remarks and references to Appendices
Hd.qrs + D/89.	25 (contd)		From 6.5 to 6.20 fired on points A3d9.1, A3d9.8, A3b8.2, A3b9.4, A5b6.5, A3b6.4. H'd rounds. At 4.15 4 rounds were fired at A4c9.9. Messages were received at 4.55. Patrons and wiring had taken the firing line intact on the right.	French maps 36 S.W.
Ave des Chavattes			The attack was held up by machine gun fire from A3 & A34. Battery fired 20 rounds into the house and wire stopped by message from Bde. HQ.	Sheet 3
A/89.			that the infantry in consequence of arty. support fire taken first line at 8.25. 8 rounds were fired on A4c04. At 9.0 shelled trench A9 c 6.4 .15	36 c N.W.
Tuning Fork			A9 b 0.8 in accordance with orders received from Inf. Div. At 9.30 received orders to shell Pope's Nose (9 rounds). Information received 7.65 INDI reports	
E. of Gorre			that our left had reached the enemy trench but that the right was held up. "At 9.0 message was received that owing to machine gun fire from the crater no supports could be got up and an infantry boot to relieve our trenches.	
			D/89. At 5.50 me section opened fire on house at the N. end of the Rue D'Ouvert to protect the left of the 58th Bde. The other section fired 30 rounds into some strong works in S28.b. At 6.10 the right section was turned on the front trenches at S27.d.1.7 until the left section was held in reserve for any opportunity offered by the enemy retiring along the Rue de Marais. Dense smoke covered everything in our front which afterwards turned to mist + rain	

WAR DIARY
or
INTELLIGENCE SUMMARY

(Erase heading not required.)

Army Form C. 2118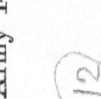

89th Bde. R.F.A.

September 1915.

Place	Date	Hour	Summary of Events and Information	Remarks and references to Appendices
Hdqtrs + Bty at RUE DES CHAVATTES.	26.		Fine after a very wet night. A/89 fired 210 rounds on point indicated by French Kmdr. 9th in as being the exit containing the machine guns, A 30 5.4. The enemy retaliated by fire from 4.4 and 4.2 how. on our support trenches and FESTUBERT. Otherwise quiet in front of IND. I. In the evening at 6 P.M. there was some heavy bombing in the south. D/89 very little doing.	Stencil maps. 36. S.W. SHEET 3
A/89	27.		Dull, showered to rain in the afternoon. There was no action.	36 C. NW. I
TUNING FORK.	28.		Dull but no rain.	
E. of GORRE	29.		Artillery more active. Some shell causing casualties fell into B/89 which was close beside D/89 and in the afternoon they searched for the Heavy battery but without success. Wet day very little going on.	
	30.		Weather improved, wind strengthened and the ground began its drying up but rain came on again in the evening. Any little happening A/89 fired 4 rounds to empty guns - into learning positions recently RUE DU VERT at VIOLAINES.	

J.M.Williames
Lt. R.F.A
Bomy of 89th Bde R.F.A.

121/7593

19th Hussars

8g th Bde: R.F.A.
Vol: 4
Oct 15

WAR DIARY
or
INTELLIGENCE SUMMARY
(Erase heading not required.)

Army Form C. 2118

89th Brigade R.F.A.
October 1915

Place	Date	Hour	Summary of Events and Information	Remarks and references to Appendices
A.89. F5b21	1		Weather bright and clear. No artillery action	TRENCH MAPS
D.89 X18a.3.2	2		Weather fine and clear. Orders were received re a change of position for A/89 and detachments were working through the earlier part of the night on gun emplacements, orders however were cancelled at midnight. The enemy 5.9 howitzer fired some shell which fell near B/88 on the left-left, D/89 at about 13 oc. Otherwise a quiet day	36 SW Sheet 3
H.Q. X17L02				36 NW Sheet 1
BETHUNE confined to 40.100	3	15	Fine cloudy and some mist, no artillery activity. No British batteries the British batting somewhat in the neighbourhood of the DISTILLERY falling just near B/88 one shell fell in a dug-out and killed Capt CHANCE 2nd Lieut HEPPLETHWAITE and 4 gunners. The first guns were HE they then changed to gas. Orders received regarding readjustment of line and change of zones – A/89 detailed and comes under orders of MEERUT Division, change of wagon lines to positions near VEILLE CHAPELLE ESTAIRE – LE BASSÉE	

WAR DIARY or INTELLIGENCE SUMMARY

(Erase heading not required.)

Army Form C. 2118

89. F.A. Brigade
October 15

Place	Date	Hour	Summary of Events and Information	Remarks and references to Appendices
A.89 F.5b 2.1	4		Rain in the morning — it cleared subsequently and kept fine for the rest of the day	TRENCH MAPS
		12	A/89 fired 12 rounds at a minenwerfer at S27 d 3.3.	36 SW Sheet 3
D.89 X18a 3.2		16	D/89. fired 52 rounds on machine guns and minen werfer at S21 D 83 and S21 D 8L.6 at 16. 0c. The fire was very effective 4 direct hits were obtained on the cupola. From 20.45 until 3 o.c. on the 5th the enemy shelled the ground in the vicinity of the battery (D 89) about 200 shell were fired.	36 NW Sheet 1
			The B.A.C. were ordered to send a section to the wagon lines of A/89	
H.Q. X17b.0.2	5		Rain all day and very thick weather. No artillery action A/89 minen werfer lines to X19b 9.4.	
Bethune Emp. maps 1/40.000	6		Fine clear weather. Work proceeding on new positions. D/89 fired 42 rounds at enemy's working party, the rounds A/89 S22 c 2.8 G S22 c 4.5. 2 enemy retaliated with 20 rounds from a 12.0 m.m. (Trench?) gun on of white fell close to Bsig H.Q.	
		17.0	Gun a very inferior cast iron shell.	
	7		Fine but rather misty. A/89. no activity.	
		16.30	D/89 fired 42 rounds at enemy trenches attacked from S22 a 2.8. to S22 c 4.6 in conjunction with 2nd group III the section of the enemy front will be bombarded. Trenches and works in rear	

Army Form C. 2118

WAR DIARY
or
INTELLIGENCE SUMMARY
(Erase heading not required.)

Sqtt Brigade
RHA
October 1915

(3)

Place	Date	Hour	Summary of Events and Information	Remarks and references to Appendices
A/89 F.56.2.1	8	14.30	Dull and misty. A/89 fired series as follows: 12 rounds at YIOLAINES 8 - A 3 b 6.5 6 - A 3 b 3.0 14 - A 3 b 3.4. 7 - trenches between A 3 d 0.6 and A 3 a 8.2 all in retaliation.	Trench maps 36 SW Sheet 3 36 NW Sheet 1
D/89 X.18.a 3.2		16.30	D/89 nothing to report.	
HQ X.17.b 0.2 Bethune Canal Wharf to H 40.000	9		Hostile howitzer battery shelled positions vacated by B/88 apparently under the impression that they were engaging a heavy battery. Dull and misty. No artillery action.	
	10	13.50 14.10 14.35	Neither Origlio, and sunny in the afternoon. Heavy firing heard to the South which continued most of the day. A/89 fired 6 rounds at a minenwerfer at the same target. At 14.35 9 rounds and at 14.10 another 11 rounds all in retaliation. D/89 were not firing were fired at A4.C 7.8 Brigade HQ changed to R 22 a 8.4.	

WAR DIARY
or
INTELLIGENCE SUMMARY

(Erase heading not required.)

Army Form C. 2118

Sqth S.O. Brigade
6 October 15

Place	Date	Hour	Summary of Events and Information	Remarks and references to Appendices
A/89	11		Fine weather. Heavy firing to the South.	Special maps
		13.15	A/89 fired 14 rounds at A 24 a 9.5 and A 17 d 5.4. Late registration	36 SW Sheet 3
F5b2.1		22.20	by aid of aeroplane. At 22.30 8 rounds were fired at A3 c 2.3.4. in retaliation.	N 36 SW Sheet 1.
D/89		15.20	D/89 fired 14 rounds for ranging seeing and destroying trenches and a	
X18a 3 2		15.45	cupula in A4 c 8. (8 and 9)	
H.Q.		15.50	4 rounds were fired at S22 B. 9. 6. (observation by aeroplane)	
R22 a 84			a failure because germans interfered with wireless	
BETHUNE Gun hut 1 40.OTO.	12	12.45 13.30	Weather cloudy but fine. A/89 fired series as follows. 3 rounds at S27b9.0. 2 at S27 d 6.8. 2 at S27 d 39. 5 at S28 a 8.3. (all registration)	
		4.10	At 14.10 it rounds were fired at S28b 1.5 and 3 at S28 a 14 at 14.30 one round was fired at S28 a 23.6. duds; with were observed at 1st 2nd 3rd 4th and 5th targets	
		15.0	D/89 fired 10 rounds at S22 c 2 8 with good results. at 15.0 the enemys howitzer fired 5 shells into the wood S of the eggaff D/89	
		6.0	enemys aeroplane was active over D/89. At 16.0.c 5 rounds were fired by D/89 with aeroplane observation at S 28 b 9.6. but again germans made it fruitless interference with wireless	

WAR DIARY
or
INTELLIGENCE SUMMARY
(Erase heading not required.)

Army Form C. 2118

No. 5

89 F.A. Brigade
October 1915

Place	Date	Hour	Summary of Events and Information	Remarks and references to Appendices
A/89	13		Rain in the morning. Turned fresh & clear about midday. Artillery demonstration by 19. Div Arty. D/89 did not take part but from 14.30 to 14.30 20 rounds were fired at machine gun emplacements in enemy FERME DU BOIS	Special Orders
F51-21		14.		36 S.W. Sheet 3
D/89			A/89 took part in the attack made by the 2 Corps and at 12 noon commenced continuous firing the afternoon. Objective CANAL ALLEY	36 N.W Sheet 1
X.18.A 3.2		12	A/7 & central N7 A 24 b-a 5. 286 rounds were fired and balloon reported good formation made by the 4.5 Howitzers	
H/8				
X17 b 0 2 R22 a 84 Bethune Canal	14.	14.50	Windy and colder. A/89 fired 35 rounds at a house in S27 2 3.6 at the request of the infantry. 19 direct hits were recorded. D/89 fired 14 rounds at the FERME du Bois at the request of the infantry with very good effect	
Junctn				
40000				
	15		Still misty and cold. No Artillery action	do
	16		do	

Army Form C. 2118

WAR DIARY
or
INTELLIGENCE SUMMARY
(Erase heading not required.)

89. F.A. Brigade

No 6

Place	Date	Hour	Summary of Events and Information	Remarks and references to Appendices
A 89 F 5 b 21	17.	13.50	Sea misty, both wind and cold. A/89 fired 10 rounds on S.27.Z.3.3. at the request of the infantry B/99.	French maps 36 SW 3
D. 89			Bright, wild weather. NE wind.	36 NW.1
X 18 a 32	18	14.0 14.35	A/89. fired 9 rounds at a suspected machine gun emplacement at S.27.Z.2.3.3. 11 rounds at a suspected obs station at S.28.b.15. and no rounds at BEAU PUITS.	
HQ		14.0	B/89 fired 16 rounds against a point at S.16 a 4.7 (BOARS HEAD) being a good deal of debris was thrown up direct hits on the parapet and a ruined house at RUE D'OUVERT S27d36 were observed.	
A/89 C/91 R22 A 84		14.50 15.20	20 rounds were fired after 6 direct hits was a small parties on a small parties.	
BETHUNE Coal Mine	19	14.35 15.15	NE wind cold. Orders were received regarding a move to fine clear weather A.89. A fighting form in A.5 entd. 7 rounds fired 5 rounds in S.29.2.4.6. and 10 rounds at a machine gun in former area. A similar form in S.27.2.3.3.(3 direct hits were reported). were reported (S.16c 7.1 b 322 a 7.8 effect	
		12.	B/89 fired 17 rounds at enemy lines good.	
40·000		15·15	25 rounds were fired at a suspected Obs Station in same area. Also fired 10 rounds at S22c 27 in retaliation for	
	20.	12.25 12.45	Cold, windy, occasional sunshine. At request of infantry – combined dummy Staffs 6. B/89 fired 14 rounds at the enemy trenches and S.22 a 17 at 17.55 when	
		15·15 17·55	request of the infantry on S22 e 18 (from lines and S.22 e 17 a 17 at 17·55 when enemy commenced bombing our trenches. 9 rounds were fired and bombing ceased.	

WAR DIARY
or
INTELLIGENCE SUMMARY

(Erase heading not required.)

Army Form C. 2118

89. 4 A. Parry[?]
hw 7

Place	Date	Hour	Summary of Events and Information	Remarks and references to Appendices
A/89	21.		Panzyle HQ returned 6 X 17 b 0 2. Misty dull toned down in the evening	Special maps
F 5 b - 2,1		12.25	A/89 fired 23 rounds. registering and connecting lines parallel A at A 3 d 0.5 and	36 SW 3
		13.20	A 3 a 6 7	36 NW 1
			D/89 nothing to report.
D/89	22		Fine, clear, and cold
X 18 a 3.2		11.45	A/89 fired 2 rounds at enemy working party at S.27.d.3.3, work ceased
HQ		16.20 }	" fired 78 rounds at Cupola S.22.c.2.8 in Registration retaliation
		16.50 }	
X 17 b . 0.2		13.30	C/89 fired 6 rounds at S.16.a.7.8 } in retaliation
Battene		14.30	6. rounds at S.16.b. 9.9
Comd		15.30	8 rounds at S.16.d.9.6
map		17.00	D/89 fired 10 rounds at the loco b'Avove at the request of Gurkhas who we being bombed, bombing shelling ceased.
1/40,000			Fine but misty arorbl.
	23	12.10 }	A/89 fired 15 rounds at a house in S.27.d.3.6 reported to be a work in course of construction
		15.00 }	
		15.30	C/89 fired 26 rounds at the salient in S.16.a a good deal of plumbing destroyed
			Enemy retaliated at 16.00 o'c
			D/89 No artillery action

WAR DIARY
or
INTELLIGENCE SUMMARY
(Erase heading not required.)

Army Form C. 2118
No. 8

89 La Belle
Oct/15

Place	Date	Hour	Summary of Events and Information	Remarks and references to Appendices
A/89 F.5.b.2.1	24		Duel turned to rain at 14.0 but cleared later	Trench Maps
		15.45? 16.10	A/89 Fired 11 shell at houses churches at ROTHESAY BAY S.27.d.1.4 in retaliation for shelling of ORCHARD trenches	36.S.W.3. 36.N.W.1
D/89		12.00 12.30	D/89 Fired 33 rounds at front line trenches east at 16.00 Fired 5 rounds at S.16.c.6.4.	
X.14.a.3.2.		16.00	N.E. gale and rain all day	
H.2. X.17.b.0.2	25		A/89 Nothing to report C/89 Withdrew from it's position with LAHORE Bri. and marched to wagon line at X.13.C.6.2	
BETHUNE Cem Bund Sheet 1 40.000	26		D/89 No artillery action. Fine clear day. The enemys aeroplanes were very active in the morning, between 14 & 15 o'clock the enemy shelled the area X.18.a. and c with 77 mm. and 120 c.m. Some shell fell in D/89 position but no damage was done A/89 Fired 5 rounds in registration, retaliation, & testing barrage C/89 Took up it's position with our action at 20.00 o'clock (X.18.C.O.2.)	
	27	14.20 15.30	D/89 Fired 10 rounds at block house S.22.d.1.3. Registered, some debris was thrown up. The/89 Rain cleared towards mid day	
		16.00	A/89 No artillery action C/89 Fired 11 rounds on S.27.d.3.6 in registration. Remaining section moved into position at 20 o'clock	
		12.45	D/89 Fired 8 rounds on Longue Church observing station, two direct hits our causing considerable damage	

WAR DIARY
or
INTELLIGENCE SUMMARY

(Erase heading not required.)

Army Form C. 2118

No. 9
89th F.A.Bde.   Oct 1915

Place	Date	Hour	Summary of Events and Information	Remarks and references to Appendices
A/89 F.3.b.2.1	28		Rain nearly all day at 16 o'clock an enemy aeroplane flew westward over FESTUBERT A/89 No artillery action C/89 No artillery action. Too misty for observation D/89 No artillery action	French maps 36.S.W.3 36.N.W.1.
C/89 A.18.C.O.8 D/89 X.18.A.3.2 H.Q X.17.b.0.2 Bethune Combined map 1/40000	29	11.30 14.00 10.45 11.30 15.35	Cold damp misty all day, cleared towards evening. A/89 No artillery action C/89 Fired 36 HE Shell in registration of the following targets. S.27.d.3.6, S.27.C.6.1 A.3.b.8.5, A.4.c.2.7, A.3.d.1.4, A.3.c.9.9. D/89 Fired 14 rounds at works in S.22.d.6 in registration. Registration carefully carried out on North and West front of work.	
	30		Cold and damp all day. A/89. Fired 12 rounds in retaliation at gun emplacement just to the right of S.28.a.8.3. Our Set see cottage. S.28.a.8.3 where very approximate to the spot where flash was located. C/89 No artillery action D/89 Just afterwards No artillery action	
	31.		Cold & damp, rain in the morning. A/89 No artillery action C/89 No artillery action D/89 No artillery action	

19th Hussars

89th Bde: R.F.A.
Vol: 5

121/7656

Nov. 15

CONFIDENTIAL

WAR DIARY

OF

89TH BDE. R.F.A.

from 1st. Nov. 1915 to 30th. Nov. 1915.

Army Form C. 2118

WAR DIARY
or
INTELLIGENCE SUMMARY
(Erase heading not required.)

89. J.A. Brigade
November 1915

Instructions regarding War Diaries and Intelligence Summaries are contained in F.S. Regs., Part II. and the Staff Manual respectively. Title Pages will be prepared in manuscript.

Place	Date	Hour	Summary of Events and Information	Remarks and references to Appendices
A/89	Nov 1.		Damp and misty all day rain at intervals	French notes
F5b 2.1 C/89.			No artillery action	36. S.W. 3 36 N.W. 1.
X 17D 9.7	2		Rain most of the day. No artillery action	
D/89	3		Damp and misty No artillery action	
X18A 3.2 HQ.	4		Weather cleared. No artillery action	
X17b.0.2 to X19d 8.8			Brigade HQ. moved to X 19d 8.8.	
Bethune Comb Map 1 40,000	5		Cold damp and misty. A/89 dispersed a hostile party with 2 rounds, at A4 c 78. C/89 fired 10 rounds at VIOLAINES registration D/89. No artillery action	
	6		Frost misty weather damp and cold No artillery action.	

Army Form C. 2118

WAR DIARY
or
INTELLIGENCE SUMMARY
(Erase heading not required.)

89. F.A. Brigade
November 15

(2)

Instructions regarding War Diaries and Intelligence Summaries are contained in F.S. Regs., Part II. and the Staff Manual respectively. Title Pages will be prepared in manuscript.

Place	Date	Hour	Summary of Events and Information	Remarks and references to Appendices
A/89 F5b 2.1	7		Fine and cold. A/89 fired 14 rounds at 14.35 on barricade in RUE DU MARAIS S28 b.1.5 and at 15.35 13 rounds at the same target. 9/89. 2/89. no artillery action	Special maps 36. SW 3 36 NW 1
C/89 X17d 9.7	8		Fine and cold. Enemy shelled left front of D/89 and road S7d from 14.15 to 16.30 with 5.9 and 77 mm about 40 shell in all — no damage done. a large proportion of duds	
D/89			At 12/40 A/89 fired 8 rounds at barricade RUE du MARAIS S28 b.15 enemy working party dispersed, stretcher requisition. D/89 from 15 to 15.45 fired 16 rounds reporting S27 e 5.6 C/89 in artillery action. 9/89 detached to 46th Division, arrived at 2 guns to S1d42 and 1 gun to M34c55	
X 18a 3.2 HQ X 17d 88	9		Fine morning showers rain at 16.30 Strong SW wind. A/89 fired 2 rounds at S27 b.82 and 3 at S27 d 33. (Confirmation of register) at 10.45 at 14.55 fired 4 rounds in conjunction with D/87 at S28 b.15 (hoc was bomraed) at 15.50 fired 8 rounds at A3 d 3.4 A/C03 A 3 b 65 and S27 d 33. detached of 87 Brigade R.F.A. D/89 fired 44 rounds at the cupola and trenches with vicinity of S22 c.4.3. Bombardment in conjunction with the 18pr batteries and II group between 14.15 and 15/30. Good effect. N eff The enemy shelled the ground occupied of the position at 14/20. 9/89 moved remaining guns to S1d42	
Battery Empl Holl? Lo oso	10		Still less wind no rain. A/89 at 15/20 fired 6 rounds at a battery in turnaware at 9/10. 2 rounds were fired were seen at S 29 b 33 Battery silenced at a workingparty at the barricade S28 b.15	

1875 Wt. W593/826 1,000,000 4/15 J.B.C. & A. A.D.S.S./Forms/C. 2118.

WAR DIARY
or
INTELLIGENCE SUMMARY
(Erase heading not required.)

Army Form C. 2118

89. F.A Brigade
November 1915 (No 3)

Place	Date	Hour	Summary of Events and Information	Remarks and references to Appendices
A/89 F.5.b.2.1 D/89 X.18a.3.2 H.Q. X.17d.8.8.	10		B/89 from 12.20 to 17.20 fired 17 rounds registering trenches from A3.2.0.5 to A3d 6.7 also houses in RUE DOUVERT (oblique fire) the effect was good many shell fell in the trenches from 15/30 to 16/30 (with aeroplane obs=) 12 rounds were fired to register numbers at S28 d 36 and S 22 b 61, this was successful at 12/30 the enemy fired 12 rounds on the Biff. front of the battery (5.9)	Search nobs 36 SW. 3 36 NW. 1
	11.		Still wind increasing from the west, rain began at dusk. A/89. fired 3 rounds at 9/30 at the barricade S28 b. 1.5 and at 11/30 5 rounds were fired at S27 b 9.0. at request of infantry. D/89. no action. The enemy shelled the obs station on the RUE DU BOIS. S15A1, known as the NOOK from 12 h/15. oc. Shell fire at about 3 min intervals from 5.9 how. Shell detonated well. 50 to 60 shell were fired and firing ceased when the forming of the loose fell. Shell detonated well as an OP. the house was infiltrated as the main wall was uninjured.	
Battime emb map ↓ LOTOS	12		Westerly gale and rain. A/89 fired 3 rounds at 10.5 at A3 b 6.7 enemy working party and at 17.30 one round was fired at the barricade. S28 b 15. D/89. no action. Hostile artillery at 15.30 fired 5 5.9 shell and about 30. 77mm shell on the RUE DU BOIS S of RR bridge.	
	13.		Northerly wind cloudy and very cold. C/89. fired 2 rounds also burst at S28 b. 1.5. D/89 no artillery action.	

Army Form C. 2118

WAR DIARY
or
INTELLIGENCE SUMMARY
(Erase heading not required.)

89. T.A. Brigade
November 15 (No 4)

Place	Date	Hour	Summary of Events and Information	Remarks and references to Appendices
A/89	14		Fine clear weather much colder. A/89 at 9/10 fired 2 rounds at a working party at S.28 d.1.6. and at 12/40 6 rounds Hospital	
F 5 b 2 1			Church and 4 at S.27 d 3 3. B/89 no artillery action.	Sketch Maps
B/89				3.I & SW 3
X 18 a 3 2	15		Fine clear day cold. A/89 fired 11 rounds at a house in VIOLAINES	36 CNW.1
HQ			B/89 no action reported. The enemy fired 9.10 cm shell on the right of the Battery on the	
X 17 d 88			RUE DU BOIS at 15.15	
	16		Fine but light rain commenced in the evening V. cold. A/89 fired 11 rounds at a house in the night of VIOLAINES between 13.25 and 14.v.e. B/89. no artillery action.	
Battews Emplmts	17		Cold, Strong North wind constant showers of rain and hail domed between 8 and 2.15 pm, then clouded over again. Fine night and frost. Heavy artillery shelled the HUMP 89 shown in diagram of enemy trenches opposite ORCHARD in evening retaliation. No action necessary at 15.20 A/89 fired 8 rounds at 15.6.6.0 where an enemy battery was reported to be in action.	
no over	18		Fine frosty very cold. & No artillery action.	

Army Form C. 2118

WAR DIARY
or
INTELLIGENCE SUMMARY
(Erase heading not required.)

89. F.A. Brigade
November 15 No (5)

Place	Date	Hour	Summary of Events and Information	Remarks and references to Appendices
A/89 F.S.2.1 C/89 X12d2q7 D/89 X18a.3.2 H.Q. X.17.d.8.8. Bethune cnds huts	19		Fine misty East wind. A/89 fired 8 rounds at 10.30 at a human wagon at A3d 67 at 14/5. 4 rounds were fired Brigader a Cheval in S27 d 33 and 4 rounds Brigader a Cheval at A3d 34 at 15.05. 8 rounds were fired at the machine gun emplmt. near A3d 22 (4 direct hits) at 15.15. 4 rounds were fired at S28 d 26.6 in retaliation and 2 rounds were fired at VIOLAINES in registration. D/89 fired 17 rounds from 15 to 15.30 at trenches S22 c 3.6 & S22 c 44 with good results.	Sketch maps 36 SW 3 36 NW 1
	20		Cold light cloud misty. A/89 fired one round at a working party at 9/30 in S28 d 5.5. 5 rounds at 11/30 at VIOLAINES church in registration. 14 rounds (including 4 direct hits) in a house at the R of VIOLAINES at 15/25. D/87 registered working party in S28 b 15 (burricoat). D/89 fired 22 rounds at trenches S22 c 36 & S22 c 44 very satisfactory the parapet was destroyed.	
	21		Cold fine (misty for observation). A/89 fired 14 rounds at VIOLAINES at 12.10 and 10 rounds at 12.30 at the HUMP. (A4 c 78) D/89, no artillery action. B/89 withdrew one section at 17/30 & relief by 1st Derby Battery and this section marched & reserve billets at & HAMET BILLET P14 a. SW. of S. VENANT	
	22		Cold fine misty. No artillery action. A/89. D/89. one section B/89 withdrew from their positions at 17/30 and marched & reserve billets at P14 a. (HAMET BILLET).	

Army Form C. 2118

WAR DIARY
or
INTELLIGENCE SUMMARY
(Erase heading not required.)

89. F.A. Brigade
November 15 No (1)

Place	Date	Hour	Summary of Events and Information	Remarks and references to Appendices
HAMEL BILLET	23		Thaw set in at 7.0 a.m. Brigade HQ and B.A.C. returned at 7.0 a.m from Reserve Billets at Pys (HAMEL BILLET)	
Map 36A/1 40.000	24		} Brigade in Reserve Billets, all ranks washing cleaning up and training	
	25			
	26			
	27			
	28			
	29			
	30			

H Williams
Lt Colonel
Cmdg 89 F.A. Brigade

8g ⁶⁸Bde. R.F.A.
vol. 6

131/790

Dec 1915

19ᵗʰ Div

CONFIDENTIAL

WAR DIARY.

OF

89TH BRIGADE, R.F.A.

from 1st December 1915 to 31st December 1915.

(Volume 6.)

WAR DIARY or **INTELLIGENCE SUMMARY**

Army Form C. 2118

89th Brigade R.F.A.

December 15

Place	Date	Hour	Summary of Events and Information	Remarks and references to Appendices
HAMET BILLET	Dec. 1		Brigade at rest in HAMET BILLET	
	2.		At 23 o'clock orders were received for Brigade Commanders. They were to meet G.O.C. R.A. at FOSSE where orders would be issued, one section of each battery was to be prepared to move into action on the afternoon of the 3rd.	MAP (One) BETHUNE 1/40,000
	3.		Weather was wet and stormy. Brigade Commanders met G.O.C. at 11 and instructions as to taking over the positions occupied by the 46th Divisional Artillery were received. One section of each battery moved off in the afternoon and took up positions as under. A/89. Two guns firing in enfilade one at PONT LOGY M.34.c.6.3 one in RUE DU BOIS at S.13.a.9. C/89 relieved one section of 2nd Derby Battery T.F. at M.32.b.4.4. D/89 relieved one section of 1st Derby Battery T.F. at X.18.A.3.2 the 4th North Midland	TRENCH MAP 36 S.W. Sheets 381
	4.		Brigade Head Quarters moved at 7.0 a.m. and relieved H.Q. Brigade at R.35.b.9.8 remaining sections of batteries relieved remaining sections of the 1st and 2nd Derby Batteries after dark. A/89 moved into position at M.26.d.9.8 (less one section) C/89 registered the distillery at S.17.c.8.8 with 5 rounds at 11.45 a.m. and at 12.15 the FERME DU BOIS with 5 rounds at 12.15 D/89 registered FERME DU BOIS with 7 rounds at 12.30 and zero line with 9 rounds at 13.0.	
	5			

Army Form C. 2118

WAR DIARY
or
INTELLIGENCE SUMMARY

89th Army de Rifle

(Erase heading not required.)

Place	Date	Hour	Summary of Events and Information	Remarks and references to Appendices
	Dec 5th		Weather dull, mild, raining at intervals. BAC relieved BAC of 4th N.M. Brigade at R25e95	Trench Maps 36 S W 1 & 3
A/89			A/89 registered zero line from new position at 14.45 with 10 rounds at 311 d 2.2	
M2bd98			C/89 registered 311 d 1.1. with 10 rounds at 10.30 and with 3 rounds at 15.15 at 0.45 2 rounds were fired on the FERME DU BIEZ in retaliation	
C/89			B/89 registered FERME du Bois with 3 rounds at 12 noon. dispersed a working party S23 d 9.1. with 9 rounds at 13.0. and registered FERME DU BOIS with 7 rounds at 13.20	
M32 b-4.4	6		Fine morning, strong wind turned to rain in the evening	
B/89			A/89. fired 12 rounds at 13.20 registering S6a64 S6a32 and MUSKRAT MOUND and at 14.15 9 rounds to register frontline trenches and FERME DU BIEZ	
X18a 32			C/89. registered S6a54 with 3 rounds at 13.0. and fired on O.P at 311 d 4.8. with 6 rounds at 14.0 one direct hit - the wind was too strong for accurate shooting	
HQ. R35 e98			B/89. from 10 till 10.40 fired 58 rounds at S16 a.5. 1/2 parapet considerably damaged at 17.40 and 19.30 2 rounds and 30 rounds were fired at S16a.77 other of group	
			Lt. Col. H.M.THOMAS. took over command of Divisional Artillery vice Br. Gen. C.B LAWRIE who took over Command of the Division, Vice Maj. Gen. FABIKEN, on sick list. MAJOR MILFORD assumed command of the Brigade. A/89 registered S17 d 9.9, S16 d 77 S16 d 69 S17 a 05 with still wet weather very windy.	
	7		8 rounds at 11.30.	

WAR DIARY or INTELLIGENCE SUMMARY

Army Form C. 2118

89. Brigade R.F.A. (3)

Serrulier

Place	Date	Hour	Summary of Events and Information	Remarks and references to Appendices
	Dec 7		Continued	TRENCH MAPS.
A/89			C/89 at 10.30 fired 10 rounds at suspected O.P. at S.11.d.1.1. at 11.30 3 rounds at S.17.a.0.5. (new trench) at 14.30 4 rounds at S.23.a.8.4 (flashes of 77mm gun) at 15 p.m. 25 rounds were fired at S.11.d.4.8. There were 10 hits. Little	36. 9. W.
M.26.d.9.8.			have been fired at often and enemy's batteries there was little displaced	Sheets 38 & I
C/89			of the nine. 4 rounds were fired at x roads T.7.d.2.6. and T.7.c.2.9. S.12.d.3.7. S.12.d.7.6. FERME DU BIEZ and from S.11.d.6.4 to LA TOUFELLE at S.20.0 and
M.32.b.4.4.			at intervals of 15 min on account of a reported relief
D/89			B/89. No artillery action.
	8		Very wet and stormy.
X.18.a.3.2.			A/89 fired 16 rounds at S.16.a.6.6 and S.22.a.5.8 registration C/89. fired 5 rounds at LORGIES at 14.0. 31 rounds at new trench S.17.a.0.5. (trench
HQ			damaged for about 100 yards) at 14.0. 2 rounds at lorne T.8.b.6.9. at 15.30 2 rounds at trench S.17.a.0.5. at 18.15. 18.45 and 21.15. to delay work in
R.35.c.9.8.			D/89. at 11 a.m. fired 12 rounds at S.16.e.5½.9½. 13 rounds at the FERME DU BOIS and 26 rounds at S.16.e.5½.9½. by order of Group Commander a good deal of damage seemed to have been done.

Army Form C. 2118

WAR DIARY
or
INTELLIGENCE SUMMARY
(Erase heading not required.)

89. S.A. Brigade (4)

Place	Date	Hour	Summary of Events and Information	Remarks and references to Appendices
A/89 M26d98	December 15 9		Windy and dull towards evening. Some rain but light. A/89 at 16.5 fired a round at S5A53 and at 20.5, 6 rounds at S5a53. By order of Group Commander C/89 at 11.10 fired 10 rounds at Salient S5d at 11.30 to 15.30 12 rounds were fired to prevent repairs and 6 rounds were fired at 20.0. to get the working party. D/89 no artillery action.	TRENCH MAPS at S13a91 fired 5 S19b46 36 SW Sheets 3&1
C/89 M32b44	10		Rain in the morning, cleared in the afternoon but heavy rain at night A/89 12.15 - 14.0 fired 48 rounds into trenches and houses around LES BRULOT and at 20.0. repeated with 6 rounds in continuation of scheme	
D/89			C/89 at 11. fired 7 rounds at the trenches S5d 2.3. at 11.30 8 rounds were fired at the DISTILLERY and QUINQUE. RUE to register the enfilade gun from its new position, at 14.0 7 rounds were fired at S5d 2.3, the enemy	
X18a32 H.Q.			trenches were full of water and quantities of mud were thrown up. 5 rounds were fired at house S6a 4. 2½ at 15.15 and 8 rounds were fired at S17a17 at 16.0 and at 20.34 rounds were fired at S5d 2.3	
R35c98			D/89. at 9.30 fired 10 rounds at the FERME. DU BOIS. at 11.30 fired 18 rounds at the orchard S16b68 at 12.15 fired 32 rounds at the FERME DU TUVLOTTE and trenches at 13.0 fired 20 rounds at the CovR DIAVOUE and round at 14.30 fired 25 rounds at the house S17a.55 at 15.0 fired 13 rounds at two works S16b.9.2 at 15.30 fired 6 rounds at the FERME DU BOIS	

WAR DIARY
or
INTELLIGENCE SUMMARY

Army Form C. 2118

89 F.A. Brigade (5)

December 15

(Erase heading not required.)

Instructions regarding War Diaries and Intelligence Summaries are contained in F.S. Regs., Part II. and the Staff Manual respectively. Title Pages will be prepared in manuscript.

Place	Date	Hour	Summary of Events and Information	Remarks and references to Appendices
A/89 M26d98	11		Fine morning turned to rain midday. A/89 fired 6 rounds at cross roads S12 C.1.2 at 19.5 at 21.5 6 rounds were fired at Cross Roads S11d 64 and at 21.45 6 rounds were fired at cross roads at S17 a 77	TRENCH MAPS Sheets 36 S.W. Sheets 3 & 4.
C/89 M32 b 44			C/89 at 13.30 fired 10 rounds at Chapel T8 b 48 where enemy were seen at 14.0 8 rounds were fired at trench T1a 93 at 14.15 12 rounds were fired at house at 3a lieut S6 b 32 6 of these were direct hits. At 14.45 20 rounds were fired at house S11 e 17	
D/89 X18c07			at 15.30 5 rounds were fired at house S11 e 17	
HQ			H/89. No artillery activity, owing to position being flooded. Battery moved to X18 c 07 in the afternoon cleared towards night.	
R35c98	12		Fine morning turned to rain A/89 at 12.20 fired 27 rounds at trench at S16 a 67 to S16 a 61 and hut in vicinity	
BETHUNE MAP 1 40000			D/M/89 at 10.45 fired 13 rounds at the DISTILLERY. This was repeated at 13.55, at 12.38 15 rounds were fired at LORGIES, at 14.10 6 rounds were fired at communication trench at and 5 rounds at 324 d 33. At 15.40 13 rounds at 329 a 9.9 and 8 rounds were fired of the same target at 16.0 at S 20.45. 21.5 and 22.5 71 rounds were fired at La FERME DU BIEZ.	
			C/89 at 11.5 fired 9 rounds at trench S17a 1.4, at 14.45 9 rounds were fired at house S11 e 17, at 15.15 11 rounds were fired at the FERME DU BIEZ and at 15.40 10 rounds were fired at the trench at 35 d 33.	

WAR DIARY or INTELLIGENCE SUMMARY

Army Form C. 2118

89th Brigade R.F.A. (6)

Place	Date	Hour	Summary of Events and Information	Remarks and references to Appendices
A/89 M26 d 98 C/89 M32 b 44	Sep. 12 13		continued. C/89 at 18.5 fired 8 rounds at LA TOURELLE cross roads. Fine. A little sunshine and colder towards evening A/89 fired 7 rounds at 18.20 and 6 rounds at 20.5 directed on cross roads S.12.a.12 C/89 fired 11 rounds at the DISTILLERY at 12.15, reported by enemy fire on group of FACTORY 10 rounds were fired at S.17.a.14, at 14/15 support trenches and 31 rounds were fired at French and emplacements by enemy infantry. at S.5 & 7.8½ at 15.10 at 15.30 8 rounds were fired at S.15.38	TRENCH MAPS 36 SW Sheets 3 & 1
D/89 X 18 d 07 HQ R35 c 98			D/89 from 10.0 till 20 fired 103 rounds at trenches in rear of BOAR'S HEAD. O.C. B/89 in reporting effect of this bombardment states Germans enemy fire about 25 yards from the GLORY HOLE was burning throughout the bombardment. 2 German who were seen, battery had to stop firing 3 times owing 6 hostile aeroplanes who were seen outside than usual. At 13.50 20 rounds were fired on trenches behind BOARS HD. The enemy retaliated freely. The bombardment of the trenches and Col. THOMAS resumed command of the division artillery	
BETHUNE MAP Pl. 1 40.000	14		resumed command of the Brigade. fine, clear. A/89 engaged trenches in front of LES BRULOTS with two salvos at 11.35 and 12.5 firing 20 and 12 rounds respectively. These which at S.5 & S.5½. 4. 10 rounds were repeated on the latter at 12.20 trenches at S.5 & S.5½. 4. 10 rounds were fired at 14.45 and 30 rounds at 14.45 were fired at S.11.c.17 and also at farm S.11.c.17 also at farm C/89. at 11.15 fired 8 rounds at 18.0. 8 rounds were fired at 37.c.38 at the farm at LES BRULOTS	

WAR DIARY or INTELLIGENCE SUMMARY

Army Form C. 2118

89th Brigade R.F.A. (7)

Beaulen 15

Place	Date	Hour	Summary of Events and Information	Remarks and references to Appendices
A/89 M26a/98	See 14	6/4/16	continued. B/89 fired 88 rounds at (communication) FERME DU BOIS and S16a 64 in conjunction with Siege battery and 18 prs, the enemy retaliated on the FACTORY and RUE DU BOIS, from 11.30 to 5.12.15	TRENCH MAPS
C/89 M32.b.44	See 15		cold clear fine. Only little gun trench evening. A/89 at 14.50 fired 22 rounds at trenches S11 a 3.3. in retaliation for shelling of our trenches.	36 SW Sheets 38
D/89 X18c07			C/89 at 11.0 fired 16 rounds at (communication) trench S17 a 2.5 where were wire in progress at 13.45 fired 30 rounds at S11 a 3.3. (group Sélarme) the parapet was breached at 18.45 and at B 3.10 wire places at 18.35. 4 rounds were fired at 8.24 B 3.10 and at 19.15 8 rounds were fired at LURGIES after which the enemy infantry bolted.	38
HQ R35c98			4 rounds were fired at the BOIS DE BIEZ. D/89. at 10.35 fired 104 rounds with enemy trenches with great volume of bombardment of German mound (S22a38) O.C. B/89 who reports station 9.2 kms got direct hit of green mound. this was immediately followed by fire from 4.5. as a result with 3.2 rounds this was knocked. the Germans retaliated at southgate was breached. fire was kept up till 11.40. the Germans fired at 11 with 77 mm on RUE DU BOIS. from 14.0. 21 rounds 10.45 on trenches and in retaliation for enemy shelling were fired on the DISTILLERY.	
BETHUNE MAP 1/40,000	See 16		Dull. turned train trench evening. A/89 fired at 21.- 21.50 - 23 - 23.45 - 24. Series of 10.6.6.6.2. rounds respectively at S6a54 to S6a78. C/89 at 11.45 fired 16 rounds at Lupus S6 e 17 a fortified house several direct hits but little damage done. at 18.30 2 rounds a fortified house several direct hits S5.B.7.0. (group under) were fired at subsequent trench.	

Army Form C. 2118

WAR DIARY
or
INTELLIGENCE SUMMARY
(Erase heading not required.)

December 15

89th Brigade
R.F.A. (8)

Place	Date	Hour	Summary of Events and Information	Remarks and references to Appendices
A/89	Dec 16		continued	TRENCH MAPS 36 S.W. Sheets 3.1
	17		B/89. no artillery action.	
M26c98			A/89 fired 8 rounds at 18.30 on S.6 a 5.4, S.6 a 7.8 and 8 rounds at 21.0 on the same objective (enemy scheme)	
C/89			C/89 fired 39 rounds at 10.0 on front line and support trenches, S.5 b 7½, 8½ to S.5 b 7.4 fire was very effective	
M32 b 44			D/89 fired 20 rounds at 11.40 in retaliation at the F FERME DU BOIS and 10 rounds at 13.30 with the same purpose at 14.15. 3 rounds were fired at the enfilade gun. at front trenches S of FERME DU BOIS from the enfilade gun.	
D/89			Still and misty	
X18c07	18		A/89 fired 8 rounds at 12.30 at S.6 a 7.8 - S.6 a 5.4 (enemy schemes) and at 21.5. 8 rounds at same at S.6 a 5.5 (SIGN POST LANE) and at 22.0 8 rounds at same at S.6 a 8.8 (enemy schemes)	
HQ R35 e98			C/89 fired 8 rounds at 14.30 on front line and support trenches at S.5 b 7.9 to S.5 b 9.3 (registration)	
BETHUNE MAP 1			D/89 no artillery action.	
40 ODD	19		Fine morning - sunshine and clear afternoon fine. enemy careful over fire. A/89. at 18.5 fired 8 rounds at S.12 c 12. S.12 c 77 at 18.30 " 12 " at x roads HALPEGARBE at 19.15 " 4 " at S.12 c 12. S.17 c 77 x roads	

WAR DIARY
or
INTELLIGENCE SUMMARY

Army Form C. 2118

89. Brigade R.F.A.
(9)

Place	Date	Hour	Summary of Events and Information	Remarks and references to Appendices
A/89 M26d98 C/89 M32b44 D/89 X18c07 H.Q. R35c98 BETHUNE MAP 1 40,000	Dec 19 20 21.		*Continued.* C/89. at 14.15 fired 6 rounds at trench S5 & 7.8 (apparent infantry at 15.20 fired 36 rounds on front line and support trench from S5 b 53 & S5 b 7.8 retaliation for enemy shelling of CHATEAU REDOUBT. D/89 at 10.0 fired 15 rounds at FERME DU TOUILOTTE and 15 at building S22b6.1. (retaliation) building S22b6.1. in unit S22 d 1.0 [S12 & 22 and 15 at S 29 a 4.5 (sniping scheme) dull tunnel train through evening. bad light. A/89 at 7.20 fired 4 rounds at S12 c 12. and at 19 u fired 6 rounds at S12 e?) at 20.15 fired 6 rounds at S12 b 12 and S12 a 77 and at 20 20 4 rounds at S 6 a 8.8. C/89 at 14.30 fired 9 rounds at house S6c18 (a suspected O.P.) D/89. no artillery action. Still running through the day. A/89 at 15:30. fired 12 rounds at S10 b 9.2 (machine gun emplacement) C/89. at 14.15 fired 6 rounds at Cm Trench S17 a 48 at 18.15 4 rounds at LATOURELLE cross roads and 4 rounds aimed near LIGNY LE PETIT at 19.40 6m rounds were repeated in LATOURELLE cross roads D/89 fired 20 rounds at 20.15 on S17 a 0.3. (right group scheme)	TRENCH MAPS 36 SW Sheet 3.1

WAR DIARY or INTELLIGENCE SUMMARY

Army Form C. 2118

(Erase heading not required.)

89th Brigade R.F.A.

December 15 — Page 10

Instructions regarding War Diaries and Intelligence Summaries are contained in F.S. Regs., Part II. and the Staff Manual respectively. Title Pages will be prepared in manuscript.

Place	Date	Hour	Summary of Events and Information	Remarks and references to Appendices
A/89	Dec 22		Dull and misty light frost. A/89 fired 25 rounds at 12.50 on S10 e 9.2 machine gun and mortar emplacement and at 13.20 fired 8 rounds at S11 e 1.9 (cramier) on hill in corner.	TRENCH MARS 36 SW Sheets 3.1
M26d98			at 22. 5-6 rounds were fired on S12 c1.2. 3.1 to 7.7 and 4 rounds at S10l-9.2	
C/89 M32l-44			C/89. at 11.50 fired 8 rounds on trench 35 & 3.1 retaliation for shelling PORT ARTHUR at 18.40-19.10 and 19.50 4 minutes were fired at each of the following LATOURELLE FERME DU BIEZ and fired E of FERME DU BIEZ 15 rounds	
D/89 X18c07			D/89. at 10.35 fired 2 rounds at FERME DU TOULOTTE at 16.50 15 rounds after some hostile retaliation. The enemy at 14.30 fired were fired at some hostile retaliation, battery and at ERNETTE 3 rounds its ground in front and rear of battery and at ERNETTE	
HQ			enemy	
R35c98			Fine raining mostly the day no artillery action	
BETHUNE M.H.P.	Dec 23		A/89. fired 7 rounds at 85 & 87 and 7 rounds at 85 l-8 3 C/89 at 14.30 fired 7 rounds at 86 & 3.1 some slight damage. at 14.35 12 rounds at S17 a 2.6 at-14.45 2 rounds and at 11.30 30 rounds at 10.40 11 rounds	
1/40,000			F/89. at 9.50 fired 5 rounds at an enemy working party attempting a work S25 a 6.4 the first two series also working parties were dispersed, the 3rd series was fired on the night times tramway party was dispersed. The fire caused the Germans to retaliate energetically (Right front salient). The fire caused the Germans to retaliate energetically on our reserve trenches and 77 mm at PRINCES RURO CHOCOLATE POST	

1875 Wt. W593/826 1,000,000 4/15 J.B.C. & A. A.D.S.S./Forms/C. 2118.

WAR DIARY or **INTELLIGENCE SUMMARY**
(Erase heading not required.)

Army Form C. 2118

89th Bde Renegade Bgde (11)

Place	Date	Hour	Summary of Events and Information	Remarks and references to Appendices
A/89	See 23		continued B/89 enfilade at 13.0 fired 14 rounds at S.23.b 2.6 enemy movement at 14.15. 10 rounds at S.25 a 5.4 (ordered by Gen 19 Div) on wiring party and at 14.20 27 rounds (ordered by G.O.C. 19 Div) on S.17 a 5.9. no direct hits little damage.	TREIVCH MAPS 36 SW Sheets 3. 1.
M.26.d 98	See 24		Showery. Some sunshine rain towards evening. high wind	
C/89			A/89. at 7.0 fired 2 rounds at S.12.b.1.2 & S.17 c 7.7 (retaliation) C/89 at 13.15 fired 12 rounds at new communic'n trench S.17.E.2.6 and dug out battery demolished at 14.15 fired 15 rounds at Soleil S.5 b 8.7 at 15.0 10 rounds at suspected OP. S.6 a.3.2 at 15.15 4 rounds at LURGIES from 18-22.0 8 rounds on trenches S.5 b 88 to prevent repairs	
D/89 X18 c 0.7 HQ			B/89 10.50 - 11.55 (49 rounds Right gun & Co Salvos) the enemy retaliated with 6 rounds of 5.9 on old battery position.	
R.35.e.9.8 BETHUNE MHP	25.		Overcast showery turned to steady rain in the evening A/89. 1.0. fired 20 rounds with HALPEGAARB	
NOOOO			12.55 / 16 rounds S.16.d.9.8 Communic'n trench 13.25 9 rounds on trenches around FERME DU BOIS 23.40 8 rounds on S.12.b.12 S.17 a 7.7	
			C/89. at 14.15 fired 15 rounds at S.8a 3.3 roof demolished	
			D/89. 1 - 1.30 fired 45 rounds LURGIES. LATOURELLE (Seaforth Rifle guns) Enemy Artillery fired several 5.9 shell shrapnel in front of old battery position.	

WAR DIARY or **INTELLIGENCE SUMMARY**
(Erase heading not required.)

Army Form C. 2118

89. Bugle RGA
December 15   12

Place	Date	Hour	Summary of Events and Information	Remarks and references to Appendices
A/89 M26d98 C/89 N32 b44 B/89 X18c07	Dec 26		Showers – sunshine mid-day – rain in the evening. A/89. 1.0. fired 30 rounds into LORGIES and HALPEGARB group Selorne. C/89. 11:45 and 14:0 fired series of 9 and 6 rounds respectively on trench S16d 2 98 14:10 fired 11 rounds into houses 86 a 3.2. Suspected OP Between 18 and 20.0. fired 20 rounds S6d 22 B/89. 1.0. fired 54 rounds into LORGIES and LA TOURELLE (group Selorne) 10·55 to 11·25 14 rounds on DISTILLERY and FERME DU TOULOTTE 14·10 fired 16 rounds on BOARS HEAD and front line trenches	TRENCH MAPS S1, 36SW Sheet 3. 1.
HQ R35 e 9 8 BETHUNE MAP 1/ 40,000	27		Stormy rain at intervals. A/89. at 12·5 & fired 37 rounds at LORGIES. retaliation for enemy shelling RICHEBOURG ST VAAST 13·30. 27 rounds at S16 a 37 & S10 c 81 front line trenches and 6 rounds at LA TOURELLE: 15·10 8 rounds at S12 a.12 the two latter series in retaliation for enemy shelling EDGEWARE ROAD. C/89. 10.0. fired 10 rounds at S16 d 9.8 15·0 " 6 rounds at same objective	

WAR DIARY or INTELLIGENCE SUMMARY

Army Form C. 2118

(Erase heading not required.)

89th Ferozepore Bgde (15)

Instructions regarding War Diaries and Intelligence Summaries are contained in F.S. Regs., Part II. and the Staff Manual respectively. Title Pages will be prepared in manuscript.

Place	Date	Hour	Summary of Events and Information	Remarks and references to Appendices
A/89 M26d98	Dec 27		Continued. B/89 at 14.0 fired 60 rounds at head of new German Communication trench, considerable damage was done at 15.20. 22 rounds were fired at houses S23d.1.1 in retaliation for enemy shelling.	TRENCH MAPS 36 SW Sheet 381.
C/89 M32 b 44	Dec 28		In morning Somewhat desultory afternoon dull. A/89 at 5/30 fired 34 rounds on houses S5 a 85 (twenty hits on buildings) fired 18 rounds on Communication trenches S11 d 01. S10 d 78 (2 machine guns) at 6/0. Shells were observed and 3 Germans killed.	
D/89 X18 c 07		16/10 19/0	Series of 6 and 23 rounds were fired at S10.1.12 FERME DU BOIS. 68 Littersens were fired by the 2 machine guns.	
HQ R35 c g 8			C/89 fired 10 rounds at 11.50 objective FERME DU BOIS. (harass registration) S5 d 85 " (same) S1b d 98 " S11 d 6.48 (many working parties seen) S8 a 32 (retaliation for shelling NEUVE CHAPELLE & FERME DU BOIS FERME DU BIEZ	
BETHUNE MAP 1/ 40.000		8 " 9 " 8 " 13 " 12 -		
			D/89. at 12.30 - 13.40 fired 51 rounds on night lines (three 61 FERME DU BOIS) Trenches in rear of BOARS HEAD (Group Schwaben)	

Army Form C. 2118

WAR DIARY
or
INTELLIGENCE SUMMARY
(Erase heading not required.)

December 15   39th Trench Battery R.A.
                                              14.

Place	Date	Hour	Summary of Events and Information	Remarks and references to Appendices
A/89	See Seq 29		Fine morning. Misty towards evening.	TRENCH MAPS No. 36 SW Sheet 32/1
M26d98 C/89			A/89 at 10.5 fired 42 rounds at S10 f 91 S10 f 93 at 14.20 7 rounds at front trenches S16 a 5.8. This series was repeated until 6 rounds at 15.55.	
M32 b 44 D/89			At 19.0 6 rounds were fired on the signpost lane Barrage and 22.0 20 rounds were fired into LORGIES. (by order different rounds)	
X18 c 07			C/89. At 11.50 fired 11 rounds at S17 c 13 at 14.0 20 rounds into the DISTILLERY & shelling of RUE DU BOIS at 19.0 9 rounds were fired at S35 & 71	
HQ	30		D/89. At noon registered S12 c 11½ (aeroplane obs'n) and fired 15 rounds	
R35 c 98			Fine cloudy towards evening. A/89 at 14.30 fired 18 rounds at S1 a 88 S1 a 5 3 in retaliation at 14.40 fired 11 rounds on trenches N. of BOARS HEAD (S16 c 37)	
BETHUNE MHQ			at 15.15 fired 14 rounds at DISTILLERY & LORGIES C/89 at 11.40 fired 19 rounds at horse S11 d 45 (several hits) at 13.15 fired	
			10 rounds at trench S11 b 34. at 14.20 10 rounds further were fired at same objective	

WAR DIARY or INTELLIGENCE SUMMARY

Army Form C. 2118

(Erase heading not required.)

SQ ? . A. Brigade. (15)

December 15

Place	Date	Hour	Summary of Events and Information	Remarks and references to Appendices
A/84 M26 d 98 C/89 N32 b 44 B/89 X18 c 07. HQ. R35 c 98 BETHUNE MAP 1/40,000	Dec 31.		Overcast a little sunshine in the afternoon A/89 became a Counter Battery A/89 at 10.50 fired 12 rounds at a 4.2 battery at S25 c 3 0 (material thrown up and battery were fine) at 12.45 13 rounds were fired at a suspected battery at S18 c 07 battery fired for at 14 0 6 rounds were fired on the FERME DU TOULOTTE S19 b 04 at midnight 12 rounds were fired into LORGIES C/89 at q.a. fired 5 rounds at S11 b 35 (retaliation) at 14.15 22 rounds at S10 d 36 at 14.30 11 rounds were fired into the DISTILLERY at an unknown pt at S25 a 5.4 B/89 at 12.30 fired 3 rounds at a working party at S25 a 5.4	TRENCH MAP 2 40 31 SW Sheets SS1

JMcLaren
Lt Col
Comdg 89th Brigade RFA

19th Division.

"A" Battery 89th Brigade R.F.A.

Vol. I.

1.4 – 31-7-15

WAR DIARY
or
INTELLIGENCE SUMMARY

(Erase heading not required.)

Army Form C. 2118

"A" Batty. 89 (H) Batt. R.F.A.

Place	Date	Hour	Summary of Events and Information	Remarks and references to Appendices
BULFORD			The Battery was raised as the 277th Batty. Royal Field Artillery on or about the 10th OCTOBER 1914 by CAPTAIN E.W. HOPE R.F.A. and Lt MOURICE R.F.A. Owing to very numerous changes in all ranks the diary to now carried forward till the battery left BULFORD as A BATTERY 89th BRIGADE R.F.A. (4.5" Q.F. HOWITZER)	T.M.
BULFORD	17.15	2 p.m.	The battery left BULFORD by train under the command of LIEUTENANT H. JOHNSTON. The other officers were LIEUTENANT E.H. BRAMHALL and 2nd LIEUTENANT A.H. WOOD. They arrived at SOUTHAMPTON at 2 p.m. Strength as under — 3 Officers, 1 Warrant Officer (2nd Class), 1 Staff Sgt, 1 Farrier Sgt, 5 Sgts, 5 Cpls, 1 Cpl Shoeing Smith, 9 Bomd"s, 2 Shoeing Smiths, 1 Wheeler, 6 Batmen, 49 Gunners, 53 Drivers, 125 horses, 4 4.5" Q.F. Howitzers, 8 Wagons, 2 Water Cart, 1 Officers Mess Cart, 2 G.S. Wagons and attached to Battery 2 A.S.C. Drivers and 2 Heavy draft horses.	V.H.
	18th		The Battery embarked on S.S. "COURTFIELD" and "LE MARGARITE" CAPTAIN T. MEREFORD 15th of the battery and took command	T.M.

1375 Wt. W593/826 1,000,000 4/15 J.B.C. & A. A.D.S.S./Forms/C. 2118.

Army Form C. 2118

WAR DIARY
or
INTELLIGENCE SUMMARY
(Erase heading not required.)

Instructions regarding War Diaries and Intelligence Summaries are contained in F. S. Regs., Part II. and the Staff Manual respectively. Title Pages will be prepared in manuscript.

Place	Date	Hour	Summary of Events and Information	Remarks and references to Appendices
LE HAVRE	18.7.15		The battery disembarked and marched to Camp No.1.	T.W.
LE HAVRE	19.7.15		The battery marched to POINT 6 and entrained. They left at HAVRE at 9 p.m.	T.W.
ST OMER	20.7.15		The battery reached ST OMER at 2 p.m. detrained and marched to BONNINGUES-LES-ARDRES, where they went into billets at 7 p.m.	T.W.
BONNINGUES	23.7.15	11 a.m.	Left BONNINGUES at 10 a.m. and marched to WARDRECQUES where the battery bivouaced	T.W.
WARDRECQUES	24.7.15		Left at 8.40 a.m. and marched to billets at BOURECQ	T.W.
BOURECQ	31.7.15		Left at 9 a.m. and marched to bivouac at MERVILLE	T.W.

12/6787

19th Division

"A"/89. Battery R.F.A.

Vol: II

August 15.

Army Form C. 2118

WAR DIARY
or
INTELLIGENCE SUMMARY
(Erase heading not required.)

Instructions regarding War Diaries and Intelligence Summaries are contained in F.S. Regs., Part II. and the Staff Manual respectively. Title Pages will be prepared in manuscript.

Place	Date	Hour	Summary of Events and Information	Remarks and references to Appendices
MERVILLE R.S.6.56.	5.8.15		The Battery marched to its wagon position R.5.b.5.6 & went into billets	√ J.M.
	7.8.15		The Battery came up at night anxious to open to a position M.10.d.4.5. into firepits that had been dug by the two preceding days & nights. At 11 a.m. the firepits were hidden in position. At 12 midday the Battery opened fire on the enemies trenches. During the day few points were registered. Thirty-nine shrapnel and two lyddite being fired. Ammunition wagons from the brigade ammunition column were attached to the 8th howitzer withdrawal munday 1/9. Two 10th charges of the horses were to be accepted for the Battery. Brig. teams & limbers kept at the Farrier.	
			The remaining Officers been up work to battery.	√ J.M. √ J.M.
M.10.d.4.3	8.8.15		The battery went on with their reparation.	√ J.M.
	9.8.15		Ditto.	
	10.8.15		Ditto. The Serjeant-Major (Snaple) was taken sick owing to a wound he had received earlier in the campaign	√ J.M.

WAR DIARY
or
INTELLIGENCE SUMMARY

(Erase heading not required.)

Army Form C. 2118

Instructions regarding War Diaries and Intelligence Summaries are contained in F.S. Regs., Part II. and the Staff Manual respectively. Title Pages will be prepared in manuscript.

Place	Date	Hour	Summary of Events and Information	Remarks and references to Appendices
M10dd3	11.8.15		Registration also by the Battery	V.M.
	12.8.15		Registration also by the Battery (?) at a direct hit on a house at N 26 c 8.4. Fired on small gun on Enemy's parapet. Got one direct hit just below observatoire from occupied watershed. Registered the here point.	V.M.
	13.8.15		Only 5 rounds were fired to find out if Battalion's find the Enemy. The cordite seems to send the shell about 4-5° short in every 100°. A fresh gun selected in case of a FO Position in case of a big battle. Used shrapnel to being put on or the secondary & primary positions. Re skins way was were brought up at night & placed near the battery.	V.M.
	14.8.15		A day of rest.	V.M.
	15.8.15		Aisne at 5am. Got everywhere heavy. Battery fired two rounds to keep down fire at our reconnoitring aeroplane. Silenced a Bosh [?] gun in the enemy front) at our trenches. Two blind by while out of Four own Parapet stale if Parapet. The Battery shot at a gun on the enemy Parapet here 252 at H.43Pm in conjunction with another (F.2). Two direct hits at first indicated were obtained. One + Mayhouse more syndicate + gun very heavily during the day. The Battery continues to improve the parados by wattle hatter disponds + overhead cover to the guns.	V.M.
	16.8.15			T.M.
	17.8.15			V.M.
	18.8.15		Communication with trenches. Fired on a registered a Communication Trench. Performed first to look out Negro pit 35° per 1000°. a to charge 435° per 1000° shrapnel short of Parapette.	T.M.

1875 Wt. W593/826 1,000,000 4/15 J.B.C. & A. A.D.S.S./Forms/C. 2118.

WAR DIARY or INTELLIGENCE SUMMARY

Army Form C. 2118

Place	Date	Hour	Summary of Events and Information	Remarks and references to Appendices
M 10 d 4.3	19.8.15		Battery retaliated in the evening against the enemy trenches as they were shelling our trenches. The enemy ceased firing. Ten direct hits were recorded.	V.M.
	20.8.15		by the forward observation officers. Battery retaliation to enemies bombarding with 3 rounds H.E. Also four rounds were registered by aid of aeroplane dropping the day.	V.M.
	21.8.15		Registration of two points in the vicinity. Rained all the morning.	V.M.
	22.8.15		Battery registered two points on the enclosure right of SORE	V.M.
	23.8.15		The Battery fired 12 rounds & point out the vicinity to the S. Entrance [?] to LESART near MERVILLE. They were relieved at 10 p.m. by D/192 Bgde RFA. They then marched into German billets R.30 — when ordered to rejoin the column & seven dropping [?] news received place sinking of Registration Bogers two cruisers & seven destroyers. [?] off Cape Argivingo [?] #79a Germans remained in burrow. The left section marched to	V.M.
LESART	24.8.15		LE TOURET with the battery staff. They moved into the 35th Battery RFA billets. The 35th Battery position & the 1st Battery RFA at 9.30 p.m. The section of the 2nd 1st Battery took but left the same place.	V.M.
LETOURET	25.8.15		Zero line reported. The right section relieved the centre section of the 35th Battery at 9.35 p.m.	
	26.8.15		The Battery went on to the 11th registration. One section of the 35th Battery moved off at about 9 p.m. remaining in position.	
	27.8.15		Registration. The remaining section of the 35th Battery moved off in the afternoon.	V.M.
	28.8.15		Registration. Weather very hot.	V.M.
	29.8.15		Registration kept of zone. Rain in the afternoon.	V.M.

WAR DIARY
or
INTELLIGENCE SUMMARY

(Erase heading not required.)

Army Form C. 2118

Place	Date	Hour	Summary of Events and Information	Remarks and references to Appendices
LE TOURET	30.8.15		Registered one point on enemies front line trench.	VZZ.
	31.8.15		Battery retaliated during the day for enemies fire about 15 rounds	VZZ.

19th Division.

"B" Battery 89th Brigade R.F.A.

Vol: I.

22-31/7/15

101/6250

Army Form C. 2118

WAR DIARY
or
INTELLIGENCE SUMMARY
(Erase heading not required.)

B. Battery, 84th Brigade R.F.A.

Place	Date	Hour	Summary of Events and Information	Remarks and references to Appendices
BONNINGUES (ez-ARDRES)	22 July 1915	5.45 a.m.	The Battery mobilised on July 16th 10/15 at BULFORD. Marching out strength. — 4 Officers — Captain & A. Dorrell Lieut. D.C. Mudie Lieut. A. Murray 2nd Lieut. E. Lumsden 130 N.C.Os & men 3 A.S.C. drivers 137 Total all ranks 129 Horses (2 short of establishment) 4 Guns - 4.5" Howitzers & Carriages. 3 Gun limbers (another limber lost from A 84 taken and returned to A 84 at Havre) 8 Ammunition Wagons 3 G.S. Wagons 1 Water Cart 1 Cooks Cart (2 wheeler) First half battery - A & C subsections with 2 G.S. Wagons & cooks wagon in charge of Captain Dorrell & Lieut Murray entrained at AMESBURY Halt at 2.45 a.m. on July 17th. Second half battery B & D subsections with 1 G.S. Wagon (Supply) & Water Cart in charge of Lieut D.C. Mudie & 2nd Lieut Lumsden entrained at AMESBURY Halt at 4.15 am of same date.	E.A. DORRELL D.C. MUDIE A. MURRAY E. LUMSDEN

Army Form C. 2118

WAR DIARY
or
INTELLIGENCE SUMMARY

B Battery, 84th Brigade. R.F.A.

(Erase heading not required.)

Place	Date	Hour	Summary of Events and Information	Remarks and references to Appendices
			The first half detrained at SOUTHAMPTON at 4.30 a.m. and the second half at 5.45 a.m. All horses and vehicles with 76 men under Capt DORRELL and Lieut MURRAY were entrained on the S.S. Cornfield and left the dock at 6.0 p.m. The remainder of the men under Lieut MUDIE and 2nd Lieut LUMSDEN embarked on the La Margurite which left at 7.45 p.m. The "Cornfield" entered HAVRE at 4.15 a.m. on July 15th and the "La Margurite" at 2.45. The vehicles were unloaded from the Cornfield from 6 a.m. and the tide rising sufficiently permitted the disembarkation of the horses at 10.25 a.m. The Battery marched from the dock at 11.30 a.m. to Point 6 Gare Maritime. A gun limber was driven from Advanced Depot HAVRE to make up deficiency of those limber belonging to "A" Bg returned to "A" Battery. The Battery entrained at the Gare Maritime at 4.0 p.m. and left at 7.30 p.m. The train stopped for fifteen minute at MONTROLIER BUCHY at 2 a.m. and again at L'ARBEYVILLE at 9.15 am July 16th. Halting 40 minutes, horses were watered & fed. Two men returned hot tea. Troops' butter 1 gm. at MONTROLIER BUCHY 4 horse lines found lying down & were unable to get up, between Sides 9 Frink & the next horse. The horses were thrown out, the breast safe undone & the horse encourses up & placed in harness again. Arrival at ST. OMER 3.15 p.m. One horse found to have been badly kicked left at Cavalry Branch. Battery marched off at 4.10 p.m.	

WAR DIARY
or
INTELLIGENCE SUMMARY

Army Form C. 2118

B. Battery 89 Brigade R.F.A.

Place	Date	Hour	Summary of Events and Information	Remarks and references to Appendices
BONNINGUES LES ARDRES	21/9/15 22/9/15	7.0 pm	After a march of 13½ miles arrived in billets at BONNINGUES LES ARDRES at 10.30 pm. Soon after leaving ST OMER a horse in A Subsection shewn signs of distress and was taken out of draught at once and replaced by Spare. Halt was made at TILQUES. Water but no Staff horse watered there, a second halt was made at MOULLE for no horse much sketche and no horse watered. In sketch from a farm 2 feet here this horse that has shewn sign of this him shein of heart failure. The Battery halting for 5 minutes each hour remaining in seated up to 12.30 am. Report to 254 Horse Transport ST OMER to try replacing him this man. One horse n Subsection Fouly ill with Pneumonia. R.D.	
WARDRECQUES		9.30 pm 23 PM	Horses died at 6.15 am at BONNINGUES thereo by Farrier Sgt Meakin guard after leaving billet. Battery marched at this rear of 19th Division with the 89th Brigade leaving BONNINGUES at 10.0 am. Halt at noon to 2.30 pm horses watered by bucket to mile off the road at EPERLECQUES. Reach WARDRECQUES at 7.30 pm Bivouaced in a field. Length of march 19 miles. The horse left Country Burnick. STOMER set up at nearest enough to travel. C.W.D.	

WAR DIARY
or
INTELLIGENCE SUMMARY

Army Form C. 2118

B Battery 39th Brigade R.F.A.

Place	Date	Hour	Summary of Events and Information	Remarks and references to Appendices
BOURECQ	24/7/15	6.30 p.m.	Marched up from WARDRECQUES at 7 o.c. a.m. halted at starting point 1 killom. the Infantry (1st Division x 55th Bde R.F.A. 9 guns). March began at 9.30 a.m. Halt at WITTES from 10.0.5 a.m. to 10.15 a.m. Horses watered by buckets from MELDE RIVER. March resumed through AIRE and ST.HILAIRE to BOURECQ arrived at 4.15 p.m. Length of march 13½ miles. Billetted in farm houses while in echelon were in the town and 2 officers in the farm. Horses and 2 officers billetted with Capt.	
BOURECQ	25/7/15		No move — Tested Gun sights by diagram – No Zero testing corners available (?) and test Winfrin with the reservoirs. Cannot get spare guns etc. from Divisns.	
BOURECQ	26/7/15		No move. Practiced gunners at laying drivers in chry & night laying out 9.0 pm.	
BOURECQ	27/7/15		No move. Tested Gun sights again no apparent defect — Clamming Plate of LILLERS 25th yard centry. Elevation to left 9 slick to right 9 right Clinemeter on front Gun 1 A.G. wheelin 40 mm. Elevation. All guns brought to the same angle. Angle of Sight on aimfs 9 sight instruments 37 mm Elevation. Error due to Sight – No spare yet available	
BOURECQ	28/7/15	6.30 p.m.	No move. Exchanged 160 rds Shrapnel for 160 rds Lyddite – 152 with D.A.C. M.Division from 8 with B.A.C. 39 Faille. 160 Tipperary No82 exchanges with Park for 160 O.A. Dryh No84. No Lyddite Trochets available when ammunition was changed, these wooden fittings in Shrapnel Trocheds had to be removed to allow room for the Lyddite Trotlet	E.W.T.

WAR DIARY
or
INTELLIGENCE SUMMARY

B. Button Sqn "B" Sqrds R.Fus

Army Form C. 2118

Place	Date	Hour	Summary of Events and Information	Remarks and references to Appendices
BOURECQ	29/7/15	6.0 pm	Sent for and have left at ST. OMER. M. MUDIE took in with Capt. Mc.HEE yesterday heard MUDIE found him for friend. He obtain 900 francs from Field Cashier at ST. OMER returned about midnight. Capt. Mc.SHEE came in with horse at 1.45 p.m. Paid out 935 francs to M. Button. Sir Douglas [?] the [?] the Dep. Regt. regds. Your afternoon reviewed. EWB / 13 Battn at 4 p.m.	
BOURECQ	30/7/15	6.20 pm	No move — one horse sent to Vet. Officer Cavalry Tronfield Section A.V.C. lately kicked in & lost. Train made things more comfortable.	EWB
LE SART (MERVILLE)	31/7/15	7.0 pm	"Brigade marched at 9.0 a.m. from BOURECQ to MERVILLE — distance 14 miles. = W. J. MERVILLE. Halted from 11.30 a.m. till 0.1 p.m. Battalion at LE SART 2 miles at ROBECQ — Weather fine without the sun.	EWB

121/6099

19th Division

"B"/89 Battery R.F.A.
Vol: II

From 1 – 31. 8. 15

"A" Form.
MESSAGES AND SIGNALS.

Army Form C. 2121.

No. of Message

Prefix **S m** Code **M CNP m** Words **21** Charge

Office of Origin and Service Instructions **F.7.S.**

Sent At ____ m. To ____ By ____

This message is on a/c of: ____ Service.
(Signature of "Franking Officer.")

Recd. at 2.41 p.m.
Date 6/8/15
From 7 Y S
By

TO { 89   F.A.   B.D.E.

Sender's Number	Day of Month	In reply to Number	
*B.M. 113	6 Aug		A A A

B Battery will march 7th
day of August Destination LOCRE
Detailed orders will follow

Copy end APPENDIX II

From
Place 19" Div. artillery
Time

"A" Form.   Army Form C. 2121.

MESSAGES AND SIGNALS.   No. of Message

Prefix M Code 337 m.	Words	Charge	This message is on a/c of:	Recd. at 4 4 m.
Office of Origin and Service Instructions	Sent At m. To By		Service. (Signature of "Franking Officer.")	Date 6 8 15 From EH 9 By 7 FS

TO { 89 FA Brigade

Sender's Number	Day of Month	In reply to Number	AAA
B.M/114	6		

Following message has been received from 19 Div AAA Begins AAA continuation my GS30 following message received from Indian Corps AAA Begins AAA B' Btj 89 Brigade RFA will march at 9.0am 7th inst AAA Destination LOCRE AAA Route ESTAIRE, LE KIRLEM, BAILLEUL AAA Officer will report in advance to Hd Qrs 2nd Corps at BAILLEUL AAA Battery will be accompanied by correct proportion of BAC GS wagons from DAC carrying established amount AAA ends AAA ends AAA Reference above the DAC have been instructed to send 3 wagons to join you tonight

From 19 Div ARTY
Place
Time 3 20

COPY APPENDIX III

The above may be forwarded as now corrected.   (Z)

Censor.   Signature of Addressor or person authorised to telegraph in his name.

* This line should be erased if not required.

(15491) S. & Co. Ltd. W 14142/641. 90,000. 4/15. Forms C 2121/10.

Original   Appendix I   BM 100   4th

Under instructions from 1st Army one battery 89 FA Bde and proportion of Ammunition Column will be transferred to Second Army AAA Wire which battery you select to go AAA 4 Ammunition Wagons of Ammunition Column should be sent under an officer AAA. Wire strength of battery in detail

19th Div Arty — 11.25 pm

139 — 5th
Your B.M. 100. I assume this does not refer to battery lent to Meerut Div. AAA. Select B battery strength four officers 128 other ranks 122 horses AAA. Section BAC one officer 26 other ranks 30 horses AAA. Above does not include ASC personnel if they accompany unit add two men 4 horses.

89 F.A Bde.

Sdp. H.M. Thomas

Army Form C. 2118

B/89th Battery 31st Brigade R.F.A.

WAR DIARY
or
INTELLIGENCE SUMMARY
(Erase heading not required.)

Place	Date	Hour	Summary of Events and Information	Remarks and references to Appendices
LE SART	1.8.15		No move.	
LE SART	2.8.15	6.10 pm	No move. Transfer of officers. Lieut. A. MURRAY from this Battery posted to the Bde Ammn. Col. 2nd Lieut V.T. O'DONOVAN posted to this Battery from the Bde Ammn. Col.	EWS
LE SART	3.8.15	6.30 pm	No move.	EWS
LE SART	4.8.15		No move. Brigade inspected by General Wilcox. Comd 2nd Indian Corps at 11.15 am	
LE SART	5.8.15	6.15 pm	No move. Officers of 89 Bde R.F.A. (Capt. DORRELL, 2nd Lieut. O'DONOVAN from (B/Bty)) attended lecture at R.F.C. H'qrs. EAST of MERVILLE at 4.0 am. Received information from Lt. Col. THOMAS Bde Comdr at 8.30 am. that this Battery is to be detached from the 2nd ARMY. No orders have yet come in. A Battery by 3rd Bde left stn. 3.0 pm today for the front under Surrey Brownlow GARDNER this GODERHAM Left tomorrow to I.O.M. at LESTRUM for mobilization until the 7 inst. 85 Bty R.F.A. marched through going to French billets S. of the Canal at MERVILLE. They had been billeted 14 miles WEST of here	I EWS

WAR DIARY
or
INTELLIGENCE SUMMARY

(Erase heading not required.)

Army Form C. 2118

Place	Date	Hour	Summary of Events and Information	Remarks and references to Appendices
LE SART	6/8/15	7.5 pm	Orders received to march 7½ August - destination LOCRE. See appendix II. at 2.50 pm Detailed Orders issued received at 4.15 pm. Inappendix. C B.S.M. B.Q.M.S. left at 2.0 pm to billet for the front. Sent Cpl. to LESTREM to bring back Bombardier GARDNER & Driver GOODERHAM who were sent Cpl. BAILEY to Div Supply Section No. 4 Coy A.S.C. to bring in Supply wagon with Bombardier TUPP and two men to rejoin. The 3 G.S. wagons to rejoin from D.A.C. arrived 7.15 pm	II III
DRANOUTRE	7/8/15	10.30 pm	Battery marched from LE SART at 4.0. am. B Subsection B.A.C. T & 13 Brigade R.F.A. & ammunition wagon — and Umi. G.S. Wagon from D.A.C. 14ᵗʰ Division. 2 x "HARPER" in charge of B.A.C. Subsection. Length of march 14 miles. Route MERVILLE, ESTAIRE, LE KIRLEM, BAILLEUL, LOCRE. Water, but halted one hour at LE KIRLEM at noon. Reported H.Q. 2 ⟨Welsh⟩ Bgde. at BAILLEUL at 1.30 pm. Reported again at H.Qrs 28ᵗʰ Division at LOCRE at 3.45 pm. Arrived at wagon line near DRANOUTRE at 5.0 pm. 8.6.4.1. (Reference map Belgium 1/3 Series 28 S.W.) Reported to O.C. B.A.C. AF.3rd Brigade R.F.A. at 6.15 pm. Commenced Battery position.	
DRANOUTRE	8/8/15	10.25 am	Made a reconnaissance of Battery position in N.27 C.4.4. Commenced work within four position to the right that buildings at 2.30 pm. Guns placed behind a hedge in rear of a Cottage Farm; position in rich entered by ridges 300 yards in front. O.P. position reached in KIMMEL HILL at N.26.C.3.7.	

Army Form C. 2118

WAR DIARY
or
INTELLIGENCE SUMMARY

(Erase heading not required.)

Instructions regarding War Diaries and Intelligence Summaries are contained in F.S. Regs., Part II. and the Staff Manual respectively. Title Pages will be prepared in manuscript.

Place	Date	Hour	Summary of Events and Information	Remarks and references to Appendices
DRANOUTRE	9/8/15	10.30 p.m.	Received verbal instructions from O.C. 31st Bde R.F.A. to bring two guns up to Inf. position that night. A.B. Subsection guns brought into position at 9.30 p.m. and prepared for action. Warned at 8.45 p.m. to have guns ready to open fire at dawn. All batteries had been ordered to open fire into SPANBROEK MOLEN at N.30.c.2.8. at 3.0.a.m. At 2.30 a.m. enemy attack commenced along the front opposite KIMMEL and 15 to 20 rounds from heavy batteries engaged them — bombardment was kept up until 4.0 a.m. when Infantry subsided. The Infantry went in for shelling SPANBROEK MOLEN when cannot not. Two enemy Shrapnel fell, one 100x left + one nearer 50x in front of battery. Received kindle immediately in front of battery were used to open fire on attackers.	ESD
DRANOUTRE	10/8/15	9.0 p.m.	Continued preparation of battery positions; arranged platform for two guns on right section using bricks from a ruined building. Two in three enemy shrapnel burst in wood on left of the battery at 10.30 a.m. Registered point in Enemy lines in afternoon, viz. KREUISSTRAAT COR 30x28. given N.36.b.3.7. and SPANBROEK MOLEN. N.30.c.2.8. Referred to guns for night firing in SPANBROEK MOLEN to enlist shouts enemy's MINEWERFER open on an trench opposite SPANBROEK MOLEN war to O.P. illuminating light. Rifle? A.D.S.S./Forms/C.2118. At N.28.c.2.5. Barometer 29.84. A Enemy Shrapnel fell 50x left of battery at 8.15 p.m. ESD

WAR DIARY
or
INTELLIGENCE SUMMARY

(Erase heading not required.)

Army Form C. 2118

Place	Date	Hour	Summary of Events and Information	Remarks and references to Appendices
DRANOUTRE	11/8/15	10.45 pm	Proceeded with preparation of Battery position. Registered two points in enemy's line – BLACK REDOUBT (3 effective) N.30.a.8.2 and WYTSCHAETE QUARRY O.19.d.1.5. at 12.30 pm & 2.0 pm. Tried ranging machine gun opposite D.3 fired at 4.15 pm. Enemy Officer observed fire. Lost two rounds up 7½" 50× new and 8.R. Range, 20× left. Two rings found of enemy's shrapnel near bullets last night – appeared An. 5.9" Howitzer Percussion Shrapnel. G.O.C. 28th Division inspected Battery position in the afternoon. [sgd]	
DRANOUTRE	12/8/15	10.0 am	Continued preparation of Battery position. Registered three points – MAEDELSTEDE FARM N.24.c.8.4.; PECKHAM N30.a.6.7. and TRESTLE BRIDGE, apparently a new German work at O.19.c.6.1. Guns firing new line. O. Salvation Guns placed in position this evening at 9.0 pm. [sgd]	
DRANOUTRE	13/8/15	10.10 pm	Reconnoitred Battery Position in the event of a retirement to reverse line (S.H.2) at M.30.d.10.2. The position good – well covered in front and good cover from aeroplane. Registered No 4 gun on SPANBRUEKE MOLEN, BLACK REDOUBT, PECKHAM and MAEDELSTEDE FARM. Also No 3 Gun on the BLACK REDOUBT. Fired two rounds of high Explosive at SPANBRUEKE MOLEN with range drum Brummitt 29.74. Weather mist with rain. [sgd]	

Army Form C. 2118

WAR DIARY
or
INTELLIGENCE SUMMARY
(Erase heading not required.)

Instructions regarding War Diaries and Intelligence Summaries are contained in F. S. Regs., Part II. and the Staff Manual respectively. Title Pages will be prepared in manuscript.

Place	Date	Hour	Summary of Events and Information	Remarks and references to Appendices
DRANOUTRE	14/7/15	9.10 p.m.	Registered with fresh fronts artillery 2 ind. my LENTER ENTRENCHMENT. O.25.d.8.0. WYTSCHAETE ROAD. N.24.a.10.6. WYTSCHAETE WOOD S.W. corner. N.24.d.7.7. 3½" Brigade laid wire to Battery O.P. at N.26.c.4.b. and from Brigade O.P. to Battery. Orchovie laid wire from Battery at N.27.c.4.3. to Wagon line at DRANOUTRE S.6.b.5.2.	End
DRANOUTRE	15/7/15	9.35 p.m.	Divisional Int. Commenting Corrieland relation 3.0 and 4.0 p.m. for the Battery. Fires three series of H.E. and Battery fire, two of H.E. shrapnel and one of shrapnel at respectively PECKHAM (W.30.a.6.7.). S.W. corner of PETITE BOIS (N.24.b.7.3.) and SPANBROEK MOLEN (N.30.c.2.8.). line was good. Range at first was excellent. Mr. McThird Good. Completed fresh wire to wagon lines.	End
DRANOUTRE	16/7/15	10.0 p.m.	Battery fired at length 14 in Enemy Trench opposite Trench 14 (N.36.a.(0.) Montgomery which trenched either side a hedge his apparition trench post at eye at rifles in the morning. Mr. O'DONOVAN forward Observing Officer. — Eleven rounds but failed to get view of communications very weak. Capt. MORRELL observed from the Inverness travel at 5.30 p.m. reported the Cutting from wire — Married a hit at Mr. 13th round and eventually fire 8 hits in to Cutting. with 22 rounds — difficulty to observe owing to the obscurity of the time of fire — observed through a mirror on a stick in front of holly field dugout. Ammunition fire from three Minute Battery today.	End

1875⁰ Wt. W593/826 1,000,000 4/15 T.R.C. & A. A.D.S.S./Forms/C. 2118.

WAR DIARY
or
INTELLIGENCE SUMMARY

(Erase heading not required.)

Army Form C. 2118

Place	Date	Hour	Summary of Events and Information	Remarks and references to Appendices
DRANOUTRE	14/3/15	9.45 p.m.	Registered KRUISSTRAAT CABINET CROSS ROADS. (N36.b.3.7) and Registered point at S.W. corner of PETITE BOIS (N24.b.2.3) Barometer 29.83	E.S.D
DRANOUTRE	18/5/15	9.15 a.m.	Second wire brought from Battery Position at N.27.c.0.43 to Observation Station at Registered WYTSCHAETE QUARRY (O14.d.1.5) wire all thro' trees. N26.c.4.6.	E.S.D
DRANOUTRE	19/5/15	9.30 a.m.	Finished laying brass wire to O.P. Relays platform in No 3 gun. Two Officers from 37 Division attached for instruction. Yesterday Captain J.L. FORRES and 2 Lieut. H.E. HOCHTON. The RED CHATEAU in O13.c.47 under No 3 and 4 gun. Each Alternat Registered front point. Three Shrapnel Shells fell at 11 o'clock this morning on the left of No 4 Lieut. Hill. battery, a fresh fissure is up set for 800 metres, from a field gun - prob S.g.mi.h Barometer 29.88	E.S.D
DRANOUTRE	20/5/15	9.0 p.m.	The usual Shrapnel fire resumed at 9.30 a.m. sent left of the batteries. 2nd O.P. for 9 & Q.2 started at N.20.b.5.5. Wind still pile - dug in each side of Ventilator 7 feet deep by 2 feet broad in the shape of a wide W. Battery did not fire to-day. Barometer 30.00 mm.	E.S.D
LANDEN HOEK	21/5/15	7.30 p.m.	Officers were mired up from Wagon line to Billeting Position. Weather all must. Barometer 29.94. Bougie test at 3.35 - Telephone Communication had Average full of mud. Shirt. Find one wire at WYTSCHAETE QUARRY, one at SPANBROEK MOLEN and one at L'ENFER ENTRENCHMENTS. Two cable cut twice. One fell very short - indicates need to test more relatively more numerous	E.S.D

1875 Wt. W593/826 1,000,000 4/15 J.B.C. & A. A.D.S.S (Forms)/C 2118.

WAR DIARY
or
INTELLIGENCE SUMMARY
(Erase heading not required.)

Army Form C. 2118

Instructions regarding War Diaries and Intelligence Summaries are contained in F.S. Regs, Part II. and the Staff Manual respectively. Title Pages will be prepared in manuscript.

Place	Date	Hour	Summary of Events and Information	Remarks and references to Appendices
LANDENHOEK 22/8	22/8	9.10 pm	Barometer 30.06. — Fair and warm — Registered new point in enemy's line — communication trench new house at O 32. C.4.5. — Parties of Germans about 50 strong first moving. Seen moving in the open to rear of trench. At 5:30 pm left arm of the line when obtaining direct hit on the heads of troops of bombers of his known at the rear of the trench. German bullets up to this opposite our front - several from NO 1 from but not from the Mine in his are hitched by the buildings immediately in front. Trench aeroplane was falling at 6:30 pm. Enemy 5 m very active in our district today. Our shells in wagon line with considerable EAST LANES 36° 84° 30 yds in bomb throwers, had a premature explosion yesterday afternoon which EWD first am our telephone dug out by an signaller with much mud in morning. Evening cloudy.	
LANDENHOEK 22/8	22/8	6.45 pm	Barometer 30.0.18. Dull cloudy with much mud in morning. Evening. Enemy trench aeroplane at PECKHAM in RITCHIEkin for German minenwerfer firing at 9.2 Wiltshires infantry officer reported that Mortar has 130° major coming from Dones trench in G.1. Trench mortars in this regiment are broken. Fire began at 11.30 am. Enemy at 6.0 pm attempt some bursts from German Trench Mortar from about Mayher westerly. Communication with trench was not the line and did not pass. — Trench mortar harassed also after firing about five rounds. Captain FORBES and 2/Lieut. HOUGHTON returned to their battn. this evening. Wiring shell was left took place in morning. Fourth splendor	

WAR DIARY
or
INTELLIGENCE SUMMARY
(Erase heading not required.)

Army Form C. 2118

Instructions regarding War Diaries and Intelligence Summaries are contained in F.S. Regs., Part II. and the Staff Manual respectively. Title Pages will be prepared in manuscript.

Place	Date	Hour	Summary of Events and Information	Remarks and references to Appendices
LANDENHOEK	24/8	9.0 p.m.	Barometer 30.09. Weather warm, dull, cloudy, little wind. At 3.30 a.m. fired 100 rounds lyddite in response to infantry call from trench Q 2 to silence Menenweg; 2 rounds repeated (1st WELSH) shrapnel repetitive & enemy slipper firing. At 12.30 pm fired 10th effect 13 rounds lyddite at BLACK REDOUBT - 8 rounds were effective - 3 shells failed to explode. Enemy replied with heavy shelling with 6 inch & 8 inch howitzers, falling well in rear of our trenches. At 3.40 pm registered MAEDELSTEDE FARM in our 7 Battery map, with 6 effective. At 5.0 pm fired one round lyddite at BLACK REDOUBT 6½ heavy howitzer fire in rear of our trenches. 5.10 pm Registered no 6 gun on RESERVE TRENCHES at O 24. a. 8.4. Enemy again shelled heavy shelling at 7.30 pm lasting until 8.45 pm.	
LANDENHOEK	25/6	9.15 p.m.	Barometer 30.06. Much warmer. Comparatively quiet day. Intermittent fire. Some heavy shelling from 6 - 7 Komm. (Luted) at 7.30 pm this continued a heavy intervals.	
LANDENHOEK	26/4	9.5 p.m	Barometer 30.01. Very warm. This has effect round of lyddite at 7.15 am at MAEDELSTEDE in reply to "Pip Squeak" sent here in German for lunch. Medical Officer inspected the wagon lines & pronounced the barn insanitary. Paid Butler. 20 inhabitants carried from	

1875 Wt. W593/826 1,000,000 4/15 J.B.C. & A. A.D.S.S./Forms/C. 2118.

WAR DIARY
or
INTELLIGENCE SUMMARY
(Erase heading not required.)

Army Form C. 2118

Instructions regarding War Diaries and Intelligence Summaries are contained in F. S. Regs., Part II. and the Staff Manual respectively. Title Pages will be prepared in manuscript.

Place	Date	Hour	Summary of Events and Information	Remarks and references to Appendices
LANDENHOEK	21/8/15	9.40 pm	Barometer 29.90. Fine storm. Airship passed over POPERINGHE last night going WEST. Hostile zeppelins heard here at 10.30 pm. Registered No 1 gun on L'ENFER — direct hit on house at 5th round. 11.30 a.m. No 4 gun having got off the line owing to track platform irregularities on reference point SPANBROEK MOLEN, fired shr 1°10' to the right. Platform has been improved during the weekend & shr has been firing greatly consistent to F. Last few days. The position was very satisfactory & very improved. Received Canvas Strips No 2308 (1 Ply), 100 Sandbags from R.E. behind hedges finished. Shewed up remains in form. One on left with cows 8am. It is 7 feet deep & with woven up earth bank is about 8½ feet deep. 4 feet broad at bottom. 12 feet at top. With Curtain about 40 mm of overseer. The Dressing is only to keep it dry, as it are 6 to 9 Marshes Cerneuits with Smoking hearts.	
LANDENHOEK	23/8/15	8.55 pm	Barometer 29.74. Fine. Very little wind. Rain falling. Registered No 4 gun on PETIT BOIS. Hand steadying by Ack of Veterinary Officer at Wagon Lines suffering from Ammonia — this broke from lifts draught horse filed to Etablishment.	
LANDENHOEK	24/8/15	8.40 pm	Barometer 29.53. Cold overcast. About 10 shells fell near our battery at 11.00 am. Shrapnel from own battery in No 2 Gun Pit — they were both 77 cm guns & 10.5 cm howitzer. A fuze picked up marked K.Z. II Sp15 and Fr 5303 anchor. Registered Sichel funnerny & trench opposite 93 (N.24 c 6.1) westerly from registration SW Corner of PETIT BOIS with ALFreekin (N.24.f. 33) Ends.	

WAR DIARY
or
INTELLIGENCE SUMMARY
(Erase heading not required.)

Army Form C. 2118

Instructions regarding War Diaries and Intelligence Summaries are contained in F. S. Regs., Part II. and the Staff Manual respectively. Title Pages will be prepared in manuscript.

Place	Date	Hour	Summary of Events and Information	Remarks and references to Appendices
LANDENHOEK	30/9/16	9.15 pm	Bombdn 29.70. Older with some rain in evening. Forced our round on BLACK REDOUBT trenchtijn line of NO 4 gun. Sketch of wire entanglement in front of Enemy trench visible from Observation Post sent to Brigade Hqrs. Spy reported in neighbourhood. Dressed as a Lieutenant R.F.A. 1st working party arrived from home.	[signature]
LANDENHOEK	31/8/16	7.30 pm	Bombdn 29.96. At M.D own front line 78. Irregulated a new front alley by the Infantry the BLACK REDOUBT, this is now the Left and between this the BLACK REDOUBT we have it thus Regulated. Shell also bisected them as before known but the town still is known as the BLACK REDOUBT. (N.30.a.4.3.) 2.30 pm fired on a working party near SPANBROEK MOLEN, (N.30.c.1.9) work stopped. Two 70's by white at BLACK REDOUBT. Enemy replied with five heavy shell which all burst. At 4.10 pm working party seen again - fired two more shrapnel & heavy trench mortar also - work stopped.	[signature]

19th Division.

"C"/89 Battery
89th Brigade R.F.A.

Vol I

101/6250

Army Form C. 2118

WAR DIARY
or
INTELLIGENCE SUMMARY
(Erase heading not required.)

Place	Date	Hour	Summary of Events and Information	Remarks and references to Appendices
Bulford	16/7/15		Mobilization of Battery completed by drawing of Ammunition from TIDWORTH. Orders received to proceed overseas.	H.R.
En route	17/7/15		The Battery left BULFORD at 3 a.m. to entrain at AMESBURY STATION where it left at 5 a.m. Arriving at SOUTHAMPTON DOCKS at 7.45 a.m. It was embarked by midday on S.S. "COURTFIELD" and left that evening	H.R.
HAVRE. No 1 Camp R.	18/7/15		En HAVRE - 5 hours were changed by A.V.C. at the docks. Disembarked in HAVRE at 5.30 a.m. after a good passage. One Sergeant Arrived in HAVRE at 10 a.m. and marched out to No 1 Camp in the afternoon. admitted to hospital.	H.R.
"	19/7/15		The Battery entrained at 10 p.m. at the GARE des MARCHANDISES	H.R.
En route	20/7/15		The En route by train. left HAVRE at 1.20 a.m. Detrained at ST OMER at 8 p.m. and marched to BONNINGUES 13 mi.	H.R.
BONNINGUES	21/7/15		Arrived in billets at 4.10 a.m.	H.R.
"	22/7/15		Rested.	H.R.
WARDRECQUES	23/7/15		Marched with 58th Infy Bde & 88th F.A. Bde to WARDRECQUES 16 miles. Started at 9 a.m. arrived 7.30 p.m. Visited by Brig. Gen. Lawrie C.B.	H.R.

Army Form C. 2118

WAR DIARY
or
INTELLIGENCE SUMMARY
(Erase heading not required.)

Instructions regarding War Diaries and Intelligence Summaries are contained in F.S. Regs., Part II. and the Staff Manual respectively. Title Pages will be prepared in manuscript.

(2)

Place	Date	Hour	Summary of Events and Information	Remarks and references to Appendices
BOURECQ.	24th		March continued to BOURECQ 15 mi from 9 a.m. to 3.30 p.m.	MR. REFERENCES map BELGIUM 1/100000 HAZEBROUCK 6A.
"	25th to 30th		Rested. Inspected in billets by Gen. Sir D. Haig G.O.C. 1st Army on July 30th.	
LE SART.	31/7/15		Marched 13 miles with 89th F.A. Bde.	

H Russell
Capt. R.F.A.
Commanding 89 F.A. Bde..

121/6787

19th Division

"C"/89 Battery
Vol. II

August 15.

WAR DIARY
or
INTELLIGENCE SUMMARY

(Erase heading not required.)

Army Form C. 2118

Place	Date	Hour	Summary of Events and Information	Remarks and references to Appendices
RICHEBOURG ST VAAST.	8/8/15	4.30 p.m.	Battery remained at Le Sart till Aug 6th on the 4th the 89th Bde was inspected by Lt Gen Sir James Wilcox Commanding Indian Corps. On 6th it left Gillells and 3p.m. and marched to Pont Ricqueul. That evening the gunners moved up to their position where they prepared gun pits. The Battery now being in the Lahore Divn remaining at Pont Ricqueul having brought their wagon line of the 89th B.A.C. with them. own section of the 89th B.A.C. The guns were brought into action on the night of Aug 8th about 10 p.m. and registration was commenced next day about 3 p.m. On the	
RICHEBOURG ST VAAST	3/8/15	—	11th the Battery was formed grouped with the XIth Brigade R.F.A. under the command of Lt Col J.McC. Maxwell C.B. and was allotted the front of the Bois du Biez. This front was found very difficult to cover owing # to the closeness of the country and it was necessary to lay out four telephone wires. On Aug 16th Capt. C.H. Tebbay was transferred to 19th D.A.C.	

Army Form C. 211

WAR DIARY
or
INTELLIGENCE SUMMARY
(Erase heading not required.)

Place	Date	Hour	Summary of Events and Information	Remarks and references to Appendices
RICHEBOURG ST VAAST	26/8/15		and was replaced in the Battery by 2nd/Lt E. CRUICKSHANK from 19th D.A.C. No event of any importance happened — the enemy remained quietly in their trenches and registration went on being used for several points. & aeroplane observation	
	27/8		On Aug the 27th the 4th Bde R.F.A. began to relieve the 11th Bde R.F.A. This move was completed by Aug 30th at 10 a.m. when the Battery was brought into "GORDON'S GROUP" under the Command Col L.A.C. GORDON C.B. R.F.A. It was now attached to MEERUT DIVISION, the LAHORE DIVISION having moved further SOUTH.	

H Russell Capt R.F.A.

Commanding 7/89 F.A. BDE.

121/6971

19th Kurram

C/89 Battery
Vol III
Sep 1. 15

Army Form C. 2118

WAR DIARY
or
INTELLIGENCE SUMMARY
(Erase heading not required.)

Instructions regarding War Diaries and Intelligence Summaries are contained in F.S. Regs., Part II. and the Staff Manual respectively. Title Pages will be prepared in manuscript.

Place	Date	Hour	Summary of Events and Information	Remarks and references to Appendices
RICHEBOURG ST VAAST.	3/9/15		11th Bde returned to action and the Battery once more came under the command of Lt Col. J. McC. MAXWELL C.B. Things still remained very quiet.	
	4/9/15		The Battery came under fire for the first time. An 18pr Battery immediately in front being heavily shelled all day. Several shells came into this position but no harm was done.	
	12/9/15	—	On the 3rd one section was grouped with 18th Bde R.F.A. under Lt Col. R.G. Ouseley Ouseley C.M.G. D.S.O. so that the battery now had to cover the whole front of the LAHORE DIVISION i.e. about 60°. By order of Group Commander No 1 gun was placed by itself to enfilade the enemy trench for about 1000+. This proved very effective and silenced enemy trench mortars. Judging by his retaliation it seemed to annoy him intensely.	
	21/9/15		The single gun was brought back, and the bombs preliminary bombardment started. This bombardment lasted till	

Army Form C. 2118

WAR DIARY
or
INTELLIGENCE SUMMARY
(Erase heading not required.)

Place	Date	Hour	Summary of Events and Information	Remarks and references to Appendices
RICHEBOURG-ST VAAST.	25/9/15		Till the morning of the 25th when the MEERUT DIVN made an attack on the line to the N. of NEUVE CHAPELLE. The Battery assisted with the artillery of the LAHORE DIVN in this The Battery as a whole was now grouped with 18th Bde RFA	
	27/9/15		and allotted the front LA BASSEE Rd to FME DU BOIS. Things now became very quiet. No firing at all taking place. The weather also was very bad high westerly winds and heavy rains. During the month the battery came completely under the LAHORE DIVN. Drawing ordnance and supplies from them	

H Russell
Capt RFA
Commanding 89

C/89 Buttery
Vol. 4

12/7678

19th Kurrein

Oct 15.

CONFIDENTIAL

WAR DIARY

OF

C/89th F.A. Bde.

From 1/10/15 to 31/10/15.

(VOLUME IV)

Army Form C. 2118

C/89 F.A.Bde
October 15

WAR DIARY
or
INTELLIGENCE SUMMARY
(Erase heading not required.)

Place	Date	Hour	Summary of Events and Information	Remarks and references to Appendices
RICHEBOURG ST VAAST.	6.10.15		After the fighting on Sept. 25th the Battery remained quiet practically not firing a round till Oct 6th when it was given the Zone from the road in S.11.a to the Salient in S.16.a. covering the front of the FEROZEPORE Bde. On the evening of the 6th the first casualty occurred – one of the telephonists being slightly wounded on while returning from the O.P. The Battery was now grouped with the 18th Bde. R.F.A.	1/10000 Trench Map 36S.W.3
	13.10/15 12.30 p.m.		The Battery took part in a very successful demonstration which covered an attack on FOSSE No 8 and the HOHENZOLLERN REDOUBT.	H.R
	19.10/15		After this the usual routine went on. The weather was very misty and gave no opportunities for observation. Several Bombthrowers were located and silenced.	
	22/15		LAHORE Divn was relieved on this front by MEERUT and the	H.R

WAR DIARY
or
INTELLIGENCE SUMMARY

(Erase heading not required.)

Army Form C. 2118

C/89 F.A. Bde.
October 15
(2)

Place	Date	Hour	Summary of Events and Information	Remarks and references to Appendices
	23/9/15		The Battery was grouped with the 13th Bde R.F.A. under Lt Col TYLER. R.F.A.	H.R.
	25/9/15		The battery received orders to rejoin the 19th Divn. and leave the Section was relieved by a section of the 60th Bty (4 Stow) at 6.30 p.m. This section marched to Locon where it billeted for the night and came into action the following night at 8 p.m. beside D/89. at X 18 c 0.7 The remaining section was relieved on the night of 26/27 and came into action on the night 27/28.	4 inch Hab. H.R.
	31/9/15		Registering went on on the 28th, 29th & 30th, but was very difficult owing to thick weather. The Battery was allotted the RUE D'OUVERT as its principal objective. The weather was very difficult not and the move was carried out in pouring rain	H.R.

H Russell Capt R.F.A
Commanding C/89 F.A. Bde.

c/89 Bulletin
Vol - 5

121/7635

19th Kwavin

Nov 15

CONFIDENTIAL

WAR DIARY.

OF.

C/89TH BDE. R.F.A.

from 1st NOV. 1915 to 30TH NOV. 1915

Army Form C. 2118

WAR DIARY
or
INTELLIGENCE SUMMARY
(Erase heading not required.)

Instructions regarding War Diaries and Intelligence Summaries are contained in F. S. Regs., Part II. and the Staff Manual respectively. Title Pages will be prepared in manuscript.

Place	Date	Hour	Summary of Events and Information	Remarks and references to Appendices
LE TOURET	1st		Very wet and muddy. No firing was done. All the time was spent in keeping gun pits in repair.	
	2nd			
	3rd			
	4th		A clear day when the opportunity was seized to do some more registration. 19 rounds being fired on the RUE D'OUVERT.	
	5th		10 also fired at VIELKINGS CHURCH.	
	6th		Battery now received orders to move, and as no definite zone had been allotted no more firing was done.	
	7th			
	8th			
	9th		No.1 gun and the left section were moved at dark. No.1 gun to do old registering position at PONT LOGY while the left section relieved two guns of the 61st Bty at RICHEBOURG ST VAAST. As usual a lost night. One gun fell into a tunnel and took two hours to extricate. Registration carried out on June 27th do first. Enemy light and heavy howitzers rather active around RICHEBOURG ST VAAST.	
	10th		No.2 Gun & freight into action in the evening. The 61st leaving for M Somewhere overseas with the MEERUT DIVN.	

Army Form C. 21

WAR DIARY
or
INTELLIGENCE SUMMARY
(Erase heading not required.)

Place	Date	Hour	Summary of Events and Information	Remarks and references to Appendices
RICHEBOURG ST VAAST.	Nov 12th		The Battery was now in the Right group of the 46th Divn T.F. The remainder of the group consisting of the 88th F.F. Bde. under command of Major TOVEY R.F.A.	
	Nov 13th	4.15pm	No 2 gun fired 10 rounds to register its lines. 33 rds fired 28 fired from enfilading gun in retaliation for enemy shelling. This gun was always very effective and generally silenced the enemy. The other rounds were employed in registering night lines.	
	Nov 13th & Nov 14 15		Very thick obscuration intensely difficult hence no artillery action.	
	16th	2.20am	4 H.E. to check registration	
		3.30pm 4.30pm 4.35pm	20 H.E. fired on enemy front line and on DISTILLERY to as retaliation for his shelling our front line and WINDY CORNER from 3pm to 4.30pm to enemy light and heavy howitzers were active.	
	17th	10.45am 1pm	4 H.E. Registration of DISTILLERY shelling our front line with field guns. A.P.E. 12 Shrapnel Retaliation for enemy. As usual the enemy hit how was busy.	
		3pm	5 rds retaliation on FHE COUR D'AVOUE. Most of FHE were fired on the FACTORY.	
		6pm	A heavy shell (5.9") fell (?) and about 200 in front of battery position.	

Army Form C. 2118

WAR DIARY
or
INTELLIGENCE SUMMARY
(Erase heading not required.)

Instructions regarding War Diaries and Intelligence Summaries are contained in F.S. Regs., Part II. and the Staff Manual respectively. Title Pages will be prepared in manuscript.

Place	Date	Hour	Summary of Events and Information	Remarks and references to Appendices
RICHEBOURG ST VAAST	Nov 18th	1.2.5pm 3.15pm	Retaliation on LORGIES for enemy shelling RICHEBOURG with A.2. Hows. 1 German seen today wearing blue forage cap.	
	" 19th	12 noon 12.30pm	9 H.E. and 4 Shrapnel (enfilade) fired on enemy front line & no retaliation for shelling of our trenches with field guns and field Hows. About noon two heavy shells (third) fall very close to position of enfilade gun. Previously Shell had fallen all round PONT LOGY - Shell of all calibres but most too close. No rise.	
	" 20th		Very misty. No action.	
	" 21st	3.45pm 4pm	16 rounds fired at German front trenches in retaliation for enemy shelling forward. Very misty.	
	" 22nd		Very misty all day. No action. At 6 o.p.m. the battery came out of action to march to out billets at HAMET near ST VENANT. It was a freezing hard and some difficulty was found in getting along the road. The route was by LOCON - CORNET MALO - ROBECQ - ST VENANT. The battery arrived in billets at 2.30 am on 23rd. No Casualties in men & horses in spite of the roads.	
	23rd to 30th		Resting.	

H Russell Cap RHA
O.C. GBQ

1875 Wt. W593/826 1,000,000 4/15 J.B.C. & A. A.D.S.S./Forms/C. 2118.

19th Division.

"D" Battery 89th Brigade R.F.A.

Vol. I.

14-30-7-15

18/1/496

"F" Battery 89th Brigade R.F.A.   Sheet No. I

Army Form C. 2118

WAR DIARY
or
INTELLIGENCE SUMMARY
(Erase heading not required.)

Instructions regarding War Diaries and Intelligence Summaries are contained in F. S. Regs., Part II. and the Staff Manual respectively. Title Pages will be prepared in manuscript.

Place	Date	Hour	Summary of Events and Information	Remarks and references to Appendices
Bulford	17/7/15	7.30 a.m	The Battery consisting of 4 Officers, 126 other ranks and 125 Horses left Bulford Camp for Amesbury	
Amesbury	"	8-30	Arrived Amesbury. Right Section entrained for Southampton	
"	"	9-15	Train left with Right Section	
"	"	10-15	Left Section left for SOUTHAMPTON	
SOUTHAMPTON	"	11-0	First train arrived with Right Section	
"	"	12-30	Second train arrived with Left Section	
"	"	1-30	Horses, Guns + vehicles shipped on the S.S. Courtfield	
"	"	6 p.m	S.S. Courtfield left with Guns, Horses, Vehicles + Battery Commander and 71 men	
"	"	7.20 pm	The remainder of the Battery with 2 Officers embarked on S.S. Margueire + left SOUTHAMPTON	
HAVRE	18/7/15	2-0 am	La Margueire arrived – Good Crossing – Fine weather –	
"	"	4.20	S.S. Courtfield arrived	
"	"	7-0 a	Commenced disembarkation	
"	"	11-30	Finished disembarkation	

"G" Battery 89 Bde R.F.A.   Sheet No 2

Army Form C. 2118

WAR DIARY
or
INTELLIGENCE SUMMARY
(Erase heading not required.)

Instructions regarding War Diaries and Intelligence Summaries are contained in F.S. Regs., Part II. and the Staff Manual respectively. Title Pages will be prepared in manuscript.

Place	Date	Hour	Summary of Events and Information	Remarks and references to Appendices
HAVRE	18/7/15	12-30	Left HAVRE for Rest Camp No 1	
		4-0	Arrived at Rest Camp No 1 – Officers billets dunder Canvas	
"	19/7/15	9-0 am	Reveille Parade – Preparation for Moving off	
		10-30	Battery left No 1 Camp for Gare des Marchandises	
"		12 md	Arrived at Gare des Marchandises & B.S commenced entraining	
		3-0 pm	Train left entraining. 2ⁿᵈ Lt Peel in all I/Asst & Correct	
		3-40	Train left Gare des Marchandises	
Buchy		9-0 am	Halted – Horses watered and fed & others of behind (Hot Coffee + Cognac from French Govt grounds)	
		9-15	Left.	
ABBEVILLE		3-50 pm	Halted. Horses watered and fed & Men Rations	
		4-30	Left.	
Auancy		7-30	Arrived + Raced for Incl orders	

"D" Battery 69th F.A. RHA Sheet No 3

Army Form C. 2118

WAR DIARY
or
INTELLIGENCE SUMMARY
(Erase heading not required.)

Instructions regarding War Diaries and Intelligence Summaries are contained in F.S. Regs., Part II. and the Staff Manual respectively. Title Pages will be prepared in manuscript.

Place	Date	Hour	Summary of Events and Information	Remarks and references to Appendices
St OMER	19/7/15	11.00pm	Arrived and commenced unloading guns, horses + vehicles	
"	20/7/15	2.00 am	Limber + left St OMER Station	
Bonningues	"	5.45 am	Arrived - after 13 miles more march from St Omer Station - Travelling on - Roads good. Horses tossed and 100 or arrival. Officers + other billeted. Guns + Horses Picketed out. Guards + Picquets mounted Stables etc.	
"	"	12 am	Battery Parade	
"	21/7/15	6.00 am	Reveille	
"	"	8.45 "	Battery Gun Drill - Equitation - Repairing Harness - Harness Cleaning	
"	"	10-30	Inspection of Rifles	
"	"	11-30	Exercise	
			1 Gunner taken to St Omer Hospital not exposed Front.	Nil.

"A" Battery 89th Bde RFA.   Sheet No. 1

Army Form C. 2118

WAR DIARY
or
INTELLIGENCE SUMMARY
(Erase heading not required.)

Place	Date	Hour	Summary of Events and Information	Remarks and references to Appendices
Bonningues	23/7/15	8-45 am	Battery Parade. Preparation for Moving	
"	"	9-30 "	Battery left. 1 horse left behind. Change of Major in new Retirement arrangement.	
Norduchen	"	11-10 "	Arrived — Horses Harness waters feed watter Released	
"	"	2-0 "	Left	
"	"	8-0 pm	Arrived — Officers Mess Bivouacs — Horses Guns	
Wardrecques	"	"	Proceeded — Guards & Piquets Mounted	
"	24/7/15	4-30 am	Roused	
"	"	5-0 "	Tea, Case to Stable up. Preparation made for Moving	
"	"	8-40 "	Battery Left & from the Squadron	
"	"	10-30 "	Halted — Horses watered.	
Bodecq	"	4-0 "	Arrived Officers under Billeted Officers quarters in Farm House. Men in Barns & Surrounding Outhouses & Guns and Horses Parked.	

1875 Wt. W593/826 1,000,000 4/15 J.B.C. & A. A.D.S.S./Forms/C. 2118.

L/89 Nympen Ptd. this to 5

Army Form C. 2118

WAR DIARY
or
INTELLIGENCE SUMMARY

(Erase heading not required.)

Instructions regarding War Diaries and Intelligence Summaries are contained in F. S. Regs., Part II. and the Staff Manual respectively. Title Pages will be prepared in manuscript.

Place	Date	Hour	Summary of Events and Information	Remarks and references to Appendices
Bourecq	25/7/15	6:00a 6:30 8:45 11:30 7:00pm	(Church Parade) Rest as usual Gym. Street Spraying Stables Church service for C of E. Men at Fynes St Queen. Service taken by Col. Thomas (Brigade Commander)	
"	26/7/15		The usual daily duties carried on as usual	
"	29/7/15		Battery Commanders arrangements. Weather continue fine and Men healthy and enjoying life. The dissatisfaction our men appear quite contented & happy.	
"	29/7/15 30/7/15	10:00a	1 Gunner sent to Hospital with Dysentery, NCO's + men get paying their ???	

121/6787

19th Division

8/89 Battery
Vol. II

August 15.

D. Battery 89th 1st RFA Sheet No 5

Army Form C. 2118

WAR DIARY
or
INTELLIGENCE SUMMARY
(Erase heading not required.)

Instructions regarding War Diaries and Intelligence Summaries are contained in F.S. Regs., Part II. and the Staff Manual respectively. Title Pages will be prepared in manuscript.

Place	Date	Hour	Summary of Events and Information	Remarks and references to Appendices
BOURECQ	31/5/15	7-30am	Battery Parade Roll Call. Preparation made for Moving	
		8-45	Left BOURECQ and joined the Brigade at 9-30. 2nd Brigade formed column of route followed by D. Battery @ 10 F.d	
Lillers		10-30	Passed through LILLERS at 10-30 a.m.	
ROBECQ		12-15	Halted - Horses watered and fed & troops rationed	
		1-0	Left ROBECQ	
		2-15	Passed through Merville	
MERVILLE				
LE SART		3-0	Arrived. Battery billeted here. Name of farm - LORIDAN SURETS LEON Rue d' and MERVILLE Heavy thunder storm experienced from a few distance (4000yrds)	
	1/6/15	Sunday	Reveille	
		5-20	Reveille	
		9-0	Horses fed	
		11-0	Breakfast	
		1-0	Lunch had arrived	
		2-30	Battery paraded for marching order to go. Canal great surprise to all men	A.M...

H Battery 69th Bde RFA Sheet No. 1 Army Form C. 2118

WAR DIARY
or
INTELLIGENCE SUMMARY
(Erase heading not required.)

Instructions regarding War Diaries and Intelligence Summaries are contained in F.S. Regs., Part II. and the Staff Manual respectively. Title Pages will be prepared in manuscript.

Place	Date	Hour	Summary of Events and Information	Remarks and references to Appendices
late SART-MERVILLE	1/8/15	6.0 am	Men of the Battery who have permission to visit MERVILLE the 3 hours from 6 to 9 am. in parties of no less than 3 in each. Members the civilians fare and men least for and well. Roo case as yet in Billets or the lines	
	2/8/15	9.0		
		9 am	Heavy gun firing heard early this morning and continues for about 3/4 hour	
		6.30	Aeroplane notices over MERVILLE under fire but got away	
		11.30	Indian Troops passed through	
		2.0	Gun fire + explosives heard audible few though	
			Heavy intermittent gunfire as though the night + showers	
			+	
	3/8/15	3.45	Reveille Horses watered 6.15	
		9.0	Retreat + several steady drills when Battery Comm. makes arrangements	
			Heavy shower we though the day. The Horses be watered at	
La Lys			Canal which is 1000 yards away from the Billets	
			Battery's Race to Andes to billeting of 20 minutes	HCle

1875 Wt. W593/826 1,000,000 4/15 J.B.C. & A. A.D.S.S./Forms/C. 2118.

Army Form C. 2118

WAR DIARY
or
INTELLIGENCE SUMMARY
(Erase heading not required.)

P Battery 69th Bde R.F.A.   Pages No 6

Instructions regarding War Diaries and Intelligence Summaries are contained in F.S. Regs., Part II. and the Staff Manual respectively. Title Pages will be prepared in manuscript.

Place	Date	Hour	Summary of Events and Information	Remarks and references to Appendices
LE SART	4/7/15	10-30 a	Inspection of the Brigade by G.O.C. Indian Corps who made complimentary remarks on the appearance of New Army.	
	5/7/15		Parade & drill as usual. Two Officers men sent to Lesbeurn for instruction and were attached to the 60th Brigade.	
	6/7/15		H. P. O. & Kitchen Band	
		10.15	Church Parade. Service held in Market Square opened first with dance of time 11.00	
	8/7/15	5-0 p	Two Officers returned from Lesbeurn. Heavy firing heard which continued as though the Enft. + up to 9 p of 16 9/15.	
	9/7/15		Two Officers + 6 at L.O.& sent to Lesbeurn & were attached to the 61st Brigade for instruction.	
	11/7/15	9.0	Battery Trees Orders. It gave not unfair to we to 10.00 under B.C. Cannander an arrived	

[signature]

Army Form C. 2118

A/89th Bde R.F.A.   Press No 9

WAR DIARY
or
INTELLIGENCE SUMMARY
(Erase heading not required.)

Instructions regarding War Diaries and Intelligence Summaries are contained in F. S. Regs., Part II. and the Staff Manual respectively. Title Pages will be prepared in manuscript.

Place	Date	Hour	Summary of Events and Information	Remarks and references to Appendices
Merville	12/8/15		2 Officers + 6 N.C.O's returned from Lestrem	
"	14/8/15		2/Lt E. Cruickshank G.O.C. 2nd from 106-29th F.A. Bde S.R. attached to B/Battery — Lt. A.L. Roby whose B/69 is detached to C/89th	
"	15/8/15	6.20	Morning Parade as usual. Battery paraded for Church. Divine Service held in Merville on plot of ground S. of Canal.	
"	16/8/15		Usual daily Parades under	
"	[22/8/15]		Battery Commanders arrangement	
"	23/8/15	2-op m	The Battery Commander, Lt. Wilks and four of Battery Staff left La Sart for the Firing Line	
"	24/8/15	6-op m	The Left Section under Lt. Stephens left for the Firing Line	

1875 Wt. W593/826 1,000,000 4/15 J.B.C. & A. A.D.S.S./Forms/C. 2118.

WAR DIARY
or
INTELLIGENCE SUMMARY

(Erase heading not required.)

Army Form C. 2118

Place	Date	Hour	Summary of Events and Information	Remarks and references to Appendices
Le Sars	25/5	6.0 pm	The L/Bty Section under Lt R Martin left Le Sars LR 16 Jenny Camp. The Major & Lieut Brown Foreden Mr reached at 0.30. The guns were taken up independently below M 30a Bailey 31st Batt.	
	26/5 to 30/5		Registration carried out - great difficulty with telephone wires. The shooting was excellent and the gun appears to have less error than the range tables show but shoots repeated charges do not shoot uniformly. Shrapnel fuzes and bullets being not agreement to the setting.	
	31/5		The Battery opened fire on the German trenches at S.22.c.3.0 to * Mar S.28.a.8.5-3.5 - The result was highly satisfactory doing severe damage to the Parapet. No. of rounds fired was 2 shrapnel percussion 30 Lyddite rg. 8. B lindo to direct hits on parapet to good bursts just behind parapet. The Layers were most accurate in their laying.	

WAR DIARY or INTELLIGENCE SUMMARY

Army Form C. 2118

1 Battery 89th Bde R.F.A. No. 11

Place	Date	Hour	Summary of Events and Information	Remarks and references to Appendices
	31/8/15		Hostile aircraft have not been as active & altogether the Germans as very quiet. Our own aircraft is particularly noticed under heavy German fire but apparently without any result. During the past month the number of casualties though without has been very slight. 3 cases only, one of which was able to rejoin the Battery. The men continued to dig in and were in cheerful conditions and in every way good and the weather has been exceptionally bright. The horses also seem to keep up condition.	

121/6971

19th Division

8/89 Battery R.F.A.
Vol III

Sept 1. 15.

"S" Battery R.H.A. ? Foss   Sheet No 1/2   Army Form C. 2118

Instructions regarding War Diaries and Intelligence Summaries are contained in F. S. Regs., Part II. and the Staff Manual respectively. Title Pages will be prepared in manuscript.

WAR DIARY
or
INTELLIGENCE SUMMARY
(Erase heading not required.)

Place	Date	Hour	Summary of Events and Information	Remarks and references to Appendices
Le Touret	1/9/15		Enemy very quiet today. Guns fired their usual flying shots at night into Rue du Bois.	
"	3/9/15	2.3 pm	Our guns opened fire and bombarded a building machine at * S.22.a.60-35 (near St Avert). This appeared very effective. A large amount of material being thrown into the air. On the conclusion however the arms of the machine could still be seen standing above the ruins. Fuze — 17.	Map. 36 S.W.I. Sheet 3
"		2.50 pm		
"	4/9/15	8.45 am 9.25 "	Hostile aircraft slightly active. A monoplane and a biplane came fire from our AA. M. LewGun. Gun was opened firing L.u. L.2. (A.A corner) at squares of infantry observed at S.22.c.00	
"	5/9/15	2.50 pm 5.40 pm 6.30 am	S.28.a.2.3. (Trenches) Enemy seems very keen at the given target.	
"		3.25	The right section opened fire on the Enemys new works from S.23.c.53 to S.23.c.84. The guns fired very effective dispersing working parties and any & new works on Rouges bas & new works.	

Allen ?

WAR DIARY
or
INTELLIGENCE SUMMARY

(Erase heading not required.)

Army Form C. 2118

Instructions regarding War Diaries and Intelligence Summaries are contained in F.S. Regs., Part II. and the Staff Manual respectively. Title Pages will be prepared in manuscript.

Place	Date	Hour	Summary of Events and Information	Remarks and references to Appendices
		5.10 pm	Registered fire on by Battery of North S. 28. d. 2.5 and road junction of communication trench 3.35 c.6.4. The enemy opened rapid rifle & machine gun fire on this as soon as the registration commenced but no shells fell in the vicinity of the Battery. One or two fell near Glencorse Wood.	
	6/5	5.45 pm to 6.15	Shells reported to be also about	
		3.30 pm & 4.0 & 2-3 & 6 to 6.15	Heavy artillery fire active throughout the day but not so apparent towards the Hun lines. By this the Boches had got the range of the Battery there were of the little damage done. Registered fire carried out by telephone and by observer. No reply from the enemy to machine gun fire in the afternoon, nothing was reported.	
	7/5	8.45 to 9.5	Enemy aircraft very active. One has been to the troops down heavily by French Artillery. Weather continues fine & hot. Part of the Battery been Pits & dug outs.	Nil.

WAR DIARY or INTELLIGENCE SUMMARY

Army Form C. 2118

(Erase heading not required.)

Instructions regarding War Diaries and Intelligence Summaries are contained in F.S. Regs., Part II. and the Staff Manual respectively. Title Pages will be prepared in manuscript.

Place: Apply La Bou

Date	Hour	Summary of Events and Information	Remarks and references to Appendices
8/15		16 enemy shrapnel supply. Enemy firing rifles on the line of the Railway short field & the front under Germans who break from our guns have been day.	
9/15	5.30p	Reported carried out of 8.16 a 10 at hour 10s grounds	
	5.55	Two of the enemys shells have been 300 yards of the Bn Hort at working Luxury of fights was seen from shelter	
		German Artillery seems to have been unusually active during the past 24 hours and also their aircraft.	
	5.15p	13 Round were fired on German support trenches opposite ORCHARD	
10/15	4 pm	A Hostile Aeroplane was brought down by our Anti Aircraft guns and fell in our lines	

Sheet No 15

S/69 A Bu RFA

Army Form C. 2118

WAR DIARY
or
INTELLIGENCE SUMMARY
(Erase heading not required.)

Instructions regarding War Diaries and Intelligence Summaries are contained in F. S. Regs., Part II. and the Staff Manual respectively. Title Pages will be prepared in manuscript.

Place	Date	Hour	Summary of Events and Information	Remarks and references to Appendices
	10/9/15	5.15 pm	At the request of the Infantry we opened fire on German trenches opposite Orchard Salient.	
	11/9/15		The enemy seems to have had reinforcements during the last 24 hours, and no hostile aircraft has been observed during that time.	
	13/9/15	12.15 pm	4 rounds were fired at what appears like a gun emplacement 50 yards E of Cour du Avoué	
		2.30 pm	At request of infantry 6 rounds were fired on German trenches Orchard Salient. The cessation of the enemy's fire was due to our effective shelling at this time	
	14/9/15	3.45 pm	} Retaliation on Orchard Salient	Kl.
	15/9/15	3.30 pm		
		7.55 am		

WAR DIARY or INTELLIGENCE SUMMARY

Army Form C. 2118

1/9th L.N. Lan. Bde. Sheet No. 16.

Place	Date	Hour	Summary of Events and Information	Remarks and references to Appendices
	15/9/15	3.45pm	O German Huns was fired up by 3/h Bennett. 20 Zara N.E. Wn. of TROCODERO. It was marked N.Z.11. Sp. 15. 82 has one of them fell and was apparently from a 15 or gun.	
		4	17 rounds on S 29. a 0 3 — S 29 L 3. 2. Rue des Maraies Piggy-baker also testing of New Shes. (AMATOL) which	
		4.45pm	proved poor: the rounds being 4 blinds & 4 very low bursts. the matter was reported to O.C 69.15th that furthwe requests tests might be carried out	
			There is less activity on the part of Hostile Aircraft to altogether things have been very mormal this loss 24 hours	
	16/9/15	4.5pm to 4.35pm	At request of Infantry 3 rounds Lyddite was fired at 26.a 3 8 and 22. C. 3. a.	
		6.30pm to	No lane search & some Lyddite was fired at points opposite Canadian Orchard	

WAR DIARY
or
INTELLIGENCE SUMMARY
(Erase heading not required.)

Army Form C. 2118

Instructions regarding War Diaries and Intelligence Summaries are contained in F. S. Regs., Part II. and the Staff Manual respectively. Title Pages will be prepared in manuscript.

F/Pg 4th Bde   Sheet No 14

Place	Date	Hour	Summary of Events and Information	Remarks and references to Appendices
	17/9/15	1-30am to 1-40	As report of infantry & bombs Lydder were fired at from opposite Orchard Salient.	
		12-10pm to 1-0pm	Registration by New Amatol Shell (9 rounds) of S.27.B.9.3.	
		11-35pm	Retaliation as German Sap Head S.22.C.0.6. (2 rounds) Hostile Aircraft was attended over Battery at 8-0am (1 Taube) and 9-0am (2 Biplanes)	
	18/9/15	1-0pm 1-50 10-0pm	Retaliation with 9 rounds Lyddite in S.22.A.3.f. Sap Head S.22.C.1.7. " " " "	

H.Q. Bde R.F.A.   Sheet No 18   Army Form C. 2118

WAR DIARY
or
INTELLIGENCE SUMMARY
(Erase heading not required.)

Place	Date	Hour	Summary of Events and Information	Remarks and references to Appendices
	19/9/15	6.30am } 7-0 " } 11.40am }	Fired 3 rounds in retaliation at S.22.A.37. Gunners service test at Battery Position.	
	"	3.45pm to 4.30pm	Test of Armstrong Rees. by Brigade Commander and G.O.C. 30 rounds fired at N. Corner Rue d'Ouvert - a full record of this test was taken by 15th Commander. It proves slightly better than the previous test but the complete detonation appears as effective as compared with shrapnel shrapnel. Enemy slightly more active today, but with no apparent result. Aircraft again here busy.	
	20/9/15	4-0 } 4-40 }	Received full instructions for the bombardment which was to commence next day.	
	21/9/15	8.40 am	Commenced Bombardment of Orchard Salient firing 104 rounds. This proved highly effective. The front line trenches were knocked down in places and the support trenches were well searched.	
		10.30 a.m.		

II/29th LO Brigade. Sheet No 19

Army Form C. 2118

WAR DIARY
or
INTELLIGENCE SUMMARY
(Erase heading not required.)

Place	Date	Hour	Summary of Events and Information	Remarks and references to Appendices
	21/9/15	2.30 pm	In Support of LAHORE - Bombarded support trenches in rear of BOARS HEAD - apparently effective. No of rounds - 24.	
		2.45 pm	Bombarded - COVERED-WAY.- Observation difficult owing to light and 18 pr Batteries wire cutting in front. effect apparently good on the EASTERN end of Covered Way - No of rounds 16	
		5.0 pm	Bombarded Junction of TRAMWAY and Communication trenches "S.23. a. 1-4" effect doubtful No of rounds 13.	
		10.0 pm	Bombarded S.22.c.5.3 - 2 rounds	
		11-0 "	" DISTILLERIE - S.1Y. No of rounds 18.	
	22/9/15	12.30 am	" S.22.C.3.0 2 rounds	
	"	3-0 am	" S.22.C.8.4 4 rounds	

1875 Wt. W593/826 1,000,000 4/15 J.B.C. & A. A.D.S.S./Forms/C.2118.

Army Form C. 2118

A/pg T. A. Tidd   Sheet No 20

WAR DIARY
or
INTELLIGENCE SUMMARY
(Erase heading not required.)

Instructions regarding War Diaries and Intelligence Summaries are contained in F. S. Regs., Part II. and the Staff Manual respectively. Title Pages will be prepared in manuscript.

Place	Date	Hour	Summary of Events and Information	Remarks and references to Appendices
	22/9/15	A.M. 9-10	Bombardment — S. 28. a. 25 — 2 rounds —	
	"	10-10 } 10 } 10-45 }	S. 22. C.17 — 16 rounds. S 22 a 31 — 14 rounds — all in the vicinity of the MOULIN D'EAU	
		12 } 10 } 12·55	S. 22. C.28. 16 rounds — S 22. a. 3 4 — 34 rounds. Moor dahs factory in several instances. Support trenches were well shelled. Shells burst in trenches themselves and much word and material was thrown into the air	
		5·0pm 3·5" 5·10"	BOARS HEAD 15 rounds ⎫ Effect highly satisfactory. Support Trenches 6 " ⎬ Huge quantity of material + BOARS HEAD 30 " ⎭ wood being thrown into the air. There was no attempt of a feint attack by the Saxon Bn. on the BOARS HEAD owing to shewn fire of German batteries, which had been very quiet slowing bombardment. In its effect so apparently failed as the German batteries hardly fired a round in reply.	Wilce

1875 Wt. W593/826 1,000,000 4/15 J.B.C. & A. A.D.S.S./Forms/C. 2118.

D/69 Z A Bde Sheet No 21

Army Form C. 21

WAR DIARY
or
INTELLIGENCE SUMMARY
(Erase heading not required.)

Place	Date	Hour	Summary of Events and Information	Remarks and references to Appendices
	22/9/15	PM 10-30	Fired 18 rounds on DISTILLERIE S.22.a 3.4 to S.22.c 1.7.	
	23/9/15	12-0 to 16 am	24 " " "	
		2-0	18 " " DISTILLERIE	
		4-0	" Cors d'Aubre + Building rear, Green Mound Front Building	
		11-40	Ouvt works, Searching + Sweeping S.22 a 3.4 to S.22.0.5.9	
		10	Went back in rear No of rounds fired 80. Effect good effective. Many direct hits on front Building and walls.	
		12-45	" Morning Range held. In searching + sweeping much damage was done to trench. Shells bursting on trench. General effect good	
		1-0 pm	BOHRS, HEAD O + Trench across La Bassée Road 30 rounds Covert Way — Hans at end of Covert Way 20 " Point 34 + ½ entrenh 53 — 12 rounds — Supposed of Hers forms	
		3-30 pm	10 rounds	

WAR DIARY
or
INTELLIGENCE SUMMARY

(Erase heading not required.)

Army Form C. 2118

Sheet No 2

2/19th Bn R Fa

Place	Date	Hour	Summary of Events and Information	Remarks and references to Appendices
		9 pm	Desultory 11 rounds	
		10 "	Head of Communication Trench 8 rounds	
		11 "	Cor d' Avone 4 rounds	
	24/5	2 AM	Trenches in rear 6 "	
		7·45 to 9·40	Rgo Cabin — House N corner of Rue d' Avone 27 rounds	
		11·40 to 12·25	29 rounds fired on "Ferme de Toulotte" — Effect apparently good. Blew up trench work & many deuces hits on Building. 4 shells were blows & 5 were very poor bursts	
		3·45	Trenches S.22.B.3.7 to 22.19.8.5. 25 rounds Brit Angle. S.23.A.0.4. 30 rounds. — Shooting very satisfactory	
		6	LAHORE — LA TOURETTE 30 rounds + horses on La Basse Rd S.11—C.2.5. 35 rounds — A number of direct hits were obtained and several horses were seen a light.	

5/89th L.A. Bde.

File No. 23

Army Form C. 2118

WAR DIARY
or
INTELLIGENCE SUMMARY
(Erase heading not required.)

Place	Date	Hour	Summary of Events and Information	Remarks and references to Appendices
	25/9	A.M. 5.30	The Battery opened fire with one Section on Houses at N. end of Rue d'Ouvert to support the left of the 56th Bde which were to advance. Later the left Section fired 50 rounds into strong points in S 28 D. Gas was noticed which in 3 minutes had obliterated everything beyond our front trenches.	
		5.36	Strange columns of smoke were noticed along the whole line of the 19th Division. The right section was turned on to the front trenches as B.I.T. which the left section was held in readiness 27.B.I.T. for relieving Germans on the Rue du Marais. The Battery was asked to to render any further assistance either in the advance or to cover the withdrawal of the leading Bns [Battalions] of the 56th Bde as orders about 8 P.M. the smoke had drifted off. A heavy rain settled in which lasted late to a heavy dew. [illegible]	

WAR DIARY
or
INTELLIGENCE SUMMARY

(Erase heading not required.)

Army Form C. 2118

Sheet No 24

1/4 69th L.A.A.

Place	Date	Hour	Summary of Events and Information	Remarks and references to Appendices
	26/9		Flag signal line referred to in former portion of LES FACONS has now been no activity on the part of the enemy during this time & no adverse influence has been noted by the Battery.	
	27/9			
	26/9	10 a.m.	The enemy started to drop their shells and to 12 pm Battery on our left & our return 30 rds. Free apparently by their Trench Mortar Battery. 30 gas envelopes has been rather expended, 10 Officers Prisoners have been taken & all troops have been Commanded to be in readiness, and men taken have been Helmets. Drops not all this. Prisoners taken have been already given & all Defence & respirators have been thoroughly examined so that every Officer & man in the Battery is in possession of the article as shown on the Knowledge of how these item.	Elle

D/184th F.A. Bde.   Ref: C.No. 25   Army Form C. 21

WAR DIARY
or
INTELLIGENCE SUMMARY
(Erase heading not required.)

Place	Date	Hour	Summary of Events and Information	Remarks and references to Appendices
	29/7/15 & 30th		Nothing has taken place either on the Part of the enemy or us during these days. The weather has been very wet. All men and horses appear very fit in spite of the unfavourable condition of the weather. Sickness amongst the men has been very slight. One case only that of pneumonia has caused the men to be struck off the strength of the Battery. Horses appear in excellent condition. The men continue to be cheerful	

121/7593

19th Khorasan

8/89 Battery RPA.
Vol 4
Col 15

WAR DIARY
or
INTELLIGENCE SUMMARY

(Erase heading not required.)

Army Form C. 2118

Sheet No. 26

D/89th F.A. Bde

Place	Date	Hour	Summary of Events and Information	Remarks and references to Appendices
	1/10/15	10.0	All the men in the Battery were sent to the Baths at Locre where they each had a good hot bath & received each a change of clean underclothing in lieu of dirty. This bath was greatly appreciated by the men. The past few days of heavy rain has necessitated a considerable amount of work being expended on gun pits & dug outs	
	2/10/15		Divine Service was held at the Battery Position at which men from the 68th Bde & men from the South sheds & attd. Lancs attended	
		3.30	The enemy dropped 5 shells into the 10-pr Battery on our left causing considerable damage & casualties. Gas shells were also sent over, the effects of which were experienced by us in this Battery. Smoke & tube helmets were at once brought into use, which prevented any serious results. A number of our men were sent to assist the 13 Battery on our left to attend to wounded casualties, and unearthing men into [illegible] become buried. Wagon horses moved on account of shelling in Billet area to *m. R.34. c.2.3	

1875 Wt. W593/826 1,000,000 4/15 J.B.C. & A. A.D.S.S./Forms/C. 2118.

D/89 N.Z. F.A Bde
Ref No 28.

WAR DIARY
or
INTELLIGENCE SUMMARY

Army Form C. 2118

(Erase heading not required.)

Place	Date	Hour	Summary of Events and Information	Remarks and references to Appendices
	4/10/15	4.0pm	52 rounds were fired at S.21.D.8.8 & S.21.D.8¾.6 to destroy machine gun emplacement (supposed) The effect of these proved very satisfactory. The following mess-age was received with regard to it:— To O.C. J/69. — Brigadier General R.A sends his congratulations on yesterdays shoot which North Lancs reported as more effective from 19th Div Arty 4/10/15	
	"	8.45pm	Enemy continuously shelled more 3 am the enemy dropped shells in the vicinity of the Battery. Some of which dropped on the Battery position. No damage what ever was done although approximately 200 shells came over. A Fuze of one which dropped at 11.45 pm near NZ mapped Z.N.11 Sp.15 this few at 11.45 P.m. Rifle fire was also reported but in the enemy which endeavor the troops close as hand. This is being investigated. Ample fuzes were picked up by a gunner above 200 yards NW night of the Battery. This was marked NZ 140 - AEG 15 on upper base and 1356 on base of fuze. This is apparently from a 3.9 Howitzer gun Please tea John French's letter to the troops was read out to the men on parade by the Battery Commander who also expressed	
	5/10/15			

WAR DIARY or INTELLIGENCE SUMMARY

Army Form C. 2118

D/84ᵗ J.O. Bee

Ref No 26

Place	Date	Hour	Summary of Events and Information	Remarks and references to Appendices
	6/10/15	10 A.M.	When the different portions of the Brigade by the Allies pointing out the places where the attacks were made and collecting grew the men a better idea of the line. The want of strong dug out rear ward posts is now being carried on. Ramps of gun pits have been lowered & enlarged to allow gun carts pass. Sides of gun revetted to give larger arc Stores have been drawn from R.E. for overhead cover and Completion of dug outs. The old 13 battery Position of A/89 is also receiving our attention. The Brigadier General R.A. visited the Battery and personally tendered congratulation on the good shooting of the 3-10-15 which was highly effective. The work on our reserved position is going forward rapidly. The trench now being thoroughly facilitated matters.	
		4.30	42 rounds were fired at enemy trench from S.22, C.2.8 to S.22, C.4.5 which proved most effective. Hostile artillery retaliated with 2 rounds from a heavy field gun apparently doing no damage. 1 shell being a blind and 1 a very fair short. A few of the shell was directed up near Brigade Head Quarters. A new race of communication	

Sheet No. 29
Army Form C. 2118

WAR DIARY
or
INTELLIGENCE SUMMARY
(Erase heading not required.)

Place	Date	Hour	Summary of Events and Information	Remarks and references to Appendices
	7/10/15	P.M. 2.30	About 2 inches of snow in Richebourg. Occupying tr. as in order of 4. It appears to be from a 5.9. 42 rounds were fired at Trenches S.22.C.2.6 to S.22.C.4.5. Effect of this proved highly satisfactory. Hostile artillery & aircraft have been very quiet during the past 24 hours, but a heavy bombardment is taking place away on our right in direction of LA BASSÉE	
	9/10/15	11.0	Gypress service was held at B. Battery Pshqrs. Trench men from several infantry regiments attended	
		3.15 to 4.10	The normal Sunday afternoon went by the enemy was described to 8 of their shells falling within 100 yards of left of B Battery & in rear of B/66° N.B. position. Fire was evidently from 10 c.m. intended to apparently delivered at S.13.C.4.6. No damage was done.	

WAR DIARY
or
INTELLIGENCE SUMMARY

(Erase heading not required.)

Army Form C. 2118

Place	Date	Hour	Summary of Events and Information	Remarks and references to Appendices
	10/11/15		Heavy Bombardment is going on & heavy rifle fire & Br. fighting apparently taking place	
		3.20 P.M	14 rounds fired for ranging & destroying — Trenches & Cupolas	
		3.45	A H C R 8 + 9 Effect good. Much work and activity appears to be going on by Germans in this neighbourhood	
	11/11/15	3.50 P.M	For Observation by Aeroplane + rounds were fired at Trenches gun trench S.22 B. 9.6	
	12/11/15	11.30 A.M	10 rounds were fired at S.22.C.2.8. offers highly satisfactory at a range of 3,3124. 1 sheep was chopped right into a thing but	
		3.0	The German artillery dropped 5 shells in their new forward position at top of Border Battery but with no effect. The Boches as the Boers of the Border seem to be recovering their attention now than any thing else + apart from sending shells over and the neighbourhood of LACOUTURE no trace of any impatience is being done by them.	
		4.15 / 4.45	Hostile Aircraft very active over Battery Position and on our right	

WAR DIARY or INTELLIGENCE SUMMARY

Army Form C. 2118

Place: 1/69 4th A Bde — Sheet No 31

Date	Hour	Summary of Events and Information	Remarks and references to Appendices
13/10		The heavy Bombardment on our right this evening was a very conspicuous one seen this continued to form all through the night. The	
"	4 p.m.	Squadron carried out by Aeroplane at 5.05 & B.96. 5 rounds being fired this time at an all observation on account of the wireless breaking down. The following messages received refer to the heavy bombardment of the past few days: "Latest News HOHENZOLLERN REDOUBT & QUARRIES now all in British hands. HULLOCH taken — no news since 10.10 to 8.7.40 a.m." French communiqué says 24 hours front number of prisoners taken N.E. of SOUCHEZ by French Artillery now 164 including 3 officers. German lines very heavily attacked in Lorraine defended by rifle and Battery fire. Strong German infantry activity in the VOSGES, repulsed. Bombardment by guns of every calibre was carried on fairly under the SPHRATZMANN ECK. After heavy Bombardment Braut Kopte of Darmi was succeeded in Fully occupied, later thoroughly evacuated by counter attack	

Army Form C. 2118

WAR DIARY
or
INTELLIGENCE SUMMARY
(Erase heading not required.)

Place	Date	Hour	Summary of Events and Information	Remarks and references to Appendices
	13th	P.M. 10	In Champagne the French have made further progress about artillery bombardment at various points of French front and also in Belgium from near Dixmude (from 19th Div Div)	
			" To 008/189th 2nd Division report 4.45 pm that the 8th Div [?] seen in little Willie L of Junction L of two trenches, also a screen of Hoh Inn further South in Little Willie. Guards are opening up new trenches, no further tanks are also unable to advance across the open enemy heavy rifle fire from 19th Div	8.30 pm
		11.40	" 17th Bde R.G.A report as follows:-	
			" We have captured the Hohenzollern Redoubt and Langes Big and Little Willie and Gump trench and are bombing along Flag-alley. We have got the Quarries and Gun trench and are pushing on throughout the night. Lose L is doubtful but not to Lane garden tech where it along its night.	

WAR DIARY or INTELLIGENCE SUMMARY

Army Form C. 2118

Place	Date	Hour	Summary of Events and Information	Remarks and references to Appendices
	13/10/15	2.0 & 2.30	"Auchy is burning, it has, when in the Outskirts of Hulluch, which is also burning - and Workshops in of Ferme du Bois. In the regard burnt out on Railway station the Loos. Progress during the past week. At X.4. C.5 & Junipers ammunition complete ready for occupation for one of fire at 60°. The position is now ready for occupation at X.10. 6. & 6. Victor No 2. Communication Trenches on today being completed and gun pits for Heavy cleaned out & detachment posted on (3769) near Points Indian Village completed. 3rd is now in course of construction & work is being still carried on.	
	14/10/15	3.40	As the request of Infantry 14 rounds were fired at FERME du BOIS effect very good. One large percentage of blind on parapet	

Sheet No 34

Army Form C. 2118

WAR DIARY
or
INTELLIGENCE SUMMARY
(Erase heading not required.)

Lt/89 L.A. Brigade

Instructions regarding War Diaries and Intelligence Summaries are contained in F.S. Regs., Part II. and the Staff Manual respectively. Title Pages will be prepared in manuscript.

Place	Date	Hour	Summary of Events and Information	Remarks and references to Appendices
	18/9/15	P.M. 2.50 6	22 rounds fired at Home S.27.D.3.6 (Thought to be an Observation post) - 6 direct hits were obtained on place which was very much ruined and full of refuse, but small portion of wall left standing, but very little damage to ruin was observed	
		P.M. 8.0 9.0	16 rounds fired at BOARS HEAD S.16.a.4.7 Repairing several direct hits on target and considerable amount of material was thrown into the air.	
	19/9/15	12 noon	At Trenches & roads S.16.c.7.1. & S.22.a.7.8 - 17 rounds for destruction of works, effect very good, much material thrown up.	
		3.15 pm	20 rounds fired on Home S.17.a.5.9 used as O.P. None but remnant standing	
		4.20	The fire at dept of 13 Battery (S.4.0) of an enemy battery from the 3.9 gun of the enemy silenced appeared at S.12.c.4.6 10 shells fired but no damage done	
	20/9/15	3.15 pm	At the request of infantry 14 rounds were fired at S.22.C.1.6 (Tube Line)	

WAR DIARY
or
INTELLIGENCE SUMMARY
(Erase heading not required.)

Army Form C. 2118

Instructions regarding War Diaries and Intelligence Summaries are contained in F. S. Regs., Part II. and the Staff Manual respectively. Title Pages will be prepared in manuscript.

Place	Date	Hour	Summary of Events and Information	Remarks and references to Appendices
			Am S 22.0.1.7 Effect fair portions of old communication trench destroyed	
		5.55	On Loos target in co-operation with E. Lancs Regt grenade throwers fire in retaliation for rifle grenade bombing. Bombing silenced. Our front casualty occurred Lt Boy O'Donnell leaving a flight scalp wound from a piece of shell. This case has attracted at the field ambulance it being nr of a serious nature.	
	21/10/15	7.15 pm	The float at top of Bailey Avon Fan Kissed 3 choppings apparently from same gun (5.9) Fans further.	
	22/10/15	2.15 pm	3 Lower shells dropped in front of Battery. They were made probably for batterie in the Rue du Bois at that line. A German aeroplane was observed at the same time.	
		5.00 pm	At request of the Gunners 10 rounds were fired at Coin d'Avro Report received Sale Halle - Pelhadron of D/89 were sale factory thus stopped shelling in bombing	

Appx. Bac R & O. Pee No 36   Army Form C. 2118

WAR DIARY
or
INTELLIGENCE SUMMARY
(Erase heading not required.)

Place	Date	Hour	Summary of Events and Information	Remarks and references to Appendices
	22/1/15		Work at our Rearward & Alternative Positions has been carried on at X.14.C.5.8. Fourth communication trenches dug to ecole plant of Battery. 2 new dug outs, 1 for earth metal completed. 3 dug outs 150 yards on R. flank of Battery dug & commenced to Battery R. flank. This position is ready for occupation at X.10.C.H.B. Communication trench dug throughout Battery trenches + to flanks. Dug one tunnel for each gun pit, platforms prepared. No overhead cover has been put up yet. Further trenches will be required for that. At Alternative Position & complete gun pits remade with overhead cover & sand-bagged. The w/off line was moved to-day to X.14.B.8.9. Orders issued for stores & ammunition at 100 for a renewed forward form was for bearer's wrute Range Line Approx 27,000 yards will be required for this purpose but as the weather continues fine & cautious we favorable the new stores is mostly occupied. Hostile aircraft has been very active to-day but a heavy ground mist prevails above to observation & access difficult.	

T/09th Bas RFA. Sheet No 37. Army Form C. 2118

WAR DIARY
or
INTELLIGENCE SUMMARY
(Erase heading not required.)

Place	Date	Hour	Summary of Events and Information	Remarks and references to Appendices
	22/10/15	5 pm	At the request of Gurkhas who were being shelled & bombed 10 rounds were fired at Cour d'Avoué. Reports on this state. Retaliation by FFG was satisfactory. Enemy stopped shelling and bombing.	
		2.30	The Rue du Bois seemed attention from hostile Artillery as this line. It was apparently much crowded with traffic & 3 shells that dropped there seemed to have done some damage. Hostile aircraft has been conspicuous by its absence lately & the report has been confirmed that the Germans do not have flash steel as generally believed when the line they are lent along was first indiscriminately they are content to drop 2 or 3 s shots.	
	23/10/15	8 pm	Hostile aeroplane afternoon the occur at this hour & from the front of Battery 2 inches light have been to pass from W to N which was immediately followed by 3 shells in the vicinity of the Rue du Bois from the Arm Rifles.	

2/59 K B₂ R.F.A.   Lut No 38   Army Form C. 2118

WAR DIARY
or
INTELLIGENCE SUMMARY
(Erase heading not required.)

Place	Date	Hour	Summary of Events and Information	Remarks and references to Appendices
	24/4/15	12 noon	Nicholas on looking 33 trenches saw lines of German from his trenches open fire - bombing without	
		to 12.30		
	"	4.0 pm	Opened fire at Cupola S.16 C.6.4.	
		1.30	reintroduced until 3.30 our Right front saw shelled by the enemy approximately 30 shells dropped	
		8.30 pm	The enemy fired shrapnel from Left front. received about 30 R.W. shells	
	Rue du Bois			
	27/4/15	10.0	5 shells fell in and near Battery position - 2 fell in Battery and 3 from 25 yards rear. The orders were given for all sections of the Battery position to 2-3 ft which was done. One shell was not exploded. The damage to house slight. 1 shell dropped but to one gun but the new day secured 20 feet out a round of ???	W⸺
		1.30		
		2.30		

WAR DIARY
or
INTELLIGENCE SUMMARY

(Erase heading not required.)

Army Form C. 2118

Week No 39

Instructions regarding War Diaries and Intelligence Summaries are contained in F.S. Regs., Part II. and the Staff Manual respectively. Title Pages will be prepared in manuscript.

Place	Date	Hour	Summary of Events and Information	Remarks and references to Appendices
	28/9/15	12.45	Lark which secured out the burst. The shots were fired by an another cheif but 30 yards away, 90 feet penetration. The fuge at of French Origin and marked E.C.P.S. 1-13 30-35-MLE 89T 37. Made of burst & graduated from O to 49 in 5 shrapnel shots spindle was of heavy wheels been broken from being handled especially in the matter of parking down the groove nut. Bore is true & clean.	
	29/9/15	10.45	8 rounds fired at Longees Church. Shrapnel shouts hole in Observation Station. The shoot hole was obtained one causing considerable damage.	
			To Reychaerom. Hounds Expended on Wards S.22 d & b. Telephone carefully carried out along the Nook & Horse Guard of the Nook. The neither this bups Larcep has been Very wet & unpleasant. Last the whole of Ruperts our forward officery has consequently greatly suffered.	

Army Form C. 2118

WAR DIARY
or
INTELLIGENCE SUMMARY
(Erase heading not required.)

Instructions regarding War Diaries and Intelligence Summaries are contained in F.S. Regs., Part II. and the Staff Manual respectively. Title Pages will be prepared in manuscript.

Place	Date	Hour	Summary of Events and Information	Remarks and references to Appendices
	31/5		The work carrying the pits & dug outs of this work is also different to others. There has been little activity on the part of the enemy during the past day or so but at 3.45 p.m. a shell from a 5.9 howitzer dropped near Road S.Y.D. The position mentioned as our Alternative Barrier is now occupied by C/79. In spite of the conditions of weather etc the case of sickness amongst the men has been very slight during the past month. There are only a driver rather present in hospital and influenza has again broken out. An excellent condition men continue to keep particularly bright & cheerful.	

8/89 Battery
Vol: 6

121/7918

19th RW

WAR DIARY
or
INTELLIGENCE SUMMARY

Army Form C. 2118.

Place	Date	Hour	Summary of Events and Information	Remarks and references to Appendices
	3/12/15	3.0 pm	The Regt. recd. small arms S.A.A. & water carts the Brigade Billets at P.14.a.9.4 and marched to Barlin. Reserve K.R. O.R.B. at 8.15 pm & later billeted in the Parker area from the 1st July. 14 R.Q.O.(T) billeting 8 x 0 men from the 23 Div. Transport no reinforcement of Officers since the last weekly return. 13 officers from 1st Bn on account of the last weekly state. 3 officers from L.C. in a bad state. X No E. 9. 4 thos. afair amount.	
	4/12/15	am 12.30	In compliance with order to rendezvous here at Heme du Bois. The 1/4 Leicester Regt. to Rond Buisson as 3 sons x arrival in action at Barling at 6 pm.	
	5/12/15	12.0 1.0	3 rounds fired at Heme du Bois be signalmen Bugnos x a: a a morning Party. 3.25 am 9.6. This was	
	6/12/15		Ampenia	

B/89th H.Q. RGA.   Sheet No 48.

Army Form C. 2118.

WAR DIARY
or
INTELLIGENCE SUMMARY.
(Erase heading not required.)

Place	Date	Hour	Summary of Events and Information	Remarks and references to Appendices
	6/12/15	10.0 am	By order of the 19th Divisional Artillery the 75ys Guns carried out a Bombardment at the Southern face of Boars Head, with the object of rendering this front useless for further standing purposes by the enemy. For registration 3 rounds were fired, and 55 rounds were fired during the bombardment at (S16.0.5.9½) Parapet was considerably damaged. Large portions of same were thrown into the air.	
		12 nn	The Hostile Artillery opened fire and retaliated high 6" shells from a 77 mm and 30 Pr. and 4.5 Howtz, on (Rosebud Villa) Came and Flew du Bois – Fired very fast for afternoon to day	
		7.30 to 9.0	At the request of Group Commander 33 rounds were fired as Communication trenches in rear of Boars Head. This was an arrangement with Infantry as a relief was reported to be taking place.	
	8/12/15	10 am	51 rounds were fired in conjunction with Divisional Observed Scheme on S.16.C.5½.9½. Green Mound. Ferme du Bois. Many direct	

Minutes

M[?] 1st D[?]W Sheet 49   Army Form C. 2118.

WAR DIARY
or
INTELLIGENCE SUMMARY
(Erase heading not required.)

Place	Date	Hour	Summary of Events and Information	Remarks and references to Appendices
	9/12/15	9.30	Hits were obtained and large quantities of bricks & timber thrown into the air. Large lead made on target. Hostile Artillery slightly active at this time — with a gun on S 9 and a 5.9 Howr.	
		6—	Observed burst of S.9 — S.22 & 6.1. Y Kite over our lines over locality of Rue du Bois and Battery O.P.	
		11—	Group Scheme carried out as follows :—	
			Ferme du Bois 10 rounds minute [?] thrown up	
		11.30 P.M.	Orchard — S.16. a. 6.6 — 16 rounds — portions of parapet breached	
		12.15 P.M.	Or. Ferme du Toulette + trenches in rear 32 rounds — where apparent — effect unobserved.	
		1.0	On [?] d'Orme + Green effond — 20 round — several direct hits	
		2.30	House — S. 17. a. 5. 5. — 25 rounds — débris blown in	
		3.0	New Works — S. 16 B. 9. 7. + Ferme du Bois 19 rounds much timber and planks thrown up	
			The [?] returned at 12.15 p.m. and 12 shells from a 77 m/m on Trowel[?] + [?] Corner. Apparent source of Hostile Weapon	W[?]

WAR DIARY
or
INTELLIGENCE SUMMARY.

(Erase heading not required.)

Army Form C. 2118.

D/89th Bar Ya Sheet 30

Place	Date	Hour	Summary of Events and Information	Remarks and references to Appendices
	11/7/15	12.20 12.30 pm 12.55	Magnetic bearing 120½ from S.H. to 9.5½ = 10 yards from Jemo Sucyer. Left at 3.43 L Dead Cow Farm and Princes Road. Magnetic bearing of Hug Pollin in flash barrel. Two dull thick observations. A.S.L shortly new F.a. Jain factory observation completed. No 6 telephone cables and communication trench at S.15.a.6.0. Wire to their Bindt.	
	12/7/15	10 a 6 4.12 pm 8.45 10 10.5	The Paris Hene Hug Selec and J Fresnoy Spur Shuken. Silenced Husband - Wernicke. Two Sohn battery and one in F. Battery Armored 24.X.17.d.9.a. G7P H Battery. Fired and Raid No 3 and 4 aspiry from bell a supplied were captured. No disturbance with Herroral Sohm Passes one to hundreds in DISTILLERY - FORMAL - communicated - train S.24.d.3 - S.29.a.89. Enemy reached to balloon. No shifts of Corps Commander of Division on account of Japanese German Relief Party. 92 rounds Wire Cut to Ferme du Bois - Halfgate Hill Gardienne C. Bosnie Pergoor at 10.10(?) the Eveline
	13/7/15			

D/89th of a Bde
Sheet No 51

Army Form C. 2118.

WAR DIARY
or
INTELLIGENCE SUMMARY.
(Erase heading not required.)

Place	Date	Hour	Summary of Events and Information	Remarks and references to Appendices
	14/12/15	midday	103 rounds were fired — Apparent of work in German trenches. Line very considerable. Early part of bombardment appeared slightly to right of intended trench, and extent left of trench and of Apple – German Coy. being fired at about 25 yds N.E. of Blue Apple. Continued turning throughout the bombardment. No Germans were seen in Salient or retiring from it. Battery shifted during 3 times owing to German Aeroplane overhead very low. Retaliation. From 10.55 a.m. eight 5.9 shell fell about Terrapod Corner.	
		1-30	20 rounds were fired at Howr. S.17 a. 5.9 – at about 1100 shell returned and large holes made in the walls.	
		11 am	In accordance with Tactical Scheme 98 rounds were fired at S.16 a.6.6 to 8.9 & 6.9. to destroy portions of trench and to harass repairs. In this the enemy was unable to any attempt to make known by the trench. Commenced at 11 a.m. to fire to Regt. Battery and Rue du Bois at row. 12 row retaliation or today stopped at 12·15 p.m. Fire open close to trench & difficult to locate.	

Recce 52
Army Form C. 2118.

WAR DIARY
or
INTELLIGENCE SUMMARY.
(Erase heading not required.)

D/89th RFA

Place	Date	Hour	Summary of Events and Information	Remarks and references to Appendices
	15/12/15	10.30	Open communication trench is being constructed - new platoon on the map - apparently running from S.16.d.7 to S.23.c.6.	
		11.30	General Scheme - With strenuous rifle fire on the front attack in conjunction with I.9 starting to 6.40 afternoon. Attack very successful. I.9 strongly garrisoned. First trench line of I.9 captured up to the line S.6.d S1/69 and as a result of application to Flatenheim large craters were made in the southern flank Sap together with bags through upper trenches communication over the "New Altrand" adjoins hole a further extension in which troops can be seen. There are no indications that it is specially prepared for defence. The trench is very bad and others seem exceedingly different owing to mud.	
		2.0	The situation 26 rounds fired fuse as bridles wire of the town tenet sent destroyed	

Wright

WAR DIARY
or
INTELLIGENCE SUMMARY.
(*Erase heading not required.*)

Army Form C. 2118.

Instructions regarding War Diaries and Intelligence Summaries are contained in F. S. Regs., Part II. and the Staff Manual respectively. Title pages will be prepared in manuscript.

Place	Date	Hour	Summary of Events and Information	Remarks and references to Appendices
	17/2/15	1.40	In Retaliation 20 rounds were fired at Ferme du Bois & 12 rounds were fired on Ferme du Toulotte — Light being bad observation nearly impossible	
		2.15	In Enfilade 3 rounds were fired on front trenches S. of Ferme du Bois.	
			At this time the Germans were firing on & shell and a few in rear of Orchard Salient, but own made it impossible to locate	
	19/2/15	10.0	On Ferme du Toulotte & Ferme 61 30 rounds expended in "retaliation"	
		2.30	On Works S 22 d. 1. 0 & 2. 2 17 rounds & on S x9 a 4 5	
		4	15 rounds fired in accordance with Group Instruction	
		4.0	Hostile Aircraft very active all the morning one passing from 10 to 11.30	
			The weather continues bad a new gun pits are in course of construction — Two cases of measles have appeared in our bays line during the past week but no further symptoms of the malady have presented themselves.	

2353 Wt. W2544/1454 700,000 5/15 D. D. & L. A.D.S.S./Forms/C. 2118.

Sheet 54

Army Form C. 2118.

WAR DIARY
or
INTELLIGENCE SUMMARY.
(Erase heading not required.)

2/89th R.F.A

Instructions regarding War Diaries and Intelligence Summaries are contained in F. S. Regs., Part II. and the Staff Manual respectively. Title pages will be prepared in manuscript.

Place	Date	Hour	Summary of Events and Information	Remarks and references to Appendices
	21/2/5	8.15pm	Orders have been given for the destruction of wire fences of the horse & cattle. As unsuitable targets could not be located the trojan lands which be left of whilst switch to eny draw country from Little Hill. In accordance with Right Group Orders 20 rounds were fired at S.7.a.0.3 (M.G.)	
	22/2/5	12.30 am	2 rounds fired on Gomm cross roads. Tendette. Taking a volume fine	
		3.50	3 Rounds 45 rounds were fired on Schelin & Shanon. Enfilade sweep to Leught	
		2.50	SOS called became suddenly absence 20 Rds at a L.L. Stop of till stop battery front Res & Junction of Rue Blanche and if she Res Buss	
		6.30	This fire as the line was Battery Force and Sm recently	
		9.30pm	After fire has ceased by S rounds of Battery as this items	

D/89th R.F.A.

Sheet No 55

WAR DIARY
or
INTELLIGENCE SUMMARY.

Army Form C. 2118.

Place	Date	Hour	Summary of Events and Information	Remarks and references to Appendices
	23/12/15	9.50 a.m.	A working party was observed at S.25 a.5.4. constructing what appeared to be a new road at it or a gravel dumping ground	
		10.40	The same party apparently assumed possession and 11 round were fired upon them which a/m dispersed them	
		11.30	Flight Group Scheme — Night Line Shoot — On Wylde Line 30 rounds fired 1-0 p.m. at S.23 L.2.6. 14 rounds on account of enemy being observed — movement was stopped	
		3.15 p.m.	S.26.a.5.4. on Working Party 10 rounds — party dispersed	
		3.20	at S.17.a.5.9. 27 rounds dispersed. Practically no aircraft. The usual — A Special Report on this scheme — Night Line Shoot — "The fire was maintained from 11.30 to 12 mn. The slow rate of "Battery fire made it difficult to judge what distribution had been "and a slight move as the line advanced the German communication "trenches. Places Reps were under fire opposed to the BOARS HEAD "Cour d'Avoué, Moulin d'Eau places which appear to be unlocated "and has no fire on them at all. From line trenches from "S.16.c.6.7 to S.16.c.5.0. - Communication trenches on right of "Ferme du Bois. The fire cause the Germans to retaliate heavily	[signature]

D/59th F.A. BDE   Sheet 56

Army Form C. 2118.

WAR DIARY
or
INTELLIGENCE SUMMARY.
(Erase heading not required.)

Place	Date	Hour	Summary of Events and Information	Remarks and references to Appendices
			"with 5.9 or larger weapon on our Reserve trenches near CHOCOLATE POST and with Shrapnell (77m.m.) about PRINCES ROAD. Copy of "extract" from Lewis received this morning"	
			"The G.O.C. R.A. was very pleased with the conduct of the guns" "Aero gun fired at his second zurichern from 19th Sn Bty.	
	Sept 23	a.m. 10.30	In accordance with Right Group Scheme 4.9 rounds were expended on "FORGIES". Shots however were observed spread well above line of buildings. But also 2 rounds were shot a little below so the Buildings.	
		11.30	Howrer 5.9 rutubuted with 6 shots on front of our Chl Bty position as X 14 a C 1.	
	Sept 25	a.m. 1.0 4.3	Firing commenced at 1.0 a.m. on Forgies 1.5 - A.O. rounds being expended on FORGIES & Lt. TOURELLE - There was no sufficient light to observe effects	
		12 p.m	X.14.a.c.1. again received attention from the same 5.9 (apparently)	

Wheatcroft

D/89'. 13 Info de R F A. Sheet 37

Army Form C. 2118.

WAR DIARY
or
INTELLIGENCE SUMMARY.
(Erase heading not required.)

Place	Date	Hour	Summary of Events and Information	Remarks and references to Appendices
	26/12/15	a.m 1-0 to 1-3	The same programme was repeated as on the previous day. 5th Army being supported in 3 minutes on STYLES + St TERESE. Two dumps could be seen on examination during the day.	
		10.55? to 11-50?	The converting line from New Gun Pit and connecting line of bay 14 Armco were inspected on DISTILLERIES Items in Tarielle	
		p.m 2-10	16 rounds engineer in careful registrations of BOARS HEAD + from Land trench opposite - about 10 yards of front parapet at S.18 a 5.8 badly damaged + top knocked in.	
	27/12/15	p.m 2.0 to 3-15	In accordance with Group Orders 60 rounds were fired at Head of new German communication trench + bridge - considerable damage done and trench knocked thrown up. The enemy have us though the day been continuing at their efforts on shelling RICHBORG + to the S.23 a.1.1 - some shells came from enemy of the shells were observed.	
	28/12/15	12.30pm to 1-40	Group Scheme - 51 rounds expended on Night Lines, House 61 from the Bois. Trenches in rear of BOARS HEAD. Bois Trenches in rear of BOARS HEAD Lid was maintained over this period	

2353 Wt. W2544/1454 700,000 5/15 D. D. & L. A.D.S.S./Forms/C. 2118.

D/29ᵗʰ & O Brigade   Sheet 55

Army Form C. 2118.

WAR DIARY
or
INTELLIGENCE SUMMARY.
(Erase heading not required.)

Place	Date	Hour	Summary of Events and Information	Remarks and references to Appendices
		12.45p	No wire cutting operations appeared very good from the Trenches.	
		3.30	Bᵗʸ 4 fields shell appeared from a sniper situated at Oᵗˢ TOURET Burst on the Battery position!! The Road. S.7 d was shelled but 2 - 5.9 Heavy shell	
	29/7/15	2.30pm	For Registration of Destroyed 15 Round was expended on S.W.C.1.12 - Non hostile aircraft over. The Burp into very tangled and several of the enemys aircraft was observed from the gun of the Batt Aircraft Guns guns in turning they have gotten own lines	
	31/7/15	P.m 12.30	At S.25. a.5.4. (working party) 3 rounds were expended. This party is continually working there	

[signature]

8/89 Battery
Vol 7

Bd/89th F.A. Brigade Sheet 59   Army Form C. 2118.

WAR DIARY
or
INTELLIGENCE SUMMARY.
(Erase heading not required.)

Place	Date	Hour	Summary of Events and Information	Remarks and references to Appendices
	1/7/16	10.30 A.M.	In accordance with Group Scheme 30 rounds were dispersed at DISTILLERIE and considerable damage was done to S/E corner of same	
		11-0	At house S.23.b.2.6 - 30 rounds were fired and several direct hits obtained	
		11-34	and 29 rounds a very good effect was observed on Head of German Trench S.6.c.9.9. The enemy has been exceptionally quiet through the day	
	2/7/16	4 PM 10.10	For the purpose of testing the ranges of my 6" Hows 15 rounds were expended. No damage was concealed	
		8 PM 3.10	For the same purpose 30 rounds were expended but no further conclusions being very unfavourable & lights very poor observation was impossible.	
	3/7/16	9 AM 10.18 6 10.45	On destruction of Tank dumps at S.23.B.93 the 13 rounds were fired at these and were obtained	
		12.0	2 rounds fired at working party at S.25.a.5.4. Considerable amount of their fire on the enemy line and the same working party to continuously being disposed	
		1-0 4 PM 3-0	A Hostile S.A. fire over 50 shells dropping them on top farm of Battery and on B/88 dir further no damage done	MDai

WAR DIARY or INTELLIGENCE SUMMARY

Army Form C. 2118.

2/59th Bde R.F.A.   Sheet 60

Place	Date	Hour	Summary of Events and Information	Remarks and references to Appendices
	5/16	1-50 to 2-55 pm	On retaliation we fired 34 rounds on Largo enemy trench. Reported much brick wall being thrown up.	
		10-30 to 12-45	On ordinary Group scheme. 92 rounds were employed as in following targets. Martin D'Eau House 142, House 51, Ferme du Trolette — some damage was done to all buildings but they are very much loops of rubble. There were many blind shells, especially with fuzes 44.	
		11-25 to 1-45	The Battery position was heavily shelled during this time from the 8" Howr that is and from the Battery. Others which answered our gun fire to show the Battery by gun flashes and casualties. Three fallen short however the Enemy shelling eased off at the end of the day again was nearer from the Enemy snipers leaving 1130 from the established position of the gun. X.17.d.9.e. (shewn of Bellew-Farm)	
	7/6	11-40 to 1-0	Group scheme to destroy activities from wire Enemy 35 rounds expended on Communication trenches S.16.d.1.7 to 5.17.c.2.3 Coml Awards S.16.d.5.8. Common Trench S.22.b.6.6. Effect good.	

Army Form C. 2118.

WAR DIARY
or
INTELLIGENCE SUMMARY.
(Erase heading not required.)

1/6th L.A. Bell   Ster 61

Place	Date	Hour	Summary of Events and Information	Remarks and references to Appendices
	8/16		Some damage done to new communication trench which is rapidly being completed. Registration of S.22.a.1.7 – of howers were registered Registration was carried out	
	9/16		The enemy have as this day been concentrating his efforts on shelling Fauvorne, and for this 25 hours were registered on Longues.	
	10/16	11.30 to 12.0	Group scheme – 40 rounds expended on new Boulevard communication trench S.16.a.1.Y to Leech grey, some S.23 L and S.6. Road and trench were mans and each thrown up. Wasted along the communication trench as dead at front. We built an thrown up on the road mark of the trench have left from the grey some trenes went about 40. Very satisfactory shot.	
		2.30	9 rounds were expended to check registration of Brow Head.	
	11/16	9 am	Offensive scheme. 66 rounds expended on S.16.a.6.6 & S.10.C.10.3 Very effective shot.	

WAR DIARY
or
INTELLIGENCE SUMMARY.

(Erase heading not required.)

Army Form C. 2118.

Instructions regarding War Diaries and Intelligence Summaries are contained in F.S. Regs., Part II. and the Staff Manual respectively. Title pages will be prepared in manuscript.

Place	Date	Hour	Summary of Events and Information	Remarks and references to Appendices
S16 a & S16 a 6&2	11th	1.50	The registration of S.16.a.6.1 + rounds were fired. Registration was effectually carried out.	
	12th	4.0	In accordance with Divisional Scheme 60 rounds of H.E. were fired on Hyma du Bois and S.16.a.6.1. Effect unknown owing to light hazy. Observation was impossible. Second shoot on battery down to Right Group H.Q. Gunners sent to Battery. Battery fired 60 rounds at 3 minute intervals on S.16.a, 6.6. + S.10.c.1.3. from North & South at Bois Hugo. Remarkably for precisely fire bursts. Very effective there on bursts at from 200 yds. Cayau about 10 m afternoon got light on S.14. Cayau huge shells at S.11 + 2 shells - Remarkable good shooting & to Hund.	
	12/6	3.0	To deepen watery early and damage dugouts & mines dugouts on S.25 o 4.4. The Hee to adverse effect.	
	14/6	1.30	In retaliation for the enemy shelling of our trenches with 77m m 6 rounds were fired at DISTILLERIE.	
	15th	10.50 pm 1.10	In accordance with Army orders to Enem nove easily 76 rounds were fired at Bn.ht shell enemy S.16.a.7.1. to S.23. &.L.S.6.	

Instructions regarding War Diaries and Intelligence Summaries are contained in F. S. Regs., Part II. and the Staff Manual respectively. Title pages will be prepared in manuscript.

WAR DIARY
or
INTELLIGENCE SUMMARY.
(Erase heading not required.)

Sheet 63

Army Form C. 2118.

Place	Date	Hour	Summary of Events and Information	Remarks and references to Appendices
			Some breastwork blown in about S 23 a 1 7. Places previously blown in on this work were noticed to be repaired today with sandbags.	
		11 30	Chocolate Menier Corner & Princes Road was shelled with 77mm about 20. A fuze picked up belonging to one of these was marked Dopp Z 96 N/A. Fired at 4.5 Howitzer [illegible] of Hostile weapon from Illies.	
		2.15	4.5 shells from a 4.2 Hostile Howitzer fell about S 5 [illegible]	
	16/10/15	10.30 to 2 50	Group scheme on O.P. to distract attention from wire cutting on House S 17 a 9 5. House S 23 c 9 8. House S 23 d 2 3. A direct hit on House S 17 a 9 5 stopped German shelling of our trenches.	
	17/10	10.45	A test on Night Lines with 4 rounds which proved satisfactory.	
		11.40	Group scheme. – 43 rounds fired on German Works S 17 [illegible] near breastwork German communication trench S 17 a 1 2 – S 17 a 5 9. Apparently satisfactory & effective. The scheme called forth a very heavy German retaliation 50 – 4.2 & 77mm being fired at O.P.s at Chocolate Menier Corner.	[illegible]

2353 Wt. W2544/1454 700,000 5/15 D. D. & L. A.D.S.S./Forms/C. 2118.

WAR DIARY or **INTELLIGENCE SUMMARY**

Army Form C. 2118.

D/64th Bde R.F.A.   Plus 64

Place	Date	Hour	Summary of Events and Information	Remarks and references to Appendices
		2.15	On all our front 18 gun + 38 guns on new approved for Corps d'Armee S.22 a 1.7. 9 hrs. further rest to be sent over the approved shell areas to enemy trenches	
	19/6	11.25	On trenches in light of 15 rounds fired in afternoon, fires on most dumps are coming from the trenches. Moving O.P. H.O.T. 13 a 6.9. HUN HOT & DISTILLERY 20 rounds each front Batteries 4 form du Bois — 8 rounds on the project of working back. DUMP S.11 c.16 20 rounds new fired. This dump appears much used & burnt wood + timber was thrown up in the extremity of front S.11 a.7.6 25 rounds new fired and half the large cottage had	
	20/6	2.0 am 6.0 3.0 10.25 15 45 12	Barrage scheme — on at 4 hour line 24 rounds 80 rounds expended on registered points	

WAR DIARY
or
INTELLIGENCE SUMMARY.
(Erase heading not required.)

Army Form C. 2118.

D/Sgn. F. A. Bde   Sheet 85

Place	Date	Hour	Summary of Events and Information	Remarks and references to Appendices
	22/10	11.35 a.m.	Bombardment of known dug outs by Group Salvos S.H.₁ & 6.H.₂ & S.H.₂ & S.H.₂. Enemy opened "Plan" fires but prisoners admitted it took effect.	
	23/10	12.55	At a suspected O.P. – 8, 17, a, 5, 9. 12 rounds were expended & several direct hits were obtained. The enemy Field Gun Pan at this time tried 6 – 4.2 s.	
	24/10	11.40	In the destruction of various communication trench S 22.d 4.5. 13 rounds were fired. Intermittent harassing fire during the night. Rue abi ays also opened at these places.	
		3.10	For the purpose of shelling registration for C/122 Brigade R.F.A. who is relieving this Batty on the 30/10/15. 70 rounds were expended on the following points – Ferme du B.H.S. – Ferme du Tom Cat House S. N. a. 5. 9. (approx 30) + Moulin D'eau.	
	25/10		The C/122 Bde took over the high section this morning and expended in accordance with orders from 11.55 am to 1.45 pm 63 rounds on the following Barbara of wire Wrecked farm	

Army Form C. 2118.

WAR DIARY
or
INTELLIGENCE SUMMARY.
(Erase heading not required.)

Instructions regarding War Diaries and Intelligence Summaries are contained in F.S. Regs., Part II. and the Staff Manual respectively. Title pages will be prepared in manuscript.

D/89

66

Place	Date	Hour	Summary of Events and Information	Remarks and references to Appendices
			S.16.C.6.6 to S.16.C.6.2. S.22.a.8.3 - Ranges of German trenches S.22.a.8.6.6 S.22.a.8.3 - Ranges of moving troops S.22.o.3.1 to S.22.C.2.8	
	26/16	11.45	2 Bullets had to come from S.22.a.10.35 or beyond & S.16.C.6 aeroplane, and the German trenches with 11 Howrs. on Tyser Farm between 2.20 pm & 3.05 pm + No damage was done known	
		12 -	For registration of S.17.a.5.9 - 5 rounds expended " " S.17.a.7.8 - 8 " "	
	27/16	11.15	Our recent trenches in S.15.b. received hostile attention apparently from the direction of DISTILLERY - 8 - 11 m m In retaliation fire Hostile Resting Work of Boom Trench S.4 rounds two expended on S.16.a.8.7 + S.15.a.2 a/c S.17. a.2.5 very efficient shoot.	
	28/6	12.15	In accordance with group scheme on Suspected OPs 5 rounds expended on Distillery.	
		12.55	Howse S.11.c.7.2 - 3 rounds - 1.15 - Howse S.11.a.4.5 - 1/2 + Howse S.11.a.5.9. 58 rounds. 4 pm - Howse S.11.c.4.5 - 1/2. 2 rounds - Several	ment

D/89th Bde R.F.A.   Sheet 67   Army Form C. 2118.

WAR DIARY
or
INTELLIGENCE SUMMARY

Place	Date	Hour	Summary of Events and Information	Remarks and references to Appendices
		12.30 6 4.30	direct hits on Houses. O.Ps were taken in turn (into German few opened with a view of ascertaining what O.sp answered to what Battery but no Indis factory conclusion was come to. The Hostile Artillery became very aggressive during this time. On the corner of the Rue du Bois + Brick Sheet 40 Shells of a H.E were dropped. Of these at least 20 were "duds". Three shells had fuzes marked Gr.Z. Gr.u. 8.2. The apparent position of the Hostile weapon whose shell dropped at S.12 a central and in line west from that from Rue de Marais - 20 shells from a Hostile 10 of these were blind. These two form a weapon situated or the line DISTILLERIE - SELLES -	
	30/6	12 noon	The Battery left its position after landing over to C/122 R.F.A. (38 x D.W.). Going to Rear moved a considerable amount of labour has been expended on the Battery position & several new Gun pits were erected and in its ferage Linen House standings + shelters were made. Slog + Lundley	

WAR DIARY or INTELLIGENCE SUMMARY

Army Form C. 2118.

Jan 11th Wind in making produce oft etc
Men have rifles and sidearms there has only it a
trench mortar Horse also — are in a good condition

The new Battery at T.29.c.9.3. were reached at 12.0 p.m. &
was found to be very comfortable, plenty of room for men
and Horses. Brick standings for Horses have to be erected

As soon as the necessary material is available
Owing to run the following programme for the term must
have to carried out. Jan 31st Morning Overhauling and
Inspection of Gun Part & Equipment. Afternoon Inspection of
Clothing and Harness Cleaning. Feb 1st Morning Repairing
vehicles who of deficient stores. Inspection of Battery Instruments
and Whip tow & equipment. Afternoon Inspection of Harness &
issue of deficiencies. In Harness. Feb 2nd Morning Physical
Exercise & Mucking Drill, arrives having Saddles.
Afternoon - Rifle Drill, Laying drill Inspection of feet
Feb 3rd Morning Physical Exercises, Gun drill
Afternoon - Laying and dialling [?]

Army Form C. 2118.

69.

WAR DIARY
or
INTELLIGENCE SUMMARY.
(Erase heading not required.)

Place	Date	Hour	Summary of Events and Information	Remarks and references to Appendices
			Range Jaeting - Lecture on what does whilst in action Feb 4th Morning - physical exercise, section gun drill, musky instruction, signalling, officers - Rifle Drill Taking of Range setting & shoulder parades. Feb 5th Morning - Inspection of 133 rd Brigade Commander by General Bruce Loring near and of Harrow officers had holiday	

Sq.Iv.Bde. PDd.
vol: 7

CONFIDENTIAL

WAR DIARY

OF

89TH BRIGADE R.F.A.

From 1st Jan. 1916 to 31st Jan. 1916

(VOLUME Y)

ORIGINAL

WAR DIARY or INTELLIGENCE SUMMARY

Army Form C. 2118

January 1916. R.F.A.

Place	Date	Hour	Summary of Events and Information	Remarks and references to Appendices
A/89 M26d9.8 C/89 M32b44 D/89 X18c0.7 H.Q. R.35c.9.8	Jan 1st		Dull & cloudy. Heavy rain at intervals, very windy towards evening. Light snow at midday. A/89. fired 29 rounds at 12.0 on Hersin Rd. Loisville X roads Crossroad - O.P. Pretoria 9 rounds at 12.20 on Communication Trench S.18.d.5.5. Pretoria 9 rounds at 13.30 on Hersin M.36.c.3.2 and S.6.a.5.4 " 5 rounds at 14.40 on Trench 2 of Boar's Head (instructional purposes) C/89. fired 11 rounds at 11.40am on Trench S.17.c.1.7 in cooperation with several other batteries to try and check shelling of windy corner. 11 rounds at 13.40 pm on Trench S.5.d.7.9 - S.5-6.9.3. registration. D/89. fired 30 rounds on the Distillery at 11.30 am and 30 rounds on horse S.23.b.2.6. at 11.am and 29 rounds on head of new trench S.6.c.99 group scheme - considerable damage done to corner of Distillery small rounds fired on new trench and horse S.23 b 2.6 had very poor effect, some damage observed.	TRENCH MAP 36 SW Sheet 3+1 1/10000
	2		Dull. Raining most part of the day. Light say wind. A/89. Fired 2 rounds on Front line trenches Boars head at 10am (instructional purposes) and at 11.am 6 rounds on Hostile Battery at S.16.c.10.7. Battery ceased firing at 12.18. 14 rounds on Horse S.6.a.S.3. and cpr. Rd Lane (retaliation) and at 14.30. 4 rounds at enemy seen working on front line trenches near Boar's head.	

W

WAR DIARY
or
INTELLIGENCE SUMMARY

(Erase heading not required.)

Army Form C. 2118

January 1916   R.F.A.

Place	Date	Hour	Summary of Events and Information	Remarks and references to Appendices
A/89 M26d.9.8	Jan 2		C/89. Fired 11 rounds towards S.5 at S.3 at 11.23 am. observation difficult owing to light. and at 15.0 fired 6 rounds on trench S.11.B.3.4.6 etc. enemy shelling our trenches.	TRENCH MAP. 36.9.W. Sheet 3+1
C/89 M32.6.4.			B/89. Fired 15 rounds at 10.10 am on enemy wire for testing ranges. and 20 rounds at 14.10.	1 / 40000
D/89	3		Fine morning. Considerable sound of MG firing. Light MG fire.	
X18.C.0.7			A/89. at 12.5 fired 8 rounds on trenches S.24.C.3.0 Registration. at 13.45 fired 39 rounds and 13.53.6 great rounds on Ferme DUBEIF and at 15.50.19 rounds on S.17.B.1.15. Being observed O.P.	
H.Q.				
R.35c.9.8			C/89. Fired 2 rounds at 9.55 am. on S.11.A.8.5½ and at 11.45 am 20 rounds at S.5.0.5½, 2½ and at 14.45". 6 rounds S.17.A.5.7. aerial effective. hits being obtained. much damage inflicted. There was most annoying by the enemy than usual today.	
			B/89. at 10.15 to 10.45 am 13 rounds fired for purpose of destroying South work at S.22.b.9/2.4½ at 12 noon 2 rounds fired on working party S.25.A.5.4.? Party dispersed. A considerable amount of work fired from a new long story at 13.50 to 14.53. 84 rounds fired at LORAIES (Retaliation) Enemy fired about 50 rounds S.9. on left front of B. of Batt. old position.	W.C.

WAR DIARY or INTELLIGENCE SUMMARY

Army Form C. 2118

R.Z.A. January 1916

Place	Date	Hour	Summary of Events and Information	Remarks and references to Appendices
A/S1 M2bd a,b,c C/S1 M226 b,d D/S9 X 19 c.0.7 H.Q. R 15 c.0.3	Jan. 4th		Still overcast, rain towards evening. Wind light, fairly good shining day. A/89. Fired 5 rounds at 13 arm in Rochester O.P. times S.18.L.2.6. and 17 rounds at 14.10. One shell hit house up considerable amount of debris at 19.40. 4 rounds fired at points S.6.a.5.4. and S.5.a.5.8. to interfere with [Sheet 31] C/89. Fired 13 rounds at 13.45 on trenches S.5.d.5.2. observed hits observed at 14.45. Fired 19 rounds on trench 11.at 4.5. D/S9 no artillery action.	Trench MAP 36 S.W. Sheet 31 Lt 0000
	Jan. 5th		Fine morning sunshine, cloudy in the afternoon, no rain. A/89. Fired 12 rounds at 11.40 a.m. on S.16.d.2.6. known as Laundry but at 12.0 to 13.30. 54 rounds fired on Houses suspected as O.P.s in LA TOURELLE DISTILLERY and at 13.35 10 rounds on LORAIES afternoon. C/89. Fired 15 rounds at 10.45 am S.11.d.4.8. Country opposite to very wet have between 14.15 to 15.40. 68 rounds were fired on the following points. S.11.c.5.2. S.6.a. 3.2. S.11.d.1.0½. S.17.a.5.9. retaliation for shelling our trenches.	

WAR DIARY or INTELLIGENCE SUMMARY

Army Form C. 2118

R 7 A

January

Place	Date	Hour	Summary of Events and Information	Remarks and references to Appendices
	Jan 5th		A/89. 10.50 to 12.45. 92 rounds were fired on the following points MOULIN D'EAU. HOUSE 42. HOUSE 34. HOUSE 61 & Ferme du Violette group Scheme & great deal of damage done to all buildings — There were many blind shells. Warmed especially with Lyddite fugs 44. Between 11.35 & 13.45. About 40 rounds were fired by the Enemy apparently on 8" Howitzer, on the Battery Position, in discovery of any inexperience about. The Shells seem to be coming from direction of Beaupont from (X17.d.7.8)	TRENCH MAP. 36 S.W. Sheet 3+1 1/40000
			B/89. Dull, light bad, Overcast, inclined to rain, mild, windy towards evening.	
			A/89. No Artillery Action.	
	6		C/89. Fired 17 rounds at 11 hrs on Hours S.5.d.5.2. Strong Point of hours (troops?) at 12.0 hrs 10 rounds on Trench S.11.5.4.8. Retaliation for shelling Port Loggy at 14.0. 10 rounds fired at Trench S.11.6.4.5 on account of carried fires seen in front line trench.	
			D/89. No Artillery Action.	

WAR DIARY
or
INTELLIGENCE SUMMARY

Army Form C. 2118

January 1918. R.F.A.

Place	Date	Hour	Summary of Events and Information	Remarks and references to Appendices
M/89 M26d.0.8 C/89 M32b.44 D/89 X18c.0.7 H.Q. R.35c.9.5	Jan 7.		Fine morning, dull in the afternoon, no a few showers. M/89. 10.30 a.m. fired 12 rounds Boars Head. 10.50 a.m. 36 rounds at Kemmel S.17 a.5.5. inspected O.P. 11.15 a.m. 12 rounds at Sandbag Hut, Ferme du Bois. Considerable damages observed at S.11.A. C/89. Fired 20 rounds at 10.46. a.m. in retaliation for Huns shelling at 12.30. Fired 25 rounds at S.12.2. at 13.10. 11 rounds trenches S.17.A.7.2/6 and at 23.30. 20 rounds. at L.28.9.1.5.8. D/89. Fired 57 rounds on communication trench S.16.A.7.9. & S.17.C.2.8. and Southwark S.16.A.3.8. Communication trench S.22.B.6.6. Good scheme for keeping to distant attention from wire cutting. Effect good. Some damage done to new front trench, which is rapidly being completed.	TRENCH MAP 36 S.W. Sheet 31 1/40,000

WAR DIARY or INTELLIGENCE SUMMARY

Army Form C. 2118

January 1916

Place	Date	Hour	Summary of Events and Information	Remarks and references to Appendices
A/89 M26d98 C/89 M32d44 D/89 M8c07 H.Q. R35c98	Jan 8		Morning fine, few showers, afternoon renewed hostility for two hours, cleared off in the evening.	TRENCH MAP. 36 S.W. Sheet 3 & 1
			A/89. Fired 32 rounds delivered 14, 20 + 15 at S10.6.9.2 (machine gun emplacement) Good effect. 16·30 fired 10 rds. S10b9.2.	
			C/89. 10·45 o'clock 10·45 if rounds at front line S11b0B. retaliation 11·12 fired 12 rounds at House S11a5.4. retaliation (shots) 12·20. rounds registration firing on ground. 13·50. 10 rounds at House S5d6.4. 15 o'clock 16 rounds at trench S11a3.2. retaliation	
			D/89. Fired 7 rds. registration between 11·35 o'clock + 11·53.	
	9th		Rained early, very fine during the day, sunshine	
			A/89. Fired 18 rds. registration at 11·40 o'clock at B'ty in action at S25d2.3. At 12·20 o'clock fired 16 rds at carpenter's O.P. at S11 a 5.5. Good effect. Fired 12 rds at DISTILLERY at 12·30 o'clock	
			C/89. Fired 4 rds. House S11 a 8.8. Good effect, 6 hits caused retaliation 14·30 o'clock 15 rds. House S6.a.3.2. S.RHS. 15 o'clock 15 rds. at House T1 a 0.3. (3 hits) 19.15 19·30 o'clock fired 12 rds. near LE PETIT. to exit ration party.	
			D/89. Fired 28 rds. on LORGIES between 14·20 + 15·20 o'clock (retaliation)	

WAR DIARY or INTELLIGENCE SUMMARY

(Erase heading not required.)

Army Form C. 2118

January 1916   89th Bde RFA

Place	Date	Hour	Summary of Events and Information	Remarks and references to Appendices
A/89 M26d 9.8. C/89 M32d.4.4. D/89 M8c.o.7. HQ. R35c.9.8.	Jan 10th		Dry morning. Sunshine in afternoon rather colder. A/89. 9.45 o'clock fired 1 rd. zero line registration. 10.45 o'clock fired 20 rds at FERME DU BIEZ and Sandbag Redt (aggressive) 11.15 o'clock 40rds thereabouts S10.d.6.4 to S10.e.4.5 (registration) 12.10 " 2.9 rds " 15.35 " 3 " FERME DU BOIS (registration) C/89. fired 8 rds registration, at 11.15 o'clock at trench S10.d.9.4 " 12 " at Mitrailleuse at 13.10 " 9 " registration at 14.35 " at SM.5.a D/89 fired 40 rds between 10.50 + 12 o'clock at trench S16.d.4.5 little grey house S.29.b.2.6. 14.30 o'clock fired 9 rds. BOAR'S HEAD good effect.	TRENCH MAP. 2.36.S.W. Sheet 34.1.
	Jan 11th		Fine morning, overcast in the afternoon. A/89 Flank gun 4.0 o'clock 20 rds CROSS ROADS, LA TOURELLE (extreme) A/89 7.5 o'clock fired 66 rds. as per scheme. do. 7 Lauke gun 8.5 o'clock 14 rounds BOAR'S HEAD (Bonnet Gun) at PUMP, BOAR'S HEAD. do. 9.5 " 2 " do. 10.15 " 19 " trench BOAR'S HEAD — do — do. 11.45 " 14 " S14.e.8.6. (suspected gun pit.)	

WAR DIARY
or
INTELLIGENCE SUMMARY 89TH Bde. R.F.A.

January 1916 *(Erase heading not required.)*

Army Form C. 2118

Place	Date	Hour	Summary of Events and Information	Remarks and references to Appendices
A/89 M.26.d.9.8. C/89 M.32.t.4.4	Jan 11th (continued)		C/89. Fired 38 rounds, at Tillerele, at S17a.2.4. to LA TOURELLE (Buroinal salient) " 34 " at 10.5 o'clock, at houses in LA BASSÉE Rd. (reprisal) " 34 " from 15.25 to 16.15 o'clock fired 111 rds at houses S11a.4.4. (salient) D/89. Fired 66 rounds, at 7.0 o'clock, at S6.a.6.6. & S10.c.10.3. (salient) " 69 " " ; " 16.0 " observation impossible owing to failing light	TRENCH MAP. 36 S.W. Sheet 34.
D/89 M.8.c.0.7. H.Q. R.35.c.9.8.	Jan 12th		D/89 with aeroplane at intervals, mainly much colder, fine evening A/89. Fired 26 rounds, at Distillery at 15-10 o'clock. +12 rds at 15-25 o'clock at BOAR'S HEAD TRENCH (approximation) C/89. Fired 10 rds, at 13-40 o'clock at S5.a.5.2 + 12 rds at 14 o'clock at S.6.a.8.9 D/89. Fired 3 rds. at FERME DE TOULOTTE. at 12.30 o'clock (German transport)	
	Jan 13th		Overcast, little sunshine, inclined to rain towards evening. A/89. Fired 4 rds registration C/89 Fired 12 rounds at 10-30 at S11.d.4.1.8, 20 rds at 14.20 o'clock at S54.6.2. a house + outbuildings with excellent effect. Fired 20 rds, at 15 o'clock at S11.c.6. also with good results. 8 rounds at 15.25 o'clock on LA BASSÉE ROAD. S17A. D/89. 5 rounds to disperse working party	

Army Form C. 2118

WAR DIARY
or
INTELLIGENCE SUMMARY

(Erase heading not required.)

89th Bde (?)

January 1916

Instructions regarding War Diaries and Intelligence Summaries are contained in F.S. Regs., Part II. and the Staff Manual respectively. Title Pages will be prepared in manuscript.

Place	Date	Hour	Summary of Events and Information	Remarks and references to Appendices
A/89 M26d.9.8.	14th		Dull morning/early. Some storm in afternoon. Evening fine. B/89 fired 8 rds at working party & aeroplane.	TRENCH MAP 36.S.W. Sheet 3+1
C/89			" 16 rds 12 o'clock at trenches S114.y. (retaliation)	
M32 b.4.5t			25 " at 14·58 o'clock at DISTILLERY & LIGNY-LE-PETIT.	
D/89 M8c.0.7.	15th		D/89. " 6 rds at 11-30 at DISTILLERY (retaliation) Cloudy, but no rain; mild, light rain. A/89. Between 9 & 10 o'clock fired 13rds at BOARS HEAD (Bombardment) 4 " " FMe DU BOIS (retaliation) T14 c 2.8. 4 " " T14 c 2.8. 12 " trenches (retaliation) at S14 b 6.5 10·30 o'clock + 30 rds at 11 o'clock	
H.Q. R35 c.9.8.			A mild 24 rds registration at LORGIES covering volumes of brick dust between 12.5 + 13.20 o'clock fired 25 rounds retaliation. At 15-30 P.M. fired 12 hrs from flank gun at FERME DU BIEZ + at 8.5 P.M. 3 rounds aggression.	
			C/89. Between 10 o'clock + 11·55 fired 26 rounds at S11 e 4.2 - 6.1. D/89 fired 46 rounds between 10-50 + 13·10 o'clock at trench S16 b.7.7. & S25 b 2.6. Group actions to enemy mine cutting.	

Army Form C. 2118

WAR DIARY
or
INTELLIGENCE SUMMARY

89th Bde. R.F.A.

January 1916

(Erase heading not required.)

Place	Date	Hour	Summary of Events and Information	Remarks and references to Appendices
A/89 M26d.9.8. C/89 M32b.4.4. D/89 M8c.0.7. H.Q. R35c.9.8.	16th		Dull overcast, some rain, light bad, observation difficult. A/89. Fired 62 rds between 12·30 + 13 o'clock at House S6c 68 ... 30 " ... at 14·30 o'clock at S5 a 91.8 suspected gunpit. C/89 ... 20 " at 14 o'clock at House S11 a 4.8 4 hits. D/89 ... 58 " between 10·25 + 12·50 o'clock at Houses S11 a 9.5, S21 a 9.6, S32 d 2.3 ... 5 " retaliation at 11·50 o'clock.	TRENCH MAP. 36.S.W. sheet 3+1.
	17th		Fine morning, dull afternoon, mild, sight very bad. A/89 Between 12·15 + 13 o'clock fired 20 rds at trench BOAR'S HEAD (good effect) C/89 11·50, 10 rds, S11 a 80. woodwork thrown up 14 o'clock, 15 rds S11 a 4.1, 4 direct hits, damaged roof. 15·50 o'clock 9 rds, T2 c 3.7, Black house D/89 19 o'clock fired 45 rds, at German trenches + wire, very effective 16 " " 36 " " at COUR D'AVOVE S22 a 14 (lightning)	
	18th		Dull morning, raining, light bad. A/89 Between 11·20 + 13·45 o'clock fired 42 rds at suspected German gun pits at S5 a 9.8, T14 e 2.9, T9 b.3.9, S5 d 9.8, T1 b 5.4. C/89 Between 15·35 + 22·40 o'clock fired 15 rds aggressive 11·20 o'clock 18 rds S11 a 3t. 8.1, 12·15 o'clock 10 rds S11 a 3t. 2. 15 " " 9 rds S11 a 3t. 8. (aggressive) light bad. NIL	

WAR DIARY or INTELLIGENCE SUMMARY

Army Form C. 2118

89th Bde R.F.A.

January 1916

Place	Date	Hour	Summary of Events and Information	Remarks and references to Appendices
A/89	19th		Very fine morning, sunshine	TRENCH MAP. 36.S.W. Sheet 2.
M3b4.98.			A/89. Between 12·30 & 13·15 fired 46 rds at enemy fronts, aeroplanes 14 & 15·30 o'clock fired on a German battery at S.6.b.6.2. & S.6.b.9.4. Return scored firing	
C/89			C/89. At 14.15 o'clock fired 25 rds at MUSKRAT MOUND, very good effect	
M3b4.44			" " 15 " Trench S.14.C.	
D/89			D/89 " " 14·30 "	
M3c.0.7			" " 11·25 " " 20 " Houses in LIGNY LE TENT (aeroplane)	
			" " 10 " Ther hut. aeroplane	
			" " 8 " DISTILLERY. wandering O.P	
			" " 5 " Fme. Dn. Bois. wandering	
			" " 20 " EARTH DUMP S.14.a.2.6. wandering	
			" " 20 " Lane S.14.d.4.8. throughout	
H.Q.				
R35.c.9.8.	20th		Fine morning, sunshine, never certain afternoon, heavy shower of rain windy A/89 Between 9 & 10·10 o'clock fired 30 rds at German trenches at 10·25 o'clock 1·5 rd at houses at S.6.c.0.8. & Bois du BIEZ (aeroplane) " 18 " active Btty C/89 Between 10 & 11 o'clock fired 30 rds at enemy trench with good effect D/89. 2·15·3 o'clock 24 rds, night fire (group silence) 10·25 & 12·30. fired 80 rds. at registered points	

Army Form C. 2118

WAR DIARY
or
INTELLIGENCE SUMMARY

(Erase heading not required.)

8978 de Rota

January 1916

Instructions regarding War Diaries and Intelligence Summaries are contained in F.S. Regs., Part II. and the Staff Manual respectively. Title Pages will be prepared in manuscript.

Place	Date	Hour	Summary of Events and Information	Remarks and references to Appendices
A/89	2 Jan		Dull misty, inclined to rain, lightened towards afternoon.	TRENCH MAP 36.S.W. Sheet 34.
M 26 d 9.8.			A/89 at 10.35 fired 12 rds at working party at S16 a 9.8	
C/89			C/89 " 10 o'clock, 6 rds " S11 b. 59 aggressive	
M 32 b 4.4			" 11.30 " 25 " S11 d 4.8 DISTILLERY	
D/89			" 14.50 " 12 " S11 b 9.1. Normal.	
			" 21 " 12 " At hostile working parties at S11 d 4 8, LIGNY-LE-PETIT	
D/89			NIL	
M Pc. 07	22nd		Dull overcast, rain at intervals, inclined to be misty, high fog.	
HQ			A/89 At 12.5 o'clock, 64 rds at MUSKRAT MOUNDS from 2 different	
			points, ran red around one mound, seemed very strong.	
R 35 c 9.8.			At 14.45 o'clock 30 rds, my flank gun at S11 c 4.8 (machine gun)	1
			C/89 11 o'clock, 5 rds, House S11 c 4.4, reported machine gun 6 hits	
			15 " " 12 rds " S11 d 4 8, 3 direct hits	
D/89			At 11.25 o'clock, 18 rds S16 a 6.4 & S16 a 6.1 (registration)	

WAR DIARY or INTELLIGENCE SUMMARY

Army Form C. 2118

89th Bde RFA

January 1916

Place	Date	Hour	Summary of Events and Information	Remarks and references to Appendices
A/89. M.26.d.9.8.	23rd		Very fine, sunshine most of the morning	TRENCH MAP 36 S.W. Sheet 3 & 4.
			A/89. 10.45 relock: fired 12 rds. at 94.4 (registration)	
			11.45 " 6 rds at LORGIES (aggression)	
C/89.			20.5 " 14 rds at Trenches S11 a 3.3. (retaliation)	
M.32.b.4.4.			C/89 13-30 " 13 " " S11 c 15.8 French mortar	
D/89.			19.45 " 10 " night wire, request of infantry	
M.P.C.0.7			D/89 12.55 " 12 " at S17 a 10.2. suspected O.P. several hits	
H.Q.	24th		Dull overcast, little rain, light trade, good towards evening	
R.35 c.9.8.			A/89. 15.10 o'clock 8 rds. at 77mm Bty. @ S6 b3.3. Bty. ceased fire	
			15.25 " 12 " S.2.b & 5.5. Y two Rds returned.	
			C/89. 10 o'clock 11 " House S11 c 4.45 suspected machine gun	
			11 " 19 " " DISTILLERY.	
			14.45 " 17 " S11 a.9.2.5 suspected machine gun	
			14.45 " 14 " S.6 a.5.3. S.6 c.11.4. registration	
			D/89. 11.40 " 13 " S.27 b 4.15.	
			15.10 " 7 " FERME DU BOIS & FERME DU TOULOTTE	
			Major K.G. Guilford assumed command of the Bde. vice Lt.Col. A.H. Thomas to the Sick list	

WAR DIARY
or
INTELLIGENCE SUMMARY
(Erase heading not required.)

Army Form C. 2118

January 1916   R.F.A.

Place	Date	Hour	Summary of Events and Information	Remarks and references to Appendices
A/89. M.26.d.9.2.	25		Fine. Mostly morning. Sunshine rest of day.	TRENCH MAP 36.S.W. Sheet 3 & 4.
		2/89. 10.25	fired 8 rounds towards S.11. C.3.8.1 (registration)	
		10.25 "	20 rounds towards N.H.C. of 4 (registration)	
		10.25 "	17 rounds –do–	
C/89. Mar.b.4.4.		11.30 o'clock	6 rounds road N.24.a.3.0. (registration)	
		14.10 o'clock	fired 16 rounds Earthwork S.23.6.6.7 (aggression)	
		14.30 o'clock	4 rounds Bty at S.28.h.a).	
D/89.			4 rounds 77 m.m. Bty at S.28.h.a).	
M.8C.0.7.			8 rounds home S.H.C.7.6 (registration)	
H.Q.		3/89. 23.45 "	24 rounds 3 shrapnel LORGIES (aggression)	
		24 o'clock	7 rounds LIGNY 6 patrol (aggression)	
		13-35 "	34 rounds S.V.a.7.7 (aggression)	
R.35.C.9.8.		2/89. 11-55 o'clock	16 rounds Parapets front line trench from S.16.C.6.8 to S.16.0.6.2	4.0000
		13-40 "	20 rounds Parapets second line trench S.22.a.8.6.6 S.22.a.8.3	
			27 rounds parapets 1st line from S.22.a.3.15 S.22.A.2.8	
	26th		Dull overcast. Little aircraft in afternoon. Enemies to the sunset.	
		4/89. 15-40 o'clock	fired 20 rounds Germ S.17.a.7.8.	
		18-15 "	6 " S.6.a.81/2.71/2.	
			6 " S.11. C.5.7	
		C/89. 11-0 o'clock	9 " trench S.11. C.4.4 1/2.	
		11-20 "	16 " home S.11. C.4.4.1/2.	

WAR DIARY
or
INTELLIGENCE SUMMARY
(Erase heading not required.)

Army Form C. 2118

January 1916

Place	Date	Hour	Summary of Events and Information	Remarks and references to Appendices
A/64 M26d98	26	11-45 o'clock fired 21 rounds trench N.S.2 5H.3		TRENCH MAP 36 S.W. Sheet 3+1
		14.15	22 rounds S.11.A.9.4.	
			8 rounds S.17.a.7.8 (regulating)	
C/89 M32b44	27	12.0		
		11-15	33 " S.16.a.8.7	
			Dull, overcast. Slight showers.	
		10.15	o'clock fired 10 rounds 77mm Bty S.6.6.7.4.	
D/89		10.25	10 " F.G. LA TOURELLE Bois Route (Retaliation)	
M&C.0.7		10.55	6 " 77mm Btys at S.6.7.7.4. (Retaliation)	
H.Q.		13.55	18 " houses S.30.a.3.9.	
R35c98		15.0	6 " 77mm Bty at S.6.6.7.4 (Retaliation)	
C/89		10 o'clock fired 15 rounds June du Bois		
		11-15	27 " Trenches S.11.a.u.3. to S.11.u.a.o.1.	
		14.0	10 " S.11.d.u.9.	
		14.45	20 " LORGIES	
		24.0	7 " S.11.a. Scheme	
D/89		13.15	o'clock fired 58 rounds houses S.11.C.4/5.4/5	
			trench S.17.a.5.9.	

WAR DIARY or INTELLIGENCE SUMMARY

Army Form C. 2118

89th Bde. R.F.A.

January, 1916

Place	Date	Hour	Summary of Events and Information	Remarks and references to Appendices
A/89	28th		Fine morning, inclined to rain in the afternoon.	TRENCH MAP 36.S.W. Sheet 3+1
M26dq.8			A/89 at 11-15 o'clock fired 6 rounds N.29.b.0.4½ (registration & aggression)	
			" 12-10 " 9 " S.29.b.0.4½ — do —	
C/89			" 13.20 " 6 " S.23.b.3.6. — do —	
M31b24			" 14.10 " 12 " M.17mm. S.6.b.6.7. + Battery enclosure fny.	
D/89			" 14.40 " 30 " Horse S.29.b.8.6.	
			" 15.4 " 8 " T.8.b.0.8	
M8c.0.4			C/89 10-0 " fires 26 rounds horse S.11.c. 7/r.5	
HQ R35e.q.8			" 11.45 " 11 rounds trench S.11.a.3.8.	1/5,000
	29th		Dull all day. light rain, mild.	
			A/89 at 11-50 o'clock fired 6 rounds S.11.a.3/r. 3	
			B/89 at 14.45 pm. fired 15 rounds at Fme du Bois	
			at 15.15 pm. fired 16 rounds at Amours S.11.d.4.8. 35d.6.3. S.11.a.7.7.	
			and S.11.a.7.7 for registration.	
			at 15.35 p.m. fired 8 rounds. at S.11.b.0.2.	
	30th		Brigade moved out to Rest Billets near Haverskerque J.29.c and D	
			Exchanging guns with 122nd Brigade.	

WAR DIARY
or
INTELLIGENCE SUMMARY

(Erase heading not required.)

January 1916   89th Brigade RFA

Army Form C. 2118

Place	Date	Hour	Summary of Events and Information	Remarks and references to Appendices
	31st		Brigade in Rest Billets. All units occupied in general cleaning up. Headquarters at J.29.d.10. A/89 J.29.d. 6.1 C/89 J.29.c. 3.3½ D/89 J.29.c. 9.3 B.A.C. J.36.a. 8.1	MAP 36 A N.E. 1/20000 1/40

W Winfret
Major
Cmdg. 89th Brigade R.F.A.

Vol. 8
20th Div
19

WAR DIARY.
89TH. BDE. R.F.A.

COMMENCING 1ST. FEB 1916 ENDING 29TH FEB 1916

VOLUME — 8.

Army Form C. 2118

WAR DIARY
or
INTELLIGENCE SUMMARY
(Erase heading not required.)

February 1916

Place	Date	Hour	Summary of Events and Information	Remarks and references to Appendices
	7th		Brigade at rest at HAVERSKERQUE. Cleaning up and re-equipping from Jan. 30th to Feb. 14th 1916	Trench map 36.S.W. Edition 2 1/10000
	14.2.16		On night of 14th C. and D/89. Each moved one section into action	
	15.2.16	7. P.M.	Renewing returns of C. & D/89. moved into action	
A/89	16th		C/89 at 2.20 P.M. fired 4 rounds at LORGIES and at 3.15 P.M. 6 rounds at S.12.c.7.6. Aggressor.	
M15d 2½.2½ C/89.			B/89. nil.	
M32 b54	17th		C/89. at 3.15 P.M. fired 11 rounds at S.16.A.4.9 & S.10.c.9.4 for registration	
D/89 M27a.0.0.			D/89. nil.	
H.Q.				
M.9.c.24	18th		A/89. moved all four guns into action at 7 P.M.	
			C/89. at 2.40 P.M. fired 38 rounds at S.17.A.6½.2.10. much damage claimed	
			D/89. at 12.15 P.M. fired 8 rounds at S.6.c.2.9	

WAR DIARY
or
INTELLIGENCE SUMMARY

(Erase heading not required.)

February 1916

Army Form C. 2118

Place	Date	Hour	Summary of Events and Information	Remarks and references to Appendices
A/89 M.15.d.2½ C/89 M.32.15.50	Feb. 19		A/89. Fired at 2. P.m. 1 round at M.31.d.9½.3 to checking repair. Between 2.45 & 3.15 P.m. 15 rounds at House N.26.c.4.6. Carrying part of house to burn. C/89. Nil. D/89. At 12.45 P.m. 8 rounds at S.15.b.5.2. reporting hand mortar.	French map 36 SW 1 Ed.6 1/10000
D/89 M.27.b.o.o H.Q. z.4 M9C.7	28th		Light out get fine day. A/89. At 9. am. 4 rounds at M.30.d.8.8. for calibration at 10.10 Am. 50 rounds at M.36.A.5-3 to M.30.c.4.5 in accordance with scheme. at 12.20 P.m. 11 rounds at House M.30.d.8.8 calibration. C/89. At 1.20 P.m. 30 rounds at Bois du BIEZ at suspected O.P. at 1.50 P.m. 15 rounds at House S.12.c.7.6. appearance. D/89. At 11.20 Am. 20 rounds at House T.2.d.3.2. appearance. at 12.40 P.m. 15 rounds at S.6.A.8.1. MUSKRAT MOUND.to. Checking registration.	

Army Form C. 2118

WAR DIARY
or
INTELLIGENCE SUMMARY
(Erase heading not required.)

February 1916

Place	Date 1916	Hour	Summary of Events and Information	Remarks and references to Appendices
	Feb 20.		D/69 Ex'td at 1.15. P.m. 9 rounds at House S.6.A.5.4. to shorten reputation	Trench Map Sheet 36SW.1 E.9.6. 1/10,000
	at 21.-		at 4.15. P.m. 7 rounds at House S.5.d.3.5. shorten reputation	
			Fine + clear but cold. Snow on the ground.	
A/89			A/89. at 11 A.m. 5 rounds at M.30.d.8.8. to calibration, also 50 rounds	
M.15.d.2½.2½			at 11.25 a.m. in accordance with scheme and in conjunction with	
O/89			Stokes mortar, much material damage done.	
M.32.b.3.4			at 5.25. P.m. 5 rounds at M.30.A.4.3	
D/89			5.45 P.m. 16 rounds do do	
			6.10. P.m. 16 rounds do do	
M.27.0.0.			7. 0. P.m. 4 rounds. N.2.5.C.0.7.+N.31.C.0.4 } in accordance
H.Q. 2.4			7.35. P.m. 4 rounds. do — do — do } with scheme.
M.9.c.2.7			8.15. P.m. 4 rounds do — do — do	
			C/89. at 11.45. A.m. 10 rounds. house S.17.A.6.7 oppressum	
			1.45. P.m. 12 " Ferme du B.1.E.3 kuepertes O.P.	
			2.30 P.m. 16 " House S.11.d.3½.8. oppressum	
			3.30 A.m. 10 " House S.12.c.7.6. oppressum	
			D/89. at 12.30. P.m. 12 rounds. at S.17.A.7.9. to reputation	
			at 2.10. P.m. 12 " at S.12.c.11.4.+S.11.d.3½.8.} to reputation	
			at 4. 0. P.m. 11 " at S.12.c.7.6.	

WAR DIARY
or
INTELLIGENCE SUMMARY

(Erase heading not required.)

February 1916

Army Form C. 2118

Place	Date 1916	Hour	Summary of Events and Information	Remarks and references to Appendices
	Feb 21		D/89. Cont. From 10 P.m. to 11 P.m. 91 rounds at Itinera in TOURELLE and LIGNY-le-PETIT. Scheme.	TRENCH MAP Sheet 36 S.W. Ed 6 1/10000
	22.		Heavy downfall of snow clearing in the afternoon.	
M/A9 M.18.d.2.5.? C/89 M.32.b.c.4 D/A9 M.27.a.0.0 H.Q. M.9.c.2.4.5	23.		A/89. at 8.10 a.m. 2 rounds 9.15 a.m. 5 rounds 9.50 a.m. 2 rounds C/89. at 3.30 P.m. 10 rounds on House S.12.C.7.6. Appresseau and (21) rounds at Ferme du BIEZ at Suspected O.P. D/89. at 3.25 P.m. 7 rounds House T.2.t.9.2. Registering. Summery light fired. A/89. at 9.30 A.M. 2 rounds C/89. at 11.20 A.M. 7 rounds at TRENCH S.11.a.7.6 for registration of FLANK Open. at 12.30 P.m. 4 rounds as per return at S.11.A.4.4. at 3.15 P.m. 22 rounds at LORGIES. Appresseau.	

WAR DIARY
or
INTELLIGENCE SUMMARY

(Erase heading not required.)

February 1916

Army Form C. 2118

Place	Date 1916	Hour	Summary of Events and Information	Remarks and references to Appendices
A/89 M&d 2½ C/89 M32 b 6·4 D/89 M27 a·0·0 H.Q. M9 c·2·4	Feb 23 to 24.		D/89. at 12.30. Pm. 3 rounds a trench S.11.A.6.4. as in scheme. Light too bad to continue. at 3. Pm 22 rounds at TIGNY. LE-PETIT. at 4. Pm 22 rounds at MUSKRAT MOUND + HOUSE T1A ½·2 Light too bad to observe accurately, near enemy. A/89. at 12.5. Pm 27 rounds at machine gun emplacement M.30 B.0.5. 2 direct hits C/89 at 12. Midday 7 rounds at S.11.A.4.2½ to registration. " at 12.35 Pm. 56 rounds at S.11.A 3.2 & S 11.A. 5. 3½. Grande Rehind. many blinds. Light too bad to observe effect. D/89 at 11.45. am. 10 rounds at front line trenches S.11.0. 5½. 3 to S.11.0. 7.1. registering. From 12.40 to 1.30 Pm. 57 shells at these trenches.	Trench map sheet 36 & W.1 Ed. 6 1/10000
	25.		Weather overcast light very bad. A/89. at 8.10. am. 6 rounds on ZERO LINE to find zero of day. at 2.40. Pm 31 rounds at IRON. CYLINDER M.30 c. 6½. 0 one direct hit.	

WAR DIARY
or
INTELLIGENCE SUMMARY

(Erase heading not required.)

February 1916

Army Form C. 2118

Place	Date 1916	Hour	Summary of Events and Information	Remarks and references to Appendices
A/189 M.18d 2.2 C/189 M32.b.5.4 D/189 M27a.0.0 H.Q. M9c.2.4	Feb 25.		C/189. at 11.30 A.M. 10 rounds at TRENCH. S.11.A.3.3 + 4.4 Dispersion. 6 Burnt repair of damaged parapet at 12.30 P.M. 19 rounds at S.10.d.2.6 } 3.4 } for retaliation 5.5 } at 2. P.M. 6 rounds at S.11.b.1.1. retaliation D/189. at 1.30 P.M. 8 rounds at TRENCH. at S.111.A.2.2. for retaliation Enemy put a heavy retaliation.	Trench map Sheet— 36 S.W. Ed. 6 1/10000
	26.		Light bad through heavily. A/189 3.30 P.M. 33 rounds front line trench Sign Post Lane M.36.c.0.5 retaliation for shelling Ebenezer Farm and 20 rounds Trenches at T.7.d.3.6. HALPEGARBE. C/189. 12.45 P.M. 13 rounds S.10.d.7.9. and S.10.d.7.4. Checking Registration 2.30 P.M. 84 rounds on S.10.D.8.9. to S.10.d.2.6. S.10.d.4.5 to S.11.d.9.8. and S.10.d.5.4. to S.11.d.0.4. Group scheme. D/189. 2.45 P.M. 88 rounds at Trenches S.11.A.2.2. to S.10.d.8.9. front line Aukpart + reserve trenches. A heck made at S.11.A.1. General bombardment very effective, + called forth heavy retaliation.	

WAR DIARY
or
INTELLIGENCE SUMMARY

(Erase heading not required.)

February 1916

Army Form C. 2118

Place	Date 1916	Hour	Summary of Events and Information	Remarks and references to Appendices
A/89 M.15.d.2½.2½ C/89 M.32.b.3.4 D/89 M.27.a.0.0 H.Q. M.9.c.4	Feb 27th		Thawed heavily during the morning. Cold wind, light daily frost M/89. 11.15 am. 4 rounds. ZERO LINE to ascertain error of day 2.20 pm. 32 " ZERO Horse Communication Trench M.30.d.8.7 4.0 pm. 14 " Front line trench S.5.b.2.3 to S.5.b.4.0 purpose of registering C/89. Nil D/89. 11.35 am. 12 rounds. T.1.A.0.2. House. Intently reported movement seen. 10 direct hits house nearly demolished. 12.35 pm. 14 rounds. 35.d.2.4 + 35.d.4.6 Registration with H.E. and Shrapnel	Trench Map Sheet 36.S.W.1 Ed. 6 1/10,000
	28th		Dull morning, mild, rain in afternoon A/89. 6.0 am. 38 rounds. Front line trench. S.5.b.2.3 to S.5.b.4.0 2 rounds seen 9.40 am. 5 rounds. Zero line Calibration 10.5 am. 9 rounds. Communication Trench. M.30.d.9.8. registered 10.15 am. 6 rounds. Zero Horse Enfilading Repela 2.10 pm. 56 rounds on Communication trenches M.30.d.9.6. in cooperation with Batt trench 3.0 pm. 4 rounds. House. M.31.b.4.4 Observation unfavourable owing to enemy shelling O.P. Stink Farm	

WAR DIARY
or
INTELLIGENCE SUMMARY
(Erase heading not required.)

February 1916.

Army Form C. 2118

Place	Date 1916	Hour	Summary of Events and Information	Remarks and references to Appendices
A/89	Feb. 28.		A/89 Cu F	Trench Map Sheet 36.S.W.1 Ed.6. 1/10000
M31d.2.2		4.30 to P.m.	34 rounds. Loop hole in mine crater M.30.a.4.6. 2 direct hits	
C/89		5.55. A.m.	39 rounds S.5.d.2½.2½ to S.5.d.3½.5" } Registrp. Scheme	
		6.8. A.m.	17 rounds. Shrapnel. 6.5.d.4.0 to S.11.b.4.8 } aeroplane series. Left too dark to observe.	
		10.30 A.m.	5 rounds. T.J.D.5.5. aeroplane series. Left too dark to observe.	
		2.30 P.m.	20 rounds. FERME du BEIZ	
		4.30 P.m.	4 rounds. S.11.B.4½.9. afflueron	
M32.b.5.4				
D/89		6.55. A.m.	58 rounds. S.5.d.2.4. to S.6. with H.E. + Knocks about S.5.b.5.0 with shrapnel. Registering line to new gun pit.	
		1.0. P.m.	10 rounds. S.6.c.1.8. horse. Registering line to new gun pit with shrapnel. Good return.	
M27.a.0.0	29.		Fine morning sunshine. Cloudy fog windy during afternoon with intervals of rain fine evening	
H.Q.				
M.9.c.24			A/89. 9.30. A.m. 4 rounds. ZERO HOUSE calibration	
		10.55. A.m.	7 rounds. Left of House N.31.b.7.6. Working Party	
		12.40. A.m.	24 rounds. N.32.c.4.8. Shrine Knapsacks O.P.	
		3.30. P.m.	12 rounds. House N.31.b.9.3 retaliation for enemy firing on Stink Farm. + RUE BACQUEROT.	
C/89		10.30. to 12.30. P.m.	16 rounds HALPEGARBE. T.7.d.3.7 aeroplane	
		2.30 P.m.	25 rounds S.11.d.5.1 afflueron	
		3.0 P.m.	15 rounds House S.17.a.7.3. do	
		8.0 P.m. 8.45 P.m. 12.30 P.m.	} 16 rounds. S.11.d.5.1. Personnel observed	

WAR DIARY
or
INTELLIGENCE SUMMARY

(Erase heading not required.)

February 1916.

Army Form C. 2118

Place	Date 1916	Hour	Summary of Events and Information	Remarks and references to Appendices
	Feb 29		Continued	Trench map sheet 36 S.W. 2 & 6 1/10000
A/89			D/89. 12.35.p.m. 12 rounds Communication Trench N.31.d.1.0. to M.26.d.7.7 Registering	
M.31.d.2.2		3.0 p.m.	34 rounds. T.2.d.3.3. Attempts a large clump of Ruling	
C/89		4.0 p.m.	Material and near cut Junction	
M.32.b.5.4		8.0 p.m.		
D/89		8.45 "	18 rounds. N. S.6.a.5.4. S.6.c.2.9. S.11.b.8.8.	
M.27.a.0.0		12.30 a.m.	Bomb Scheme.	
H.Q.				
Mar 2.4			F.R. Hanway	
			Lt Col.	
			Comdg 89 Bde RFA	

89 RFA
Vol 9

CONFIDENTIAL

WAR DIARY

of

89TH BRIGADE RFA.

from 1st March to 31st March 1916.

VOLUME 9

WAR DIARY or INTELLIGENCE SUMMARY

Army Form C. 2118

Title Pages March 1916 **89th Bde. R.F.A.**

Place	Date	Hour	Summary of Events and Information	Remarks and references to Appendices
	1st		Fine morning, a little overcast in the afternoon, light very good	
N.8.L.d.2.1/2		B/89. 8.50 o'clock 11 rds Hones Tr 31.b 8.4 (smoke seen issuing)		
M.15.c.		16.00 – 51 " about M 30 a 9.5, mine shaft, German reserve my	Trench map.
M.15.c.5.4.		C/89. 11.15 o'clock 8 rds S11.A.4.4. aggression	shot.
		14.00 – 29 " S11.D.2.9. suspected O.P., much thatch torn off	36.S.W.1
		16.00 – 18 " S11.A.1.4. damaging top part of wall severely	
		16.40 – 14 " House S11.11/2.4. Part of wall knocked down	
M.32.β.		D/89. 11.45 – 13 " S 6 0 central retaliation	Ed. 6.
D/89. A.O.P.		12.30 – 29 " trenches at Les BRULOT.	
		13.15 – 26 " T1 D 3.9 to T1 B 2.3	11.0000
M.27.a.		16.25 – 20 " T2 D 8.35 trenches at LES BRULOT. 2 direct hits German working party dispersed	
H.B. 2nd & 2ND			apparent O.P.	
M.9.	2nd		Fine morning, cloudy during afternoon, light good	
		A/89. 9.55 o'clock 4 rds ZERO trial barrel reg'n	
		15.15 – 38 " Horses N 32 A.1.2 aggression	
		" – 16 " on communication Trench M 30 D M.1	
		18.56 – 4 " "	
		19.15 – 4 " "	
		C/89. 11.15 15 12 o'clock 31 rds at SNIPER'S POST (S 5 c 9.1.) + House S11.B.8.5	
		15.25 o'clock 16 – " trench S11 A 4.1. retaliation	

Army Form C. 2118

WAR DIARY
or
INTELLIGENCE SUMMARY

89th Bde RFA

(Erase heading not required.)

MARCH 1916

Instructions regarding War Diaries and Intelligence Summaries are contained in F.S. Regs., Part II. and the Staff Manual respectively. Title Pages will be prepared in manuscript.

Place	Date	Hour	Summary of Events and Information	Remarks and references to Appendices
			(CONTINUED)	
A/89 M.15.b.2.h.2	2ND		D/89. 11-30 o'clock 10 rds. 2nd line trenches S6 A 6.6 registration, good effect.	Trench Map Sheet 36. S.W.1 Ed. 6 1/10000
			12.5 " 6 " " " S6 A 6.8 — do —	
C/89. 4.5.4	3RD		13.30 " 5 " Front " " S.5 A. Suspected gas attack	
M.32.6.5.4			14.30 " 14 " Houses S'A 4.3 strongly fortified. 2 hits	
D/89			Overcast, rain in afternoon, visibility light moderate.	
M.27.a.6.0			A/89. 11-40 o'clock 6 rds. emplacement M 24 D 6.3.	
H.R.c.2.4			13.30 " 6 " BLOCKHOUSE M 30 B 9.1.	
M.9.c.9			15.00 " 14 " Communication trench behind MOULIN DE PIETRE	
			C/89. 12.00 " 13 " S11 D 5.1. Aggressive	
			14.00 " 5 " S 5 B 4.1 & S 5 D 5.8 group scheme	
			15.30 " 8 " S 12 c 4.6	
			16.00 " 14 " S 12 c 5.9	
			D/89 14.00 " 50 " S 5 B 5.3 & 8.6 group scheme	
			Apparently very satisfying. The 4TH round emerged from volumes of smoke as if a front line had been exploded. Parapet appeared much damaged	

Army Form C. 2118

Instructions regarding War Diaries and Intelligence Summaries are contained in F.S. Regs., Part II and the Staff Manual respectively. Title Pages will be prepared in manuscript.

WAR DIARY
or
INTELLIGENCE SUMMARY

89th Bde. R.F.A.

MARCH 1916

(Erase heading not required.)

Place	Date	Hour	Summary of Events and Information	Remarks and references to Appendices
	4th		Heavy fall of snow during the night, continuing during the day	
A/89.		14.50 o'clock	10 rds commn. trench M30 D 8.4.	fresh map sheet 36. S.W.1. 36.6. 1/10000.
M.15.d.2½.2		— do —	— do — " BAS POMMERAV	
C/89.		16.5 o'clock	24 " Houses N31 A 1.3 + N31 B 4.6 registration	
M.32.6.5.4		20.15 to 20.55 o'clock	19 rds commn. trench M30 D 8.8. Salvoes	
D/89.		12.00 o'clock	5 rds S30 c 5.5 tim area	
		12.30 —	6 — S18 c 9.6	
M.27.a.0.0		14.30 —	5 — FERME DE BIEZ	
N.Q.		16.30 —	6 — S30 c 5.5.	
M.9.c.2.4.			NIL	
	5th		Fine morning. Cloudy, light rain in afternoon	
A/89.		13 o'clock	9 rds emplacement M30 B 7.4. Registration	
		14.56.46 "	28 " PIETRE X trench + house BAS POMMERAV (total 37)	
		16.45 "	28 " LACHOUVERTERIE FARM + houses N 31 D 4.8.	
		16.50. "	4 " Commn. trench M30 d 8.8 aggression	
C/89.		15.30 o'clock	5 rounds FERME DE BIEZ	
D/89.		9.45 "	19 " T2 c 5.3 small wood, possibly telephone dugout	
		10.10 "	19 " T 8 B 3.9½ possibly an O.P.	

Army Form C. 2118

WAR DIARY
or
INTELLIGENCE SUMMARY

(Erase heading not required.)

89th Brigade HQr

Title Pages MARCH 1916

Place	Date	Hour	Summary of Events and Information	Remarks and references to Appendices
A/89 M.15.d.2.h.2	6		Fine day, light very good, either towards evening, inclined to freeze	Trench Maps Sheet 36 S.W.1. Ed 6. 1/10000
			A/89 14-30 o'clock 6 rds at Huze x Roads N33 e.8.3 retaliation	
			15-10 " 4 " 60mm Trench Mor od 8.8. aggression	
			15-20 " } 83 " N33.e.8.5 + House N31.e.4.6 Scheme	
			to 14-10 " }	
C/89 M.22.6.5.4			20-15 " 6 " LA CLIQUETERIE FARM aggression	
			20-35 " 6 " N33.e.8.5 aggression	
D/89 M.10.D.8.7			C/89 15.0 o'clock 30 " S5 4.2 annual bus on parapet	
			16-30 " 29 " do — do	
HQ M.9.c.2.4			D/89 12-30 " 13 " } farm at N25 a 6.6	
			13-0 to 15-30-26 rds }	
			Reg. + enfiring line of fire.	
			D/89 changed their gun position to M10 D 8.4	
			Lt. Bde. Hennessy slightly wounded, observing in front of trench. A German rifle bullet penetrated parapet, causing slight flesh wound in hand + face	

WAR DIARY or INTELLIGENCE SUMMARY

Army Form C. 2118

MARCH 1916 — 89TH Bde. R.F.A.

Place	Date	Hour	Summary of Events and Information	Remarks and references to Appendices
	4th		Snow fell during night & continued during day, light frost thawing	trench maps
A/89 M.15.d.2½.2			A/89. 11 o'clock 9 rds. at machine gun M30 a 4.1. Registration	Sht 36.S.W.1
			13·15 " 9 " " M30 B 2. W. working party	52.6
C/89			C/89. 15·30 " 34 rds. S11 B 5·4. Henee & S11 c 5·5·5 to S11 d 4·3	1/10000
M.32.b.5.4			22·00 " 20 " S12 a 72 & HALPEGARDE to entil ration parties W	
D/89.			D/89. 16·00 " 1 rd. to test light & range	
			Fine day, sunshine, freezing at night	
M.10.3.d.O.1	5th		A/89. 8·30 o'clock 18 rds M 24 d 4.1. Comm. trench retaliation	
H.Q.			9·40 " 6 " M 30 D 5·10 — do —	
M.9.C.24			19·30 " 6 " MOULIN DE PIETRE, scheme	
			16·45 to 17·30 o'clock do	
			C/89. 11·30 o'clock 11 rds. S11 f. 0·3. Observation difficult owing to snow	
			13·30 " 20 " S11 c 4·3 House. Enemy seen leaving post on road	
			15·15 " 30 " House S6 B. 4.9.	
			16·25 " 9 " S6 A. 4.2. retaliation at request of infantry	
			D/89. 10·05, 12·45 " 52 rds. x roads N26 c 8·4.	
			14 o'clock 18 " N25 A 5·5. 15 o'clock 8 rds x roads N15 A 3·3. registration	
			16·20, 25, 14·10 o'clock 28 rds Wireless house N31A 9·5. 21 x roads PIETRE	
			19·20·15, 9·0 " 10 " PIETRE X roads eventp scheme	

Army Form C. 2118

WAR DIARY
or
INTELLIGENCE SUMMARY

(Erase heading not required.)

89th Bde. R.F.A.

MARCH 1916.

Place	Date	Hour	Summary of Events and Information	Remarks and references to Appendices
A/89. M.15.d.2h.2.	9th		A/89. Fine morning, sunshine, cloudy during afternoon, colder.	Trench Maps Sheet 36. S.W. 1. So. C. 1/10,000.
		9.45 o'clock	12 rds Zero range Registration	
		10.20 to 12 "	170 " OC Blockhouse + Comm: trench M30 D & 8. Group scheme. Parapet breached in 4 places.	
C/89. M.32.b.5.4.		13.0 to 13.30 "	39 rds front line at M30 A 5.7. to M 30 A 5.B. Fairly good	
		13.40 o'clock	80 " Comm: trench N 3 a 8.8. & 4400 yds to rear. caused much dislocation in our communications	
C/89.		15.00 o'clock	20 rds work in trench S11 D4.1 direct hits obtained	
D/89.		10.30 "	54 " CUPOLA M 36 a 5.9. Bomb scheme. See below.	
M.10.D.8.7.			The scheme was carried out as ordered commencing at 10.30 A.M. in CUPOLA situated at M36 A 5.4. and the fire of the parapet from M36 a 5.8 & 5.6. the parapet was blown away for 3 feet from the lip at the nose of the salient at A 5.8 and another breach was made just 10 yds south of the CUPOLA. The CUPOLA stands about 5 yds out from the parapet + is connected by a covered way which was destroyed. After 5 or 6 more rds of 4.5. + what appeared like a direct hit by B/89. a man came out from the CUPOLA from the front; ran 5 yds in the open + disappeared into the trench in front of the parapet. The enemy	
H.Q.			churned in agony + were no cert.	
M.9.C.2.4.			The CUPOLA after the firing ceased no signs of being destroyed (report continued overleaf)	

Army Form C. 2118

WAR DIARY
or
INTELLIGENCE SUMMARY 89th Bde R.F.A.
(Erase heading not required.)

Instructions regarding War Diaries and Intelligence Summaries are contained in F.S. Regs., Part II. and the Staff Manual respectively. Title Pages MARCH 1916. will be prepared in manuscript.

Place	Date	Hour	Summary of Events and Information	Remarks and references to Appendices
A/89. M.15.d.2.h.2.	9th	Continued	D/89 Report on group scheme. the German retaliation with MM + H.E. was all along our front line but must if their shooting was even	Trench Map Sheet 36. S.W.1. 20. 6.
C/89. M.32.b.5.4			D/89. only fired 54 rounds of the 100 rounds, when our telephone line were cut & it was too late to continue when communication was restored.	1/10000
D/89. M.10.D.8.7.	10th		The trench mortar fired simultaneously with the Battery almost 6 rounds with good effect. Wet, light frost etc.	
H.Q. M.9.C.24.			A/89. 13 o'clock 39 rds. front line trenches M 30 a 25.5 several Lib 13.40 to 14.30 o'clock 60 rds Communication trench M30 D 8.3 + 400 yards new group scheme.	
			C/89. 15 to 15.40 o'clock 96 rds Group Scheme 15.50 " H " S11 B4.5 retaliation	
			D/89. 12.25 o'clock 15 rds checking line + range on zero point 13.00 " " 120 " PIETRE X roads. W31 a 4.4 and Rouen in vicinity group scheme. Observation difficult while other Batts were firing	

Army Form C. 2118

WAR DIARY
or
INTELLIGENCE SUMMARY 89th Bde. RFA

MARCH 1916

(Erase heading not required.)

Instructions regarding War Diaries and Intelligence Summaries are contained in F. S. Regs., Part II. and the Staff Manual respectively. Title Pages will be prepared in manuscript.

Place	Date	Hour	Summary of Events and Information	Remarks and references to Appendices
A/89	11th		Dull morning rest of the day.	French Maps Sheet No 36 S.W. 1- S.E. 6. 1/10000
M.15.d.2½.2.			A/89. 16.45 o'clock. 12 rds at LA CLIQUETERIE FARM (aggression)	
C/89			C/89. 11.30 — 26 " S11 c 3.9 suspected O.P.	
N.32.b.5.4.			14.00 — 7 " S6 B½ a remnant of infantry	
			15.45 — 15 " S11 B½ 7 suspected sniper post	
			16.00 — 20 " S11 A 8.5 sniper post	
			16.30 — 14 " S11 A 9.4 retaliation	
D/89.			D/89. 28.45 — 18 " M 24 d 7.25, M 24 d 5.0, M30 a 9.4.2, M30 d 8.8.	
M.10.b.87	12th		Raining most of the day, misty. Reign of night time turn direct hits on parapet	
HQ.			A/89. 10.40 & 14.40 o'clock, 23 rds in enemy trenches M30a 8.8 & N 25	
M.9.C.24			15.10 to 16.3 — 46 " House BAS POMMEREAU N 31 B ½.4 aggression	
			14.40 " 18.30 — 8 " common trench M30 d 4.4. enemy relief	
			16.10 — 12 " MOULIN de PIETRE retaliation	
C/89.			C/89. 13.30 o'clock. 19 rds House S11 d 4.8 suspected O.P.	
			14-16 " 15 " S11 A. 14.45 o'clock 5 rds. S11 d 4.1 working party	
			15.15 " 9 " S11 d 4.1 working party	
			16.00 " 14 rds S11 d 2.0 to S11 d 4.1. got of work hewing down with roar	
			19.00 " 12 " S11 d 4.1 to enemy working position	
D/89.			D/89. 14.20 " 24 rds night lines (retaliation)	

WAR DIARY

Army Form C. 2118

Instructions regarding War Diaries and Intelligence Summaries are contained in F.S. Regs., Part II. and the Staff Manual respectively. Title Pages will be prepared in manuscript.

INTELLIGENCE SUMMARY 89TH BDE R.F.A.

MARCH 1916

(Erase heading not required.)

Place	Date	Hour	Summary of Events and Information	Remarks and references to Appendices
A/89	13-		Fine day, sunshine, hardly any wind.	
M.15.d.2½.2.		9.55 o'clock	11 rds Common" french M30 d.8.8 retaliation for enemy shelling WINCHESTER trench	
		12.15 to 12.55	43 " Howzr M36a4.8; in 2 vols totally demolished	
C/89.		13.35 o'clock	M30 d.8.8 retaliation 14.35 o'clock 23 rds BAS POMMEREAU retaliation	
		15.0 to 15.55 o'clock	30 rds Howzr N31B8.8 BAS POM? Howzr T2 B1.4 aggression + reg	Trench Map
M.32.b.5.4.		16.0 renew to 16.40. 13 "	" N31c69 " N21d1.9 aggression	Sheet 36.5.N.
		17.0		1.
		20.25 o'clock	9 rds M30D8?1 emplacement M30D4.8 retaliation + reg.	Ed. 6.
D/89		12 o'clock	35 rds S11 A 8.5 sniper post. 12.45 o'clock 20 rds S11 A 9.4.	1/10000.
M.10.D.9.7.		12 " to 14 o'clock	25 rds LA TOURELLE X road S24 c 4.1, T14 c 1.9, B Length replied by aeroplane	
		14 "	22 rds S11A2.2 retaliation 16 o'clock 26 rds Fme. DE BIEZ	
H.Q.		16.45 "	22 " S5B4.5 + M36e2.4 at regiment of infantry	
M.9.c.2.4.				
D/89		9.30 o'clock	14 rds M24D4 24, M24D50 retaliation	
		12.30 "	3 " M24D4.2 check night firing	
		13.50 "	58 " Howzr AUBERS x roads retaliation + checking Zero line	
	14:-		Very fine day, sunshine, little wind	
A/89.		10 o'clock	16 rds Howzr. M30 d 8.4 aggression	
		11-20 to 12 o'clock	34 rds PIETRE X roads Common" Emma? trench M30 d 8.5	
		13.0 o'clock	BAS POM? M36 e 0.4. aggression	
			31 rds M30 a 5.4., M30 c4.5, M30 w 4.5", aggression	
		14.40 "	28 " N 32 c 0 2. N25c4.2	
		23.35 "	11 " Salient M30a retaliation	

WAR DIARY
or INTELLIGENCE SUMMARY

Army Form C. 2118

MARCH 1916. 89th Bde. R.F.A.

Place	Date	Hour	Summary of Events and Information	Remarks and references to Appendices
A/89. M.15.d.2½.2. C/89. M.32.b.5.4. D/89. M.10.d.8.7. H.Q. M.9.c.2.4.	14th	continued		
			C/89. 14-30 o'clock 11 rds. 6.23.B.2.6.	Trench.
			15-15 " 10 " FERME DE BIEZ enemy O.P.	Map Sheet 36.S.W.1
			D/89. 11-20 " 4.2 " M.30.D.88 retaliation	5.6.
			13-0 " 2.6 " front line trenches	1/100000
			15-30 to 17-0 wire 10 rds. registration	
	15th		Dull overcast, inclined to rain changed to sunshine in afternoon.	
			A/89. 8-0 to 8-50. 8 rds at Germans trench M.30.D.6.6. + road N.26.c.O.5.	
			10-25 – 11-35. 25 " Strong point between M.30.A.6.2 + M.30.A.3.8. reserve	
			11-0 o'clock 14 " to LA ELIQUETERIE FARM	
			11-35 to 12 " 20 " Houses N.31.B.4.E. to ditto followed by shrap.	
			C/89. 15-30 o'clock 8 rds. S.11.D.5.1. enemy working party	
			D/89. 11-30 o'clock 25 rds. M.10.D.8.8 + vicinity front to return	
			12-0 " 14 " T.1.b.6.5. + N.31.D.9.2. registration	
			12-15 " 44 " front line M.24.D.4.1. to M.30.A.5.5. destruction of parapet + seals with cordite + lyddite.	

Army Form C. 2118.

WAR DIARY
or
INTELLIGENCE SUMMARY

MARCH 1916   89th Bde RFA

(Erase heading not required.)

Instructions regarding War Diaries and Intelligence Summaries are contained in F. S. Regs., Part II. and the Staff Manual respectively. Title Pages will be prepared in manuscript.

Place	Date	Hour	Summary of Events and Information	Remarks and references to Appendices
A/89. M.15.d.2/2.2. C/89. M.32.6.5.4. D/89. M.10.D.8.7. H.Q. M.9.C.2.14.	16th		Very fine, sunshine, rather strong wind, very good light.	
		A/89. 11-35 o'clock.	16 rds. at House N.31.B.4.4. BAS POMMEREAU + MOULIN DE PIETRE.	Trench Map Sht. 36. S.W.1. S.3.6. 1/10000
		12-15 "	14 " " BAS POMMEREAU + MOULIN DE PIETRE	
		16-00 "	5 " " House N.26. & 4.5 evening working party.	
		C/89. 12-30 "	8 " " FERME DU BIEZ evening O.P.	
		D/89. 14-0 "	24 " N.25.B.5.5 request of infy	
			This not intended to be duel	
		A/89. 6-40 o'clock to 10-35	20 rds. M.36.e.4.9 retaliation at request of infy	
		16-30 "	4 " " + M.36.a.9.1 regestration	
		23-35 "	19 rds at M.36.a.9.1 at request of infy	
		C/89	NIL	
	17th			
		D/89	NIL	

Army Form C. 2118

WAR DIARY

INTELLIGENCE SUMMARY 89TH BDE R.F.A

MARCH 1916

Instructions regarding War Diaries and Intelligence Summaries are contained in F. S. Regs., Part II. and the Staff Manual respectively. Title Pages will be prepared in manuscript.

(Erase heading not required.)

Place	Date	Hour	Summary of Events and Information	Remarks and references to Appendices
	18th		Dull in morning, brightened up to sunshine in afternoon	Trench Map Sheet 36.S.W.
A/89.			A/89. 24·30 & 9·45 o'clock 16 rds about M36a at request of infy.	1.
N.15.d.2/2.2.			10·15 " 2 " do ————	50.6.
C/89.			12·30 " 4 " M36.c.4·5 at request of infy	1/10000.
M.32.6.s.4.			C/89. NIL	
D/89.			D/89. 13·30 & 14·30 19 rds registering M30B8.32, M30B8.34, M30B8.8.1, M30DD8.8, & M30D4.4	
M.10.d.3.7.Q.5	19th		Dull in morning, sunshine in afternoon, light good	
+ Q.			A/89. 14·15 o'clock 1 rd M36 a 5·5 retaliation	
M.9.C.2.4.			21·5 " 5 " M36 e 3·7 — do —	
			C/89. NIL	
			D/89. 12·0 & 12·30 o'clock 18 rds. M30 a 4·6 & M30 a 5·6 retaliation	
	20th		Sun & rain all day. slight sunshine	
			A/89. 16·15 o'clock 16 rds re-gistering M30 e 8·95, & M30 a 4·1 — do ———— group scheme	
			22·50 & 23·55 - 21 rds " M36 a 6·1 retaliation	
			C/89. NIL. — do ————	
			D/89. 14·10 & 14·30 o'clock 16 rds. M30 a 3·7. at request of infy	

Army Form C. 2118

Instructions regarding War Diaries and Intelligence Summaries are contained in F.S. Regs., Part II. and the Staff Manual respectively. Title Pages will be prepared in manuscript.

WAR DIARY or INTELLIGENCE SUMMARY

89th Bde. R.F.A.   March 1916

(Erase heading not required.)

Place	Date	Hour	Summary of Events and Information	Remarks and references to Appendices
A/89	21st		Dull inclined to rain	
M.15.d.2/h.2			A/89. 24.50 to 2-10 clock 92 rds at DUCK'S BILL. M36a61 + M30e60 at request of infy.	Trench map Sheet 36.
C/89.			10.35 – 11.0 " 38 " " M30D887 + M30a9.5	S.W. 1.
M.32.B.5.4.			11.35 clock 3 " " M30e60 + M30e61 at request of infy	S.6.
D/89.			C/89. 12.30 " 4 " S5B83 retaliation	116000
M.10.D.8-7	22nd		D/89. 1.0 to 12.35 relief H1 " M30B02, M30e7.9½ + M24D50 retaliation at request of infantry	
H.Q.			Dull inclined to rain, light frost	
M.9.C.2.4.			A/89. 12.5 clock to 13.30. 50 rds at trenches opposite DUCK'S BILL M30a61 + trenches M30 a 9.1	
	23rd		Dull all day, light very tread	
			A/89. 6.55 clock 4 rds M36a61. C.5.6.3 aggression	
			8.10 " 5 " M30B87.4 enemy working parties	
			8.30 to 10.40 clock 36 rds M36a61 5.6.3	
			C/89. NIL	
			D/89. NIL	

Army Form C. 2118

WAR DIARY
or
INTELLIGENCE SUMMARY

89TH Brigade
R.F.A.

MARCH 1916

(Erase heading not required.)

Instructions regarding War Diaries and Intelligence Summaries are contained in F.S. Regs., Part II. and the Staff Manual respectively. Title Pages will be prepared in manuscript.

Place	Date	Hour	Summary of Events and Information	Remarks and references to Appendices
A/89	24th		Snow during the night & morning, very cold, light lead.	Trench Map Sheet 36. S.W. 1 20.6 1/10000
M.15.d.2/4.2.			A/89. Fired Strks during afternoon at Hences N°31 D	
C/89.			C/89. NIL	
M.32.b.5.4/25th			D/89 NIL	
	25th		Cold, dull, light lead.	
D/89.		8-50 o'clock	A/89. 15 9.30. 8rds M30 a 4.1 retaliation	
		10-15	" 12-00 4" Trench opposite DUCK'S BILL retaliation	
M.10.D.8.7		3-30	C/89. 10 rds S5 b 4.1 retal.	
H.Q		13-50	" 15 rds 10 rds S11 a 5-3½ + S10 a 4.9 retaliation	
M.9.C.2.4.		10-45	D/89. 4 rds registering T2 B 9.5	
		11-00	" 14 " retaliation M36 a 6.6	
		14-00	" 13 " registering LA CLIQUETERIE Fme	
	26th		Dull inclined to rain.	
		4.5 o'clock	A/89. 6 rds LA CLIQUETERIE Fme witch	
		12.15	" 8 " Hence T1 B 8½. 6. reg"	
		14.30	" 8 " trench opposite DUCK'S BILL	
		19.50	" 4 " HALPEGARBE	
		22.15	" 6 " Hence N 31 B4.4 retal"	

Army Form C. 2118.

WAR DIARY
or
INTELLIGENCE SUMMARY

89th Bde RFA

MARCH 1916

(Erase heading not required.)

Place	Date	Hour	Summary of Events and Information	Remarks and references to Appendices
A/89	26" (continued)		C/89 NIL	
M.15.d.2.2.			D/89. 15.15 rds/hr 9 rds. S5b 5.2. registration	Lieut Maypo Shut No 26. S.W. 1. 30.2. Y Horns.
			16.15 " 15 " S5a 2.4. "	
			16.50 " 15 " N32 ~ 5.1 retaliation	
C/89	27.		Cold, some rain, dull	
N.32.4.5.4			A/89. 15.15 minute 8 rds ZERO HOUSE S30a Y.8t.	
D.189.			15.30 " 5 " N32 & 8.9. CROW'S NEST	
M.10.C.3.7			C/89 NIL	
N.Q.			D/89 12.45 rds/hr 13 rds. T2 & 1.7.	
M.9.c.2.4			14.45 " 6 " N26 4.4	
	28.		Fine sunshine, strong wind, light good	
			A/89. 8.5 & 8.45 rds/hr 9 rds. T8 & 4.0 retal?	
			9.50 rds/hr 2 rds. N31 & 4.4 Horns — AM	
			11.30 " 8 " retaliation fire at LIGNY-LE-GRAND, HALPEGARBE, LIGNY-LE-PETIT.	
			C/89 NIL	
			D/89. 14.30 rds/hr 4 rds. Road N32 d.	

WAR DIARY
or
INTELLIGENCE SUMMARY

Army Form C. 2118

89th Bde. R.F.A.

MARCH 1916

(Erase heading not required.)

Place	Date	Hour	Summary of Events and Information	Remarks and references to Appendices
A/89.	20th		Fine, warm, light excellent	Trench map Sheet 36. S.W. 1 S.D. 6 1/10000
M.15.d.7.4.2.			A/89. 13.30 ranged 4 rds trenches near SIGN POST LANE retaliation	
			15.54 " 9 " House N 32 c 0.2 nil	
C/89.			15.25 " 9 " LIGNY-LE-GRAND nil	
M.32.b.5.4.			15.30 " 4 " Enemy party on railroad at N 32 c	
D/89			C/89. 9 rds registering S 21 d 1.4	
M.10.D.8.7.30.			D/89 14.40 ranged 4 rds at X roads N 26 c 8.3 enemy infantry & S.S. wagon dispersed	
			Fine, warm, slight haze	
N.Q.			A/89. 10.55 ranged 5 rds MOULIN DE PIETRE	
M.9.c.2.4			14.55 " 10 " Trenches M 30 d 6.4 retal.	
			15.15 " 6 " House N 31 d 4.8 opening	
			15.30 " 9 " Trenches M 36 a 4.1 - M 36 a 5.3	
			14.8 " 2 " " M 30 a 6.4	
			C/89. 3 rds registration S 12 c 6.5	
			D/89 11 & 12 minute 13 rds. registering M 30 a 8.4	
			M 30 d 6.2	
			M 30 c 8.8	

Army Form C. 2118.

WAR DIARY
or INTELLIGENCE SUMMARY

89th Bde. R.F.A.

MARCH 1916

(Erase heading not required.)

Place	Date	Hour	Summary of Events and Information	Remarks and references to Appendices
A/89.	3/3/15		Fine, sunshine all day, light excellent.	Trench map Sheet. 36.S.W.
M.15.d.2.2.			A/89. 11-30 rounds 5 rds. M36.c.2.5 - M36.e.4.4. } registration	1.
C/89.			12.5 & 12.30 rounds 18 rds. M36.a.5.8 - M30.c.6.6 }	2 & 6.
M.32.b.5.4.			14.30 rounds 6 rds. Hun. N31.v.4.4. } retaliation	1/0000
D/89.			18.20 " 1 rd. trench N31.A.8.0 }	
M.10.D.2.7.			C/89. NIL	
H.Q.			D/89. 14.15 & 14.45 enemies 10 rds registering N31 d 6 3	
M.9.c.2.4.			15.20 rounds 8 rds. M2d d 4.1 retaliation	

J. S. Hanson
Lt. Col. R.F.A
Commanding 89th Bde R.F.A

89RFA
VOL 10

XIX

CONFIDENTIAL
WAR DIARY
OF
89TH BRIGADE. R.F.A.
APRIL. 1916.
VOLUME. 9.

Army Form C. 2118

WAR DIARY
or
INTELLIGENCE SUMMARY   89th Brigade R.F.A.
(Erase heading not required.)

Place	Date 1916	Hour	Summary of Events and Information	Remarks and references to Appendices
	April 1		Fair, mild, slight mist in morning. Dull & bright in afternoon	
A/89 N.15 a 2½.½		A/89. 11-5	robust onto M.30 d 1.9	
		16-0	" " N.31 b 4.4	
C/89 M.32 b 5.4		16-25	" unexpected O.P. M.36 a 5½ .6	
D/89 N.10 d 8.7				
		C/89 16.30	Home S 11 C 2-8.	
A/89 N. LINE M.20 a 4.8		17-0	" S 12 d 1.2 registration	
C/89 N. LINE R.11 a 1.1	2nd		Same but rather hazy cool	
B/89 W.LINE L.36 c 5.4		B/89 11-0	15" do unexpected HQ at M.31 b. 8.7.	
		16-45	10 " LA CLIQUETTERIE FME.	
B.A.C. R.10 b 2.5		17-45	13 " do — good effect	
			21 " do — retaliation	
		C/89 7-15	10 " approache [?] group scheme	
		15-20	8 " M 30 C 7.9 ½ retaliation	
		D/89 15-20	11 " T. 6. 96.	
		16-40		

Army Form C. 2118

WAR DIARY
or
INTELLIGENCE SUMMARY — 89th Brigade R.F.A.

(Erase heading not required.)

Place	Date 1916	Hour	Summary of Events and Information	Remarks and references to Appendices
A/89 M.15.d.?.?	3rd		Fine warm, slight haze.	
C/89 M.32.b.5.w.			A/89 16.35 o'clock 9 rds shrapnel N.31.d.8.8	
D/89 M.b.d.8.7			16-34 " 7 " OLD BLOCK HOUSE M.30.c.6.5. 1 hit	
A/89 W. LINE M.2.a.4.8			16-50 " 8 " M.30.c.6.8 chestnut night hutts	
C/89 W.LINE R.11.a.1.1.			" " 4 " shrapnel S.11.B.17. S.11.A.9.6 S.11.A.8½.6	
A/89 W. LINE L.36.C.5.w.	4th		C/89 14.30 " 42 " shrapnel S.11.B.17.	
B.A.C. R.10.6.2.5			Cool. dull. very cloudy.	
			D/89 17.30 shoot 5 rds M.30.t.7.7.	
	5th		Misty, fair, some showers. cold	
			A/89 14-55 o'clock 20 rds reported trench mortar at M.36.a.53	
			19-40 " 20 " x roads at M.36.a.8.7. N.31.a.0.3 bombardment	
			16 " S.6.8½.9½ aeroplane covers	
			C/89 12-35	
	6th		Cold. Some slight hail.	
			A/89 3.20 shoot 15 rds shrapnel N.31.a.4.7.	

Army Form C. 2118

WAR DIARY
INTELLIGENCE SUMMARY 89th Brigade R.F.A.
(Erase heading not required.)

Instructions regarding War Diaries and Intelligence Summaries are contained in F.S. Regs., Part II. and the Staff Manual respectively. Title Pages will be prepared in manuscript.

Place	Date/1915	Hour	Summary of Events and Information	Remarks and references to Appendices
A/89 M15 d7 h7 N4 1/2 C/89 M32 65.4 D/89 M10 d 8.7 A/89 W. LINE M2 a 4.8 C/8 W. LINE R11 a 1.1 B/89 W. LINE L36 c 5.4 B.A.C. R10. b 2.5	6th 7th 9th 10th		C/89 12 o'clock 20 rds FME DU BIEZ 12.15 – 17 " Trench S11 c 6.0. D/89 19.40 20 " MOULIN DU PIETRE & M20 c 6.8. A/89 Wady weather. Brigade moved to new Billets at G32 a 7/2.2. Cold, dull, bright not very good for observing. A/89 15.5 o'clock 14 rds the house N31 a 4.7 retaliation D/89 14.55 " 11 rds house N32 a/b. 5 approach Bde H. Quarters Mainly fair, cool in morning, bright sunshine in afternoon H/89 14.10 o'clock 6 rds house N.31 a 4.7 Same Brig't D/89 20 – 15 o'clock 8 rds Road junction at N26 c 8.3 & 6.8. Quiet interval	

Army Form C. 2118

WAR DIARY
INTELLIGENCE SUMMARY
(Erase heading not required.)

89th Brigade R.F.A

Place	Date	Hour	Summary of Events and Information	Remarks and references to Appendices
A/89 M.15d.2/b.1/a.9/b C/89 M.30.d.5.4 D/89 M.30.d.8.7	10/6	11.15	Showery & cloudy all day. Enemy slow to observe well.	
A/89 W.LINE M.2.a.4.8		12.6	A/89 16.50 rds at 5 rds WINDOW HOUSE T.1.f. 6.6. Continuous rain, very dull	
C/89 W.LINE R.11.a.1.1			A/89 Nil C/89 Nil D/89 Nil Some bird observing. Light good in between	
D/89 W.LINE L.36.C.5.4		13.6	A/89 16.25" rds at 5 rds PHANTOM trench M.36.a.6.6.	
B.A.C. R.10.b.2.5			C/89 Nil D/89 Nil	

WAR DIARY

INTELLIGENCE SUMMARY

(Erase heading not required.)

Army Form C. 2118

89th Brigade R.F.A.

Place	Date Hour	Summary of Events and Information	Remarks and references to Appendices
A/89 M/S 4.4 A4 C/89 M3 6.5.4.14 B/89 Mod 8.7 A/89 W Line M2 # 8 B/89 W Line R 11.a 1.1 C/89 W Line L 23.b.25.4 B.H.C. R.10.b 2.5 HAVERSKERQUE	19/6 15th	Observing light good in between A/89 nil C/89 11-15 October 6 rds fuze S11 c 7.3 14-15 " 35 " Fme. DU BIEZ 15-0 " 29 " Communication trench S11 d 4. 3 & S11 d 7.4 15-30 " 20 " Trench S18 c 5. 4/12 B/89 nil Brigade moved into rest billets at HAVERSKERQUE, + were occupied in general cleaning up + renovation of equipment until April 21st 1916, when they went into billets at ELARQUES (1st army training area), + commenced training in Bttry. + Bde. + Divnl training. All units received recuperation.	

Signature

MEMORANDUM.

Army Form C. 348.

From C.O.
       89th F.A. Bde.

To D.A.G.
   3rd Echelon

From

To

ANSWER.

3rd June 1916.

Herewith War Diary of the 89th Brigade R.F.A. for the month of May, 1916.

F.P. Harvey Lt Col
Comdg 89th F.A. Bde

_____ 191 .

89 RFA
vol II

WAR DIARY
OF
89TH BRIGADE R.F.A.
for month of MAY 1916
(VOLUME II)

CONFIDENTIAL

Army Form C. 2118

WAR DIARY
or
INTELLIGENCE SUMMARY

MAY 1916

8 9th Brigade, R.F.A.

(Erase heading not required.)

Instructions regarding War Diaries and Intelligence Summaries are contained in F.S. Regs., Part II. and the Staff Manual respectively. Title Pages will be prepared in manuscript.

Place	Date	Hour	Summary of Events and Information	Remarks and references to Appendices
CLARQUES	1st-6th		Divisional Training	HAZEBROUCK 5A 1/100000
	7th		Entrained and moved to YZEUX in Divisional H.Q. Reserve	
	8th & 9th			
YZEUX	25th		The Divisional Artillery was re-organized	AMIENS 57 X/100000
			A/89 became D/86 D/86 became A/89	
			C/89 became D/87 D/87 became B/89	
			D/89 became D/88 D/88 became C/89	
			Headquarters remained unchanged	
			A/89 and B/89 prepared gun position at the front. Remainder of batteries and C/89 continued training under Brigade Cmdr.	

J.P. Harvey
Lt Col
Comdg. 89th F.A. Bde

WAR DIARY
MAY 1916
or
INTELLIGENCE SUMMARY

Army Form C. 2118

89th Brigade R.F.A.

Place	Date	Hour	Summary of Events and Information	Remarks and references to Appendices
CHARMES	1st-6th 7th 8th 9th		Divisional Training	HAZEBROUCK 5A 1/40000
YZEUX	25th		Entrained and moved to YZEUX via Divisional HQ RAINNEVILLE. The Divisional Artillery was re-organized. A/89 became D/86 D/86 became A/89 C/89 became D/89 D/89 became D/89 D/89 became D/89 Headquarters remained unchanged. A/89 and B/89 prepared gun positions of the front. Remainder of Batteries and B.H.Q. continued training under Brigade Comdr.	AMIENS 17 1/40000

Comdg. 89th A.B. R.F.A.

CONFIDENTIAL

WAR DIARY

OF

89TH BRIGADE R.F.A.

from 1st June 1916 to 30th June 1916

VOLUME 12.

Army Form C. 2118

WAR DIARY
or
INTELLIGENCE SUMMARY
(Erase heading not required.)

80TH BRIGADE R.F.A.

JUNE 1916

Place	Date	Hour	Summary of Events and Information	Remarks and references to Appendices
	1st to 2nd	—	At YZEUX in Headquarters Divisional Reserve. G.H.Q.	
	3rd 4th 10th 11th	—	Undergoing training at CAOURS	
		—	Returned to YZEUX. C/89 occupied a new billet at BOURDON	
	15th	—	Moved to BEHENCOURT. Carried out further scheme of training, including firing & bridging practice.	
	29th	—	Marched to LONG VALLEY & took up position of readiness in Divisional Brigade in pending operations, remaining there until 30th.	

J. P. Kearney
Lt. Col. R.A.
Commanding 89th Bde. R.F.A.

19th Div.
III. Corps.

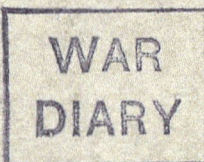

Headquarters.

89th BRIGADE. R.F.A.

J U L Y

1 9 1 6

WAR DIARY or INTELLIGENCE SUMMARY

Army Form C. 2118

89th Bde. R.F.A.

July 1916

Place	Date	Hour	Summary of Events and Information	Remarks and references to Appendices
DENANCOURT	1st to 5th		Groups in position for DENANCOURT. Attached for two days under Lt Col Jonny's Granate 83 Bde RFA	M&P Reference 62 N E 1/20000
A/89. X20B 8.1	5th–6th		Firing Battr. occupied the following positions, taking items from 34th Divisional Arty. (X20B 8.1 B/89 X20B 4.2 C/89 X20B.1.5 D/88. Waggon lines remained at DENANCOURT. H.Q. established at X20B.1	57 D.S.E. 1/20000
B/89 X20B 4.2	6th		Day spent in registering, strengthening positions etc. Casualties "NIL"	
C/89 X20B 8.1	7th		In conjunction with 23rd Div. & the 19th Div. attacked enemy at 8 a.m. with a view to establishing itself on the line X14 B 5.2 – X 14 D 1.0 – X 14 D 5.8 – X15 c 2.4 – X15 c 8.9 – X15 B 1.2 – X15 B 4.2 – X16 A 1.0.	
D/88.			Groups carried out following programme of barrages:	
HQ. X20B 8.1			7-20 to 8 o'clock	9-30 onwards
			D/88. X.14 d 4.5 – 5.8 – 3.8. – 0.8 – 1.4.	9.5 to 9.30 onwards X 14 B 9.4. X 15 A 3.3 – X.15 A B.4. X 9 c 9.1.
			18pr. Battr. the triangle X14 d 0.8 – 3.8 – 5.8 – 4.5 – 1.4 – 8 X14 d.5.8 X 15 c 2.4.	lift gradually along X14 B 3.0. – 4.2 – 3.2. lift gradually + form barrage X 14 B 9.4 5 X 15 A 3.3 – X 14 B 9.4 X 15 A 8.0 5.2 – 8.0 Remain and continue barrage
			Following programme for night barrages allotted to Group. Two. Hows. X 8 B 4.8 – X 2 D 9.2. " " X 8 D 4.8 – X 3 c 0.2. 18pr. Battr. X 15 A 8.5 to X 14 B 8.4	lift and form barrage on line X 15 a D 4.5 – X 15 A 5.6 – X 15 B 0.5
			Fired in these barrages as previous mentioned between hours of 22 and 4 o'clock. D/84 attached to LEFT GROUP in place of D/88. Casualties "NIL"	

Army Form C. 2118

WAR DIARY
or
INTELLIGENCE SUMMARY

(Erase heading not required.)

Instructions regarding War Diaries and Intelligence Summaries are contained in F.S. Regs., Part II. and the Staff Manual respectively. Title Pages will be prepared in manuscript.

Place	Date	Hour	Summary of Events and Information	Remarks and references to Appendices
	8.		Quiet day. Very little artillery activity on either side. Casualties "NIL"	
	9.		Following gun allotted to front – X9c 6.8, X9d 2.3, 100 rd 18pr. Shrapnel and 30 rd 4.5" How. H.E. expended on these guns between 10 P.M. & 4.0 A.M. 10% most. Casualties 2 wounded	
	10.		Quiet. Very little activity. Situation normal. 1 O.R. wounded	
	11. & 12.		Two days bombardment commenced at 12 o'clock on following points. 4.5" Hows. X9b 5.1, X9d 5.9, X9d 5.8, X9b 6.6, X9b 4.3. 2 O.R. wounded on 11th. Group also bombarded with 18pr. Shrapnel + H.E. the enemy's ground within its own zone N.E. of the road running from X10c 0.8 to X9c 9.8 for half an hour after similar was allotted for How. bombardment. The bombardment was repeated at 4.0 a.m. interval from time originally fixed for a space period of 48 hours from 12th "NIL" front. Army attacked the enemy's second line between LONGUEVAL and BAZENTIN-LE-PETIT WOOD. Group gun's allotted as follows:	
	13.		X10 A 1.2 & X10 c 6.9. The 80 Bde. partially manning the 11th by Bde and its Bde. on its left (4th Bde. 2.5-B6) Casualties "NIL"	

WAR DIARY
or
39th Bde R.F.A. INTELLIGENCE SUMMARY   JULY, 1916

(Erase heading not required.)

Place	Date	Hour	Summary of Events and Information	Remarks and references to Appendices
HQ. W.23.D.3.65.	14.		Frontage allotted to group X10c6.9 X5 X10A1.2. At 3P.M. a bombardment of ordinary rate was commenced on the undermentioned line, and was quickened up to an intense bombardment at 3.20 for five minutes. Trench X4D8.2.25 X4D.1.1. and enfilade X4D4.1 5 X10B1.4-4.2. One 18 m Bty and one two Btys on the trenches and area included in X10 c 6. 9., X10A4.2. X10A5.3., X10A4.2., X10A3.0.	
A/89 W.23.D.3.6.	15.		Fire then slowed down to an ordinary bombardment for some time. The attack fails. At night moved into new positions in the mungu Bazentin. I.O.R. Killed (gas). These positions were in OLD GERMAN FRONT LINE. Divisional artillery rearranged for all Bdes to have their own batteries grouped together. D/84 therefore returns to 84th Bde. Use of term "group" discontinued. Bazentin	
B/89 W.23.D.3.57			The 1st Division attacked at 9 A.M. astride the enemy's second line of defences from W. edge BAZENTIN-LE-PETIT wood northwards with the object of consolidating that line from S4D3.2 X5 X5B24. Bazentin	
C/89 W.23.D.3.17			2 5th Bn attacked POZIERES from the west 3 5th " " " " " " Initial bombardment from 8.20 to 9.35 o'clock. 89th Bde X4D3.6.5 X5 e.O.6. Zone at 9.35 o'clock this was lifted with left along railway line and right along in line from X5 e 1.65 X5 X5 B 2.1. at 11 o'clock all Btys lifted the front trench is supposed slowly, line 200 yds new enemy trench slowly. Bazentin "nil" No operation of any amount. Bazentin "NIL"	
	16.			

Army Form C. 2118

WAR DIARY
or
INTELLIGENCE SUMMARY

80TH BDE. R.F.A.

JULY, 1916.

(Erase heading not required.)

Instructions regarding War Diaries and Intelligence Summaries are contained in F.S. Regs., Part II. and the Staff Manual respectively. Title Pages will be prepared in manuscript.

Place	Date	Hour	Summary of Events and Information	Remarks and references to Appendices
	14th		Bombardment was carried out during evening. Zones as follows:- 80th Bde. 18 pr. Battu X.11.1. to X.4.D.8.2. from 6.30 PM to 8.5 PM. at 8.5 PM all guns lifted to a line through X.4.c.9.6 - X.4.D.3.5 - X.4.a.5.5 - X.5.c.1.4. expended about 1,200 rds. Casualties "NIL"	
	18th		34th Division attacked POZIÈRES at 3-30 AM in conjunction with simultaneous attack by II Corps. Zone allotted to 89th Bde & D/88 (How Bde.) Left boundary X.4.D.5.5 - X.4.B.6.1 - X.4.B.8.3 - R.34.D.6.4 Right boundary X.4.D.9.6 - X.4.B.9.1 - X.5.A.2.3 - R.35.C.2.6. Bombardment continued till 4.20 AM making backwards & forwards. Casualties "NIL" 2,500 rds. expended.	
SHEET 57D S6.1/20000. A/89. X.17.6.9.6. B/89. X.17.6.7.9. C/89. X.17.e.9.7. Hd QFS. X.29.A.7.4. LOWER WOOD.	19th & 20th 21st		Relief of 19th Divisional Arty. by 1st Australian Divisional Artillery commenced & was completed, Bde. Communications handing over, at 9 am 20th. 680 rds expended on 19th. 20th NIL Rds positions & HdQrs were established as per margin. Building parapets around of guns, making dug outs, establishing communication with Right Brigade of 1st Division and intercommunication within Bde., registering targets (see on survey line) zones allotted as follows: 89/Ta Bde (i) for enfilade of line M.33.B.5.0 - M.33.c.4.2 - S.2.B.5.4. S.2.a.5.2. and (ii) sylvan of line M.32.c.e+D and S.2.A+D	
			Casualties I.O.R. wounded	

Army Form C. 2118

89th Bde. R.F.A. WAR DIARY or INTELLIGENCE SUMMARY   JULY 1916

(Erase heading not required.)

Place	Date	Hour	Summary of Events and Information	Remarks and references to Appendices
	22nd – 23rd		Fourth Army attacked German switch line. Objective of 19th Division Switch line M33D0.3 to attack at S2 a 5.8 Fire commenced at 10.30 pm 22nd & following forms programme was carried out:—	
		10.30 PM – 10.45 PM	Rake backwards and forwards with fire ground preparing special attention to NEW TRENCH	
		10.45 PM – 12.25 AM	Rounds of fire in Switch line & new trench, the zone 100 in front of, and the new trench	
		12.25 AM – 12.27 AM	New trench (time shrap.)	12.27 AM – 12.30 AM New trench (Percussion shrapnel only)
		12.30 AM – 1.25 AM	Fire quiet 100x and then rake slowly back to SWITCH LINE trench	
			Odd guns of Battle go to P.S. and remain in SWITCH LINE sweeping so as to cover the whole Battery zone. Even guns firing T.S. lift 100x + remain sweeping so as to cover the whole Batty zone.	350 rds expended on 22nd 3800 rds on 23rd
		1.25 AM – 1.30 AM	1.30 am onwards	
			lift to back ground + rake backwards and forwards, covering the whole zone. All guns return to T.S.	
			Wagon line timely shelled during 14 OR to wounded + 5 killed and 5 killed German Battn location following positions RECORDED.	had 5 men buck
			A/89 from M32 d 9.6t along road to M33 d 2.9	
			B/89 " M32 d 3.4 " " M32 d 2.9	
			C/89 " M32 a 4.2.0 " " M32 a 4.9	
	24"		Fire commenced at 2.40 P.M. with H.E. Batty fire 10 sec. for 10 minute	
			All batteries fired in Battery in MARTINPUICH Patty fire 5 sec. for 5 minute 10 sec for further 5 minute and then 2 rds gun fire. Expended 400 rds.	
			I.O.R. wounded in course of day.	

1875   Wt. W593/826   1,000,000   4/15   J.B.C. & A.   A.D.S.S./Forms/C.2118.

Army Form C. 2118

Instructions regarding War Diaries and Intelligence Summaries are contained in F.S. Regs., Part II. and the Staff Manual respectively. Title Pages will be prepared in manuscript.

WAR DIARY
or
INTELLIGENCE SUMMARY

(Erase heading not required.)

89th Bde R.F.A.   JULY 1916.

Place	Date	Hour	Summary of Events and Information	Remarks and references to Appendices
D/86 along side C/89.	25th		D/86 handed over to 89 Bde for attachment. Much firing in enemy batteries in retaliation for heavy shelling which our batteries were subjected to. Our men wounded 4 O.R.s. 1 wounded + 2 killed. Ammn. expended 739 rds.	
	26th		Quiet day. Expended 548 rds in retaliation on enemy front line zone. No casualties.	
	27th		13th Corps attacked DELVILLE WOOD and GUILLEMONT, to meet diversion. III rd Corps artillery bombarded enemy's lines in their own front successfully. From 6.10 a.m to 7.10 a.m 89 Bde enfilade INTERMEDIATE trench " 7.10 " 7.40 a.m " " " " " 7.40 " 7.45 a.m shelled orchard + roads in and around COURCELETTE " 7.45 " 8.0 a.m enfilade INTERMEDIATE trench " lifted to objective at 7.10 a.m & 7.40 a.m 3 killed enemy batteries during day (retaliation) 40 th Div men killed + 2 men wounded of D/86 Expended during day 1159 rds. During night kept ground between intermediate trench + switch line under fire 25 rds per hour for 18 hour batteries.	
	28th		During night of 28th B/89 shelled COURCELETTE in square M25B. intermittent bursts of 25 rds per hour, 18 pdr and 20 rds per hour 4.5" D/86 " M30A. F/89 " The whole intermediate line M27 & 32 E/89 2 guns shelled M27 & 32 M28 D 54	
			Expended 474 rds. no casualties.	

Army Form C. 2118

WAR DIARY
or
INTELLIGENCE SUMMARY

80TH BDE. R.F.A.

JULY 1916.

(Erase heading not required.)

Place	Date	Hour	Summary of Events and Information	Remarks and references to Appendices
	29th		From 3 P.M. to 3.15 P.M. bombarded intermediate trench in morning intensely, & from 3.15 P.M. to 3.30 P.M. continued slowly. D/86 bombarded S 2 c 8.4 + S 2 a 5.3. 980 rds expended. No casualties. During night fire on intermediate trench, switch trench & N.W. corner of HIGH WOOD. D/86 recorded MARTIN PUICH 50 rds per hour 18 pdr How. 40	
	30th		Bombardment as for 29th repeated commencing 4.40 a.m. At 6.10 P.M. the 5th & 6th Div. Infy attacked between the German intermediate line between S 3 D 0.4 + S 2 c 8.4 also the new line between S 2 D 1.7. 6½ and S 2 c 4.5½. 8gun Bde fired as follows: A/89 on trench from S 3 B 5.5 to S 3 B 8.0. 1 gun in support at S 3 B 2.8 commencing at 6.9 pm. 2 guns of B/89 on road from S 3 B 2.4 to S 3 B 8.2 (18 ers ready) Remainder on area S 3 B 8.0 – S 4 A 5.4 – S 4 A 0.6½ – S 3 D 7.4. D/86 Redoubt in S 3 c + d from 6.28 P.M. to S 6.10. + from 6-10 P.M. onwards lifted direct to the four barricades in S 2 a, b, c + d. 3,100 rds expended. Casualties 1 officer (2nd Lt Ivor Jardine) wounded, 3 O.R. wounded. Night arrangements as before.	
	31st		Situation normal. Very little artillery activity on either side during afternoon. Enemy started to bombard our front line at 10 pm Bombardment slacked down within 30 minutes. All Btys were turned on to be switched line at a quicker rate of fire. C/9 reported 1 killed 2 O.R. wounded on the 28th inst.	

F. Rainsford.
Lt Col R.F.A.
Comdy. 80th Bde R.F.A.

19th Divisional Artillery.

89th BRIGADE R. F. A.

AUGUST 1 9 1 6

Army Form C. 2118

WAR DIARY or INTELLIGENCE SUMMARY

(Erase heading not required.)

89TH BDE, R.F.A.

AUGUST 1916.

Instructions regarding War Diaries and Intelligence Summaries are contained in F.S. Regs., Part II. and the Staff Manual respectively. Title Pages will be prepared in manuscript.

Place	Date	Hour	Summary of Events and Information	Remarks and references to Appendices
Sheet 57D. S.E. 1/20,000 A/89 X14 b 9.6 B/89	1st.		Aug 31/1st Very quiet owing to relief taking place during the night of note occurred during the morning. Major Van Suidich B/89 killed in front line whilst attending also one gunner of A/89 killed at gun position. Enemy artillery very active between 8 & 10 pm. All Btties retaliated.	
X14 b 4.4 C/89 X14 c 9.7 H.Q. X19 A 7.4	2nd.		Morning quiet. Very little artillery, machine gun or rifle fire on either side. B.O. 155th Bde & 40th Bde, 15th Div. called and witnessed fire with reference to taking over. 4 P.M. enemy shelled valley road behind B/89 for about 15 minutes.
Preparatory to attack on Switch line opened bombardment with heavier Bom. Btt in fire at 018 as follows;
A/89 in bursts– S3 a 2.4, 8.2 & S3 a 8.0.
B/89   S3 a 8.0   S3 a 3.5.2
C/89   S3 a 3.5.2   S3 a 0.4
fire after 50 yards every minute until range was in Switch line. Rate of fire 80 per gun for 5 ones. At 3.25 the same rate of fire but lifted 300 yards beyond the Switch line searching ground during lifts one hundred yards at a time. At 3.30 pm Btties fired an extra minute on Switch line.
B/86 at 3.18 pm fired a slow bombardment on Switch from S4 a 3.4.2 to M 28 d 0.6. At 3.25 pm intense fire on Switch line at 3.30 pm fire lifted 300 yds in 100 yds at a time and continued at slow rate. Range for C/89 found to take this very command of 86 + BDE. Capt Valpar posted to temporarily command of B/89 there.

1875 Wt. W593/826 1,000,000 4/15 J.B.C. & A. A.D.S.S./Forms/C. 2118.

WAR DIARY
or
INTELLIGENCE SUMMARY

Army Form C. 2118

Title: 89 Bde. R.F.A.
Month and year: AUGUST 1916

Place	Date	Hour	Summary of Events and Information	Remarks and references to Appendices
	3rd		Morning and afternoon very quiet. About 11 P.M. the enemy put a short tremendous burst of shell fire, the enemy retaliated for about 20 mts along MAMETZ Valley otherwise night quiet. Right section of 40" Bty. arrived at the Bde wagon lines and stayed for the night.	
	4th	4 am.	Right section of 40" Bty moved up to its gun position. Notes were from A, B + B/89 and D/86. These sections moved back to the wagon lines + left under command of the Adjutant to FRECHENCOURT. But for a little shelling during morning and afternoon day was very quiet. The new section of the 40" Bty arrived at wagon lines during the evening. Bombardment at 8pm and were again coming into its later. Its shooting intervals of INTERMEDIATE attempt was again made to forward ammunition but were driven back. Our infantry got a footing in the Bde. gunners during day. No casualties during day.	
BECORDEL	5th		At 5 am. The new section of 40" Bty. relieved the Rt. Section of 40" Bty. Out personnel then relieved at wagon lines. These relieved men at went 9 am and much new section to FRECHENCOURT at 9 am arriving at 3.30 pm. One casualties during day. at 5.30 hrs Capt. Bourn inspected 89 Bde. Total casualties while not the in the Somme Operations 4+3	

Army Form C. 2118

89 ⁴ᵗʰ Squadron

WAR DIARY
or
INTELLIGENCE SUMMARY
(Erase heading not required.)

Instructions regarding War Diaries and Intelligence Summaries are contained in F.S. Regs., Part II. and the Staff Manual respectively. Title Pages will be prepared in manuscript.

AUGUST 1916

Place	Date	Hour	Summary of Events and Information	Remarks and references to Appendices
FRÉCHENCOURT	6-		Orders received for entraining in morning of 7. 1/89 marched from FRÉCHENCOURT at 19 midnight to entrain at LONGEAU leaving at 6.45 am and detraining at GODWAERSWELDE. Remainder of Bde. either at FRÉCHENCOURT for the night with motors to take in the entrainment the morning. 4 m/Bn. orders were received from 19ᵗʰ Bde. that B/89 B/89 relieving B/253 in Centre Group gun position at N27 & 82.4 goes into action by sections in night 8/9 to 9/10. C/89 relieving C/253 in left Group gun position N10a 3. & 7.une 15 were struck D/3 & K2. B A/89 relieving A/253 ...were not in action	
EECQUES	7-		1/89 left FRÉCHENCOURT at 1.40 am, trains to entrain at LONGEAU, leaving Kur at 8.28 am detraining at CASSEL. C/89 left FRÉCHENCOURT at 3.30 am. At entrain at LONGEAU, leaving Kur at 10.18 am; detraining at GODWAERSWELDE No. 1 left FRÉCHENCOURT at 2.30 am. D at entrain at SALEUX, leaving Kur at 9.36 am. detraining STEENBECQUE On arrival at detraining stations units marched independently to EECQUES and carried out arrangements for the night. A.D. visited HQrs of 250ᵗʰ Division with reference to maintaining all arrangements for relief, and taking over charge from 27 Divn	

Army Form C. 2118

WAR DIARY
or
INTELLIGENCE SUMMARY

89th Brigade R.F.A

(Erase heading not required.)

Instructions regarding War Diaries and Intelligence Summaries are contained in F. S. Regs., Part II. and the Staff Manual respectively. Title Pages will be prepared in manuscript.

August 1916

Place	Date	Hour	Summary of Events and Information	Remarks and references to Appendices
	8th		Bt section of B/89 - C/89 went into action during night. A/89	moved from ECOIVRES
HQ. N15 B 8.9	9th		up to Wagon lines at A/253rd Bde at M12 a 8.0. HQ stayed at ECOIVRES awaiting orders from C.O.	
A/89 M12 a 8.0			Rear section of B/89 - C/89 went into action during night. Bde HQ moved from ECOIVRES to N15 B 8.9 Relief of 253rd Bde completed today.	SHEET 28 SW2
B/89 N17 a 8t.4	10th		Special work allotted to Bde. Inflicted enfilade enfilade & wiring of new proposition for new defensive scheme. A/89 also out of action & resting at Wagon lines.	1/10/1916 28.NW 1hr avo
C/89 N106 3.8	11th		Special work on gun positions continued A/89 still resting	
	12th		Continuation of special work, arranging dumps for machine, transport &c. One enemy AMC anti aircraft shell splinter	
	13 to 21st		Continuation of special work & general routine working parties to reports	

1875 Wt. W593/826 1,000,000 4/15 J.B.C. & A. A.D.S.S./Forms/C.2118.

Army Form C. 2118

WAR DIARY
or
INTELLIGENCE SUMMARY

89 Bde RFA

August 16.

(Erase heading not required.)

Place	Date	Hour	Summary of Events and Information	Remarks and references to Appendices
A/89	21/22		On the 22nd a group known as "Kenway" group, consisting of the following batteries was formed. A/89 B/89 B/154 C/154 D/88. This group relieved the "Dodo" group of the 3rd Canadian Divisional Artillery on the afternoon of the 25th from the VIERSTRAAT rd. to the DIEPENDAAL BEEK. Bty position as detailed in margin. Heavy air bomb. was placed near the return of the Hd Qtrs. Canadian Divisional Divn. which was evening its front. Also orders of the Left Group 19th Bde Arty.	Map of 1/20,000 sheet 28 S.W. and Sheet 28 N.W. Belgium 3.D
H/SE 1.4				
B/89				
N.u.d 25.5				
B/154				
N.15.131.9				
C/154	23rd		Situation remained unchanged.	
N.16.a.4.8				
D/88				
N.14.e.9.8	24th		All batteries registering	
HQ	25th		Registration continued	
N.7.c.3.6	26th		A/89 fired 18 rds on Chambrin farm on observed burst of machine gun fire during the night.	
	27th 28th		Another summary to report. Front very quiet. B.T.C.s fired about one hundred rounds in retaliation for machine gun & T.M. fire. Reg. continued	
	29th		Own trenches were heavily bombarded with minenwerfer and a little shelling by 4.2" for which we retaliated, firing about 350 rds.	

WAR DIARY
or
INTELLIGENCE SUMMARY

89th Bde. R.F.A.

August 16.

Place	Date	Hour	Summary of Events and Information	Remarks and references to Appendices
	30.		310 rds were fired at intervals in rear of BOIS QUARANTE and a line 07.d.25.7 and LOUWAEGE Fm. In the am working parties had been seen for some days. Enemy retaliated in DICKEBUSCH	
	31st.		C/154 were shelled by 4.1in. & 10.5 c.m. throughout the day. About 150 rds. fell round their position. No casualties received. A/89 expended 15 rds on PICCADILLY Fm. in retaliation for intermittent fire.	

J.R. Harrison (?)
Lt. Col. R.F.A.
Comdg. 89th Bde. R.F.A.

Vol 15

CONFIDENTIAL

WAR DIARY
of
99th BRIGADE RFA
from Sept 15th 16 to Sept 9th 16

VOLUME 15

Army Form C. 2118

89th BDE. R.F.A.   WAR DIARY or INTELLIGENCE SUMMARY   September 1916.

(Erase heading not required.)

Instructions regarding War Diaries and Intelligence Summaries are contained in F.S. Regs., Part II. and the Staff Manual respectively. Title Pages will be prepared in manuscript.

Place	Date	Hour	Summary of Events and Information	Remarks and references to Appendices
	1st.		36 hrs expended in registering & in retaliation for enemy T.M. fire.	Ref sheet. 28 SW 2. 1/10,000 28 SW. 1/40,000
	2nd.		Night quite light had few trench mortar bombardment all day. This established for enemy T.M. Tried trench bombardment. On Ridge Sal — Ridge. There were a few alarms on our right — a false alarm given on our front at 2 a.m. (?)	
	3rd.		LA CLYTTE was shelled by 77 c.m. gun apparently no registration.	
	4th.		This group became No 3 group under 19th Divine Artillery at 10 a.m. Very quiet during the whole day.	
	5th.		Very quiet day. As soon as reported the Germans were relieving on our front. A heavy barrage was put on their trenches & approaches from 8.30 to 12.30 a.m. One short intense burst was also fired on the front line at 3 a.m. The enemy retaliated with very little shelling.	
	6th.		The first section of the relieving Bde (112th Bde R.G.A.) 3rd Divisional relieved no section of each of the Groups in the night 6/7. A/89 relieved by H/89 and B/89 relieved by H Bty C/89 relieved by 33rd Bde	

89th Bde. R.F.A.

WAR DIARY
or
INTELLIGENCE SUMMARY

Army Form C. 2118

SEPT 1916

Place	Date	Hour	Summary of Events and Information	Remarks and references to Appendices
	7-		Section relieving Batty carried out registration afterwards a very quiet day. Relief of A/89, B/89, & C/89 were completed at 10:30 p.m. Bde moved to rest camp at SENSEXXEN, R 35 a.	Ry sht 27.
	8-		After mid day in my owing action of the Divisional Arty commenced. Right section A/89 forming a one gun Bty. Left section — C/88 " " " " " Right section B/89 " " " " " Left section B/89 " " " " " C/89 Bde with one section formed a one gun Bty and were renumbered A/88. Head quarter Staff 89 Bde was incorporated with HQ 86: Bde forming the HQ's of the new 86th Bde. It left HB Harvey taking command of the 89 Bde. R.F.A. was thereupon up & disbanded.	A/88.
	9-		R.I.P.	

F.C. Harvey.
Lt Col RFA
Comdg 89 Bde. RFA

19TH DIVISION

TRENCH MORTAR BATTS

JUN 1916 - OCT 1918

Army Form C. 2118.

WAR DIARY
or
INTELLIGENCE SUMMARY

(Erase heading not required.)

June '16 Y/119 T M By
Cor 18 Cor 1

Place	Date	Hour	Summary of Events and Information	Remarks and references to Appendices

Army Form C. 2118.

WAR DIARY
or
INTELLIGENCE SUMMARY

(Erase heading not required.)

Instructions regarding War Diaries and Intelligence Summaries are contained in F. S. Regs., Part II. and the Staff Manual respectively. Title Pages will be prepared in manuscript.

Place	Date	Hour	Summary of Events and Information	Remarks and references to Appendices

2449 Wt. W14957/M90 750,000 1/16 J.B.C. & A. Forms/C.2118/12.

Army Form C. 2118

W/19 Heavy Trench Mortar Battery.

WAR DIARY or INTELLIGENCE SUMMARY

"W"/19 HEAVY TRENCH MORTAR BATTERY.

(Erase heading not required.)

Place	Date	Hour	Summary of Events and Information	Remarks and references to Appendices
LOCRE	1/7/17 to 3/7/17		13 Battery parades	
	4/7/17		Moved camp from LOCRE to VIERSTRAAT	
VIERSTRAAT	5/7/17 to 8/7/17		Collecting Camouflage under orders of 19th D.A.C.	
"	9/7/17		Prepared position & put one gun in action at 0.22.a.30.25. 30 rounds of ammunition taken to position at night	
"	10/7/17		Fired 15 rounds at DRUID FARM. 0.23.a.14	
"	11/7/17 to 13/7/17		13 Battery parades	
"	14/7/17 & 15/7/17		Prepared position & moved gun to 0.16.d.10.55. 30 rounds of ammunition taken to position on night of 15/7/17	
"	16/7/17 8 pm		Fired 14 rounds on JUNCTION BUILDINGS. 0.17.C 70.5.5. 30 rounds of ammunition taken to gun position at night	
"	17/7/17		13 Battery parades. 30 rounds of ammunition taken to gun position at night	
"	18/7/17 8.30 pm		Fired 15 rounds on JUNCTION BUILDINGS 0.17.C. 70.55. 30 rounds of ammunition taken to gun position at night	

Army Form C. 2118

WAR DIARY
or
INTELLIGENCE SUMMARY
(Erase heading not required.)

Place	Date	Hour	Summary of Events and Information	Remarks and references to Appendices
VIERSTRAAT	19/7/17		Moved gun to position No O.22.b.10.90. to engage RIFLE FARM. O.23.d.10.90.	E. Gibeorah. Capt. R.F.C. Comdg: W/19 Heavy T.M. Br.
	20/7/17 App 23/7/17		Put a second gun in the line. This gun was put in position at O.22.b.10.75. to engage GROENELAMDE CABt. O.17.C.90.80 30 rounds of ammunition taken to gun position on the night of 23/7/19	
	24/7/17	3am	Fired 15 rounds on BAR. FARM. O.23.d.58.90	
		5am	Fired 15 rounds on GROENELAMDE CABt O.17.C.90.80 26 rounds of ammunition taken to gun position during the night.	
	25/7/17		Battery paraded	
	26/7/17	2pm	Fired 18 rounds on RIFLE FARM O.23.d.10.90.	
	27/7/17	4pm	Fired 30 rounds on JUNCTION BUILDINGS O.17.C.70.55. + GROENELAMDE CABt O.17.C.90.80. (During this about 40 of the enemy were flushed.)	
	28/7/17	2pm	Fired 28 rounds on RIFLE FARM O.23.d.10.90.	
	29/7/17 + 30/7/17		Battery paraded.	
	31/7/17	4.45pm	Fired 20 rounds on JUNCTION BUILDING G.S. O.17.C.70.55. During this short period the duration of TINY FARM. O.17.C.90.40 30 rounds of ammunition taken to gun position at night.	

Army Form C. 2118.

WAR DIARY
or
INTELLIGENCE SUMMARY of X.19 T.M. Bty.
for July 1917.
(Erase heading not required.)

Instructions regarding War Diaries and Intelligence Summaries are contained in F. S. Regs., Part II. and the Staff Manual respectively. Title Pages will be prepared in manuscript.

Place	Date	Hour	Summary of Events and Information	Remarks and references to Appendices
LOCRE	4/7/19	9 a.m.	Moved into Camp at Vierstraat (July 1st & 4th at rest – Battery Parades)	
VIERSTRAAT	July 5th			
	6			
	7			
	8			
	9		Salvaging Camouflage under the orders of 19th D.A.C.	
	10			
	11			
	12			
	13			
	14			
	15			
	16			
	17			
	18		Battery Parades	
	19		ditto	

Army Form C. 2118.

WAR DIARY
or
INTELLIGENCE SUMMARY

(Erase heading not required.)

X.19 T.M. Battery
for July 1917

Place	Date	Hour	Summary of Events and Information	Remarks and references to Appendices
VIERSTRAAT	July 20	9.15 am	7 Bhp Working on Gun position at 28 O 16 d 25.75	
		7.45 pm	Took up Ammunition to Gun position for 6" Newton	
	21	9 am	Battery Parades	
	22	9.30 am	Carrying Ammunition from Dump to Gun for 6" Newton 219. 28 O 16 a 30.95	
	23	9.0 am	Battery Parades	
	24	9.0 pm	Took up Ammunition to 2.19 forward Dump 28 O 16 a 30.95	
	25	9 am	Battery Parades	
	26	9 am	Work on Gun Pit 2.19 at 28 O 16 d 25.75	
	27	9 am	Battery Parades 2 N.C.O.s. to 2.19 for work on Pit	
	28	9 am	Working for 2.19 on position 28 O 16 d 25.75	
	29	9 am	Took over 1. 6" Newton Gun & Position at 28 O 10 d 10.75	
		7.45 pm	Took up Ammunition to forward Dump at 28 O 16 a 30.95	
	30	9 am	Battery Parades Took Amm. 6" Dump.	
	31	9 am	Work on Gun Pit at 28 O 10 a 10.75. Laying telephone wire & improving O.P. at 28 O 10 d 75.65.	

Farquharson L.M.
O.C. X.19 T.M.B.

Army Form C. 2118.

WAR DIARY
or
INTELLIGENCE SUMMARY. of X/19 T.M. Battery R.A.
(Erase heading not required.)

Place	Date	Hour	Summary of Events and Information	Remarks and references to Appendices
LOGRE.	4/7/17 July	9 am	Moved into Camp at Vierstraat.	1/7/17 to 3/7/17 at rest in LOGRE — Battery Parades
	5/-			
	6/-			
	7/-			
	8/-			
	9/-			
VIERSTRAAT.	10/-		Salvaging Camouflage, under the orders of 19th D.A.C.	
	11/-			
	12/-			
	13/-			
	14/-			
	15/-			
	16/-			
	17/-			
	18/-	1.30pm	Put two 2" M.L. Trench Mortars to in action at N.26 O. 16 D 70.35".	
		6.30 =	Took up 60 rounds 2" Trench Mortar Ammn. to position at 28 O 16 D 70.35".	
	19/-	10 =	Working on gun positions at 28 O 16 D 70.35".	

Army Form C. 2118.

WAR DIARY
or
INTELLIGENCE SUMMARY of X/19 T.M. Bty. R.A.

(Erase heading not required.)

Instructions regarding War Diaries and Intelligence Summaries are contained in F. S. Regs., Part II. and the Staff Manual respectively. Title pages will be prepared in manuscript.

Place	Date	Hour	Summary of Events and Information	Remarks and references to Appendices
VIERSTRAAT	20" 1"	6.15am	(July contd.) Working on gun position at 28.016 D 40.55" and completed same.	
"	21 "	6.30"	Physical Drill. 9.15 am. Reddling for all N.C.O. & men. 11.0 am. Gas Release inspection and target drill.	
"	22 "	6.30 "	Ditto	
"	23 "	10.0 "	Fired 40 rounds 2" T.M. Ammunition from 28 O 16 D 40.55" on JUNCTION BLDGS. (28 O 17 a Central)	
"	24 "	9.0 "	Put 6" NEWTON T.M. into action at 28 O 16 D 25.75".	
"	25 "	9.0 "	Fired 25 rounds 6" NEWTON Ammunition from 28 O 16 D 25.75" on Enemy dugouts about 28 O 17 B 35.40.	
"	26 "	6.0 "	Carried Ammunition (6" NEWTON) to gun position at 28 O 16 D 25.75". Fired on Enemy dugouts at 28 O 17 a 90.80 — 15 rounds (6").	
"	27 "	9.0 "	Carried 6" NEWTON Ammunition to gun position at 28 O 16 D 25.75". Fired 45 rounds 6" Ammunition on S.P. at 28 O 17 B 15.65, Dugouts at 28 O 17 B 35.45, and Farm at 28 O 17 B 90.30. Enemy retaliated very heavily, the detachment having to be withdrawn five times. Trench above position much down Rd.	
"	28 "	6.0 "	New gun position (for 6" NEWTON) dug at 28 O 16 D 20.40, ready for opening firing at 4.0 p.m. Did not shoot owing to Infantry's relieving.	

Army Form C. 2118.

WAR DIARY
INTELLIGENCE SUMMARY.

1st Y/19 T.M. By. R.A.

(Erase heading not required.)

Place	Date	Hour	Summary of Events and Information	Remarks and references to Appendices
VIERSTRAAT	29.7 (July Contd.) 8.0am		Fired 8 rounds 6" ammn. from 28.o.16.D.20.40. on dugouts at 28.o.17.B.35.45.	28.o.17.B.35.45.
			also 10 rounds 2" ammn. from 28.o.16.D.90.55 on Junction Blos. (26.o.17.C.Cent.).	(26.o.17.C.Cent.).
			Very heavy rain prevented further shooting.	
"	30 "	10.am.	Fired 50 rounds 6" ammn. at 2 p.m. from 28.o.16.D.20.40 on S.P. at 28.o.17.B.15.65.	o.17.B.15.65.
			dugouts at 28.o.17.B.35.45. and Farm at 28.o.17.B.90.35.	
"	31 "	6.30"	Physical drill 9.15 am. Raining; 11 am. Box respirator inspection + drill	
			Casualties 1/7/17 to 31/7/17 : Nil.	

3/8/17.
[signature] Lieut. R.F.A.
O.C. Y/19 T.M. By. R.A.

WAR DIARY
INTELLIGENCE SUMMARY.

Of Y/19 T.M. Bty. R.A.

Army Form C. 2118.

Place	Date	Hour	Summary of Events and Information	Remarks and references to Appendices
MÉTEREN	August 27th	6.30"	August (cont'd) Training	
"	28th	6.30"	ditto	
"	29th	6.30"	ditto	
"	30th	6.30"	ditto — 9.0 am Inspected by C.R.A. Battery gun drill.	
"	31st	6.30"	Training	

31/8/17.

[signature] Lieut. R.A.
O.C. Y/19 T.M. Battery R.A.

Casualties for Month of August — NIL.

Army Form C. 2118.

WAR DIARY
or
INTELLIGENCE SUMMARY. 1/1st Trench Mortar Battery R.A.

(Erase heading not required.)

Instructions regarding War Diaries and Intelligence Summaries are contained in F. S. Regs., Part II. and the Staff Manual respectively. Title pages will be prepared in manuscript.

Place	Date	Hour	Summary of Events and Information	Remarks and references to Appendices
Zuidstraat	Aug 1	6.30 am	Battery Parades	
"	2	6.30 "	Removing Siege from Ravine Wood 28 O.10 d 10.75 to forward dump.	
"	3	9.0 "	Preparing 2" Bombs at York House Dump on Vierstraat Ropt	
"	4	9.0 "	Unloading 2" Bombs at York House dump on Vierstraat Road.	
"	5	9.0 "	Removing 6" Bombs from Ravine Wood 28 O.10d 10.75 to forward dump.	
"	6	9.0 "	" "	
"	7	9.0 "	Salvaging 2" Bombs in the vicinity of camp & taking same to York House dump.	
"	8	9.0 "	Working party of Siener detailed forward 1/19 Battery to work on gun emplacement. The remainder salvaging up Bombs as in the 7th inst.	
"	9	6.30 "	Battery Parades	
"	10	9.0 "	" "	
Caudescure	11	6.30 "	Moved out of camp into rest billets at Caudescure. Old billets taken over by 87th Division	
"	12	6.30 "	Battery Parade.	
"	13	6.30 "	"	
"		10.0 "	Inspection in S.M.O by C.R.A.	
"	14	6.30 "	Training as per weekly programme	
"	15	6.30 "	" "	
"	16	6.30 "	" "	

Army Form C. 2118.

WAR DIARY
or
INTELLIGENCE SUMMARY of Z/19 T.M.B. for July 1917

(Erase heading not required.)

Instructions regarding War Diaries and Intelligence Summaries are contained in F.S. Regs., Part II. and the Staff Manual respectively. Title Pages will be prepared in manuscript.

Place	Date	Hour	Summary of Events and Information	Remarks and references to Appendices
LOCRE	4/7/17	9 a.m.	Moved into Camp at Vierstraat	
VIERSTRAAT	July 5			
	6			
	7			
	8			
	9		At Rest - Batty Parades	
	10		Salvaging Camouflage under the orders of 19th D.A.C.	
	11			
	12			
	13			
	14			
	15			
	16			
	17			
	18		Battery Parades & digging in 6" Newton at 22.O.16.d.25.75.	
	19		Ditto	
	20	9.15	Work on Gun Position at 28.O.16.d.25.75. 6" Newton.	
	21	9.15	Fired 10 Rounds at THEETWINS 28.O.11.d.9.3. from 28.O.16.d.25.75.	
	23	9.15	Fired 5 Rounds at S.1.28.O.11.d.05.20, from 28.O.16.d.25.75.	
	24	9.15	Work on gun pits & carrying ammunition	
	25	9.15	Work on gun pits & carrying ammunition & material	

Army Form C. 2118.

WAR DIARY
or
INTELLIGENCE SUMMARY of 2/19 T.M.B.
(Erase heading not required.) for July 1917

Place	Date	Hour	Summary of Events and Information	Remarks and references to Appendices
VIERSTRAAT	26	9.15	Fired at arm of Green Wood O.17.b.15.80 to O.17.b.15.55. 10 Rds.	
	27	9.0	Built new emplacement at 28 O.10.d.10.75.	
	28	9.am	Bombed Gun & position at O.10.d.10.75 to X 19 TMB.	
	29	—	Battery parades.	
	30	9 pm	Took ammunition to forward dump at 28.O.16.a.30.95.	
	31	—	Battery parades.	

Casualties from 1.7.17. to 31.7.17.
Nil.

Wyman 2/Lt R.F.A. (S.R.)
for O.C. 2/19 T.M.B.

Army Form C. 2118.

WAR DIARY
or
INTELLIGENCE SUMMARY.
(Erase heading not required.)

WO 95/1771/4
19th TM Bty
Vol 2

Place	Date	Hour	Summary of Events and Information	Remarks and references to Appendices
VIERSTRAAT (Parrot Farm)	August 1917			
	1st		Battery Parades.	
	2nd		Raining Battery Parades.	
	3rd		Selected new position for guns at O.16.d.9.2 and collected material for making new gun platform.	
	4th		Battery Parades	
	5th		Battery Parades - Party went up to gun line to clean old position	
	6th		Battery Parades	

Army Form C. 2118.

WAR DIARY
or
INTELLIGENCE SUMMARY.
(Erase heading not required.)

Instructions regarding War Diaries and Intelligence Summaries are contained in F. S. Regs., Part II. and the Staff Manual respectively. Title pages will be prepared in manuscript.

Place	Date	Hour	Summary of Events and Information	Remarks and references to Appendices
	August 1917			
Vierstraat (Pond Farm)	7th		Battery Parade. Started new positions behind Signallers Dugout at O.18.d.9.2	
"	8th		Cleaned up positions and bombs ready to hand over to 37th T.M's.	
"	9th		Went to Wytschaete to meet 37th T.M. Battery Commanders to show them round positions and front.	
Locrehove	10th		Handed over to 37th T.M's and moved at 11 am in 3 Lorries – Arrived at Caudescure at 3 pm. Our battery is billeted at a farm near the church.	
	11th		Battery Parade.	
	12th		Battery Parade.	
	13		Battery Parade.	

Army Form C. 2118.

WAR DIARY
or
INTELLIGENCE SUMMARY.
(Erase heading not required.)

Instructions regarding War Diaries and Intelligence Summaries are contained in F. S. Regs., Part II. and the Staff Manual respectively. Title pages will be prepared in manuscript.

Place	Date	Hour	Summary of Events and Information	Remarks and references to Appendices
	August 17			
Caudescure	14th		Battery Inspected in F.S.M.O. by C.R.A.	
	15th		Battery Training Parades (as per weekly Training programme)	
	16th		Ditto	
	17th		Ditto	
	18th		Ditto	
	19th		Ditto	
	20th		Ditto.	
	21st		Marched with G.S. Wagon to Meteren.	

Army Form C. 2118.

WAR DIARY
or
INTELLIGENCE SUMMARY.
(Erase heading not required.)

Place	Date	Hour	Summary of Events and Information	Remarks and references to Appendices
Meteren	Aug 21			
	22nd		Continued Training Programme.	
	23rd		Training	
	24th		— Ditto —	
	25th		— Ditto — [struck through]	
	26th		— Ditto —	
	27th		— Ditto —	
	28th		Bty. helped to pick hops which had been blown down by wind.	
	29th		— Ditto —	

Army Form C. 2118.

WAR DIARY
or
INTELLIGENCE SUMMARY.
(Erase heading not required.)

Instructions regarding War Diaries and Intelligence Summaries are contained in F. S. Regs., Part II. and the Staff Manual respectively. Title pages will be prepared in manuscript.

Place	Date	Hour	Summary of Events and Information	Remarks and references to Appendices
METEREN	Aug 17			
	30th		Hop Picking — Received No 3 Section of 5th Batt — Lost 4 —	
	31st		Hop Picking —	

WAR DIARY or INTELLIGENCE SUMMARY

Army Form C. 2118.

X 19th Trench Mortar Battery R.A.

For August 1917

Place	Date	Hour	Summary of Events and Information	Remarks and references to Appendices
VIERSTRAAT	Aug 1st	9.0 A.M.	Battery Parades	
"	2	9.0 "	New Gun Positions reconnoitred at 28 O.17.d.25.55. Work begun on same	
"	3	9.0 "	Work on Gun Position at 28 O.17.d.25.55	
"	4	9.0 "	Regaining Ammunition from abandoned Gun Position at 28 O.10.d.10.75	
"	5	9.0 "	Battery Parades	
"	6	9.0 "	Working on Gun Position at 28 O.17.d.25.55	
"	7	9.0 "	ditto	
"	8	9.0 "	ditto	
"	9	9.0 "	Battery Parades. 6" How. on Temp. Red. Accumulators and Emplacement at 28 O.17.d.25.55 handed over to relieving Division. (No 39th)	
"	10	9.0 "	Work out of action. 6 Ry. Posts at CAUDESCURE Battery Parades. Inspected by S.T.M.O at 10.30 a.m.	
CAUDESCURE	11	9.0 "	Battery Parades	
"	12	9.0 "	Battery Parades	
"	13	—	10th Inspection by D.S.M.O by C.R.A. Battery Parades	
"	14	6.30 A.M.	Parades as per training programme	
"	15	"	ditto	

Army Form C. 2118.

WAR DIARY
or
INTELLIGENCE SUMMARY

(Erase heading not required.) X 19 TMB for August 1917

Place	Date	Hour	Summary of Events and Information	Remarks and references to Appendices
CAUDESCURE	16 Aug	6.20am	Battery Parade as per Training Programme	
	17	"		
	18	"		
	19	"		
	20	"		
	21	11.30am	Moved to billets near Meteren	
METEREN	22	6.30	" "	
	23	"	Training	
	24	"	"	
	25	"	"	
	26	"	"	
	27	"	"	
	28	"	"	
	29	"	"	
	30	9am	Inspection by C.R.A. at Gun Drive — Battery Parades	
	31	6.30	Training Casualties for August — NIL.	

OC 19th TMB

Army Form C. 2118.

WAR DIARY
or
INTELLIGENCE SUMMARY.

Y/19 Trench Mortar Battery R.A.

(Erase heading not required.)

Place	Date	Hour	Summary of Events and Information	Remarks and references to Appendices
Verinchoot	August 1st	8.30am	Physical Drill 9.0 am. Rebilling for all N.C.O's and then 11.0 am Stock Check and Inspection and drill	
	2nd	9.0"	New Gun Position reconnoitred at 28 O 17 c 25 45: Work begun on same	
	3rd	10.0"	Working on advanced gun position at 28 O 17 c 25 45. Two 2" T. Mortars at 28 O 16 D 70 55 brought out of action	
"	4th	9.0"	Working on position at 28 O 16 D 20 40 — Improving gun pit and building an Ammn. store. Gun pit in action. Ones round fired at Farm at 28 O 17 } 6" Howitzer T.M.
			b g5.35. Had to cease firing owing to gun being out of action.	
"	5th	—	Battery Parades. Gun (6" Howitzer) at 28 O 16 D 20 40 fut into action	
"	6th	9.0 am	Working on Gun position at 28 O 17 c 25 45.	
"	7th	9.0"	ditto.	
"	8th	9.0"	ditto.	
"	9th	—	Battery Parades. 6" Howitzer Gun, ammn. and Emplacement handed over to relieving division — 37 Division	
"	10th	9.0 am	Moved out of action to rest billets at Oudescure.	
Oudescure	11th	—	Battery Parade. 37 Div. took over billets at Yerstraat.	

D, D, & L, London, E.C.
(A7833) Wt W809/M1672 39,000 4/17 Sch 823. Forms/C/2118/14

Army Form C. 2118.

WAR DIARY
INTELLIGENCE SUMMARY.
Jr. X19 Trench Mortar B͟y. R.A.

(Erase heading not required.)

Place	Date	Hour	Summary of Events and Information	Remarks and references to Appendices
			(AUGUST Contd.)	
CAUDESCURE	12/k	—	Battery Parade.	
	13/k	—	ditto.	
"	"	10 a.m	Battery inspected in F.S.M.O. by C.R.A.	
"	14 "	6.30 "	Battery Parade (as per weekly training programme)	
"	15 "	6.30 "	ditto.	
"	16 "	6.30 "	ditto.	
"	17 "	6.30 "	ditto.	
"	18 "	6.30 "	ditto.	
"	19 "	6.30 "	ditto.	
"	20 "	6.30 "	ditto.	
"	21 "	11.30 "	Moved by march route to MÉTEREN.	
MÉTEREN	22 "	6.30 "	Training	
"	23 "	6.30 "	ditto	
"	24 "	6.30 "	ditto	
"	25 "	6.30 "	ditto	
"	26 "	6.30 "	ditto	

Army Form C. 2118.

WAR DIARY
INTELLIGENCE SUMMARY.   Z/19 Trench Mortar Battery. R.A.
(Erase heading not required.)

Instructions regarding War Diaries and Intelligence Summaries are contained in F. S. Regs., Part II. and the Staff Manual respectively. Title pages will be prepared in manuscript.

Place	Date	Hour	Summary of Events and Information	Remarks and references to Appendices
Caulaincourt	Aug 17	6.30 a.m.	⎫ Training as per weekly programme	
"	18	6.30 "	⎬	
"	19	6.30 "	⎭	
"	20	6.30 "	Marched to marshalls at Heilly.	
"	21	11.30 "		
Pretoria	22	6.30 "	⎫	
"	23	6.30 "	⎪	
"	24	6.30 "	⎪	
"	25	6.30 "	⎬ Training as per weekly programme.	
"	26	6.30 "	⎪	
"	27	6.30 "	⎪	
"	28	6.30 "	⎭	
"	29	6.30 "		
"	30	6.30 "	Training Pat 9.0 a.m. Inspection by C.R.A. at Battery Gun Drill. Training.	
"	31	6.30 "		

31/8/17.   W.R. Sheasby Lieut R.F.A.
O.C. Z/19 T.M. Battery R.A.

Casualties for month of August — NIL.

Army Form C. 2118.

"W"/19
HEAVY TRENCH
MORTAR BATTERY.
No.................
Date................

WAR DIARY
or
INTELLIGENCE SUMMARY.
(Erase heading not required.)

Instructions regarding War Diaries and Intelligence Summaries are contained in F. S. Regs., Part II. and the Staff Manual respectively. Title pages will be prepared in manuscript.

Place	Date	Hour	Summary of Events and Information	Remarks and references to Appendices
	Sept.			
METEREN	1st	6.30am	Training	
STRAZEELE	2nd	11	Training	
"	3rd	"	Ditto	
"	4th	"	Ditto. Inspection by G.O.C. 19th Division.	
"	5th	"	Ditto & Batt.	
"	6th	8am	Marched to Camp at VIERSTRAAT (Laiterie) No 1811 Filer & Smith R.F.A. awarded military medal	
VIERSTRAAT	7th	"	Camp Fatigues	
"	8th	6am	Building Battery Position for 18 pdrs. No RG5 at 0.3.a. 95.75	
"	9th	"	Ditto	
"	10th	"	Ditto	
"	11th	"	Ditto	
"	12th	"	Ditto	
"	13th	"	Ditto ————— for 4·5 How. No RG2 at 0.3.a. 80.40	
"	14th	8am	Camp Fatigues.	
"	15th	6am	18 pdr & 4·5 How. Ammunition Supply to Rt. Group	
"	16th	"	Ditto	

Army Form C. 2118.

WAR DIARY
or
INTELLIGENCE SUMMARY.
(Erase heading not required.)

Place	Date	Hour	Summary of Events and Information	Remarks and references to Appendices
VIERSTRAAT	Sept 17th	6 am	Ammunition Supply to Rt. Group.	
"	18th	5 am	Ditto	
"	19th	"	Ditto	
"	20th	"	Ditto	
"	21st	"	Ditto	
"	22nd	"	Ditto	
"	23rd	6 am	Ditto	
"	24th	5 am	Ditto	
"	25th	"	Ditto	
"	26th	"	Ditto	
"	27th	"	Ditto	
"	28th	6 am	Ditto	
"	29th	"	Ditto	
"	30th	"	Ditto	

Army Form C. 2118.

WAR DIARY
or
INTELLIGENCE SUMMARY
(Erase heading not required.)

X 19 Trench Mortar Battery
for September 1917

Place	Date	Hour	Summary of Events and Information	Remarks and references to Appendices
STRAZEELE	1 Sept	11 a.m.	Moves to new billets in STRAZEELE area.	
"	2	6.0 a.m.	Training	
"	3	6.0 a.m.	"	
"	4	6.0 a.m.	"	
"	5	10. a.m.	Inspection by C.O.C. 19th Division at MORRIS	
"	6	11 a.m.	Left rest billets, marched to the line going into bivouac at off York Road near Vierstraat. No. 2 Cadet, RGA awarded Military M—	
VIERSTRAAT	7	6.30	Camp fatigues.	
"	8	5.30	Supplying Ammunition to Field Batteries	
"	9	"	do.	
"	10	"	do.	
"	11	"	do.	
"	12	"	do.	
"	13	"	do.	
"	14	"	do.	
"	15	"	do.	
"	16	"	do.	

WAR DIARY
or
INTELLIGENCE SUMMARY

of X19 J.W. By R.A.

Army Form C. 2118.

SEPTEMBER

Place	Date	Hour	Summary of Events and Information	Remarks and references to Appendices
VIERSTRAAT	17th	5:30am	Supplying Ammunition to Field Batteries	
"	18	"	do.	
"	19	"	do.	
"	20	"	do.	
"	21	"	do.	
"	22	"	do.	
"	23	"	do.	
"	24	"	do.	
"	25	"	do.	
"	26	"	do.	2Lt. R.H. Dove, R.F.A. Wounded in Action
"	27	"	do.	" " Died of wounds same night
"	28	"	do.	
"	29	"	do.	
"	30	"	do.	
			Casualties for September. 1 Officer.	1 R.F.A.

Farquharson T.W.B.
O.C. X19

Army Form C. 2118.

WAR DIARY
INTELLIGENCE SUMMARY of Y.19 T.M. Bty, R.A.

(Erase heading not required.)

Instructions regarding War Diaries and Intelligence Summaries are contained in F. S. Regs., Part II. and the Staff Manual respectively. Title pages will be prepared in manuscript.

Place	Date	Hour	Summary of Events and Information	Remarks and references to Appendices
	SEPT.		SEPTEMBER.	
Méteren	1st	6.30 AM	Training. 11 AM. Moved by march-route to STRAZEELE.	
STRAZEELE	2nd	"	ditto.	
"	3rd	"	ditto.	
"	4th	"	ditto. Inspection by G.O.C. 19th Division.	
"	5th	"	ditto. Baths.	
"	6th	"	Marched to Camp at VIERSTRAAT. No. 171904 Gd. Marl, RFA awarded Military Medal.	
VIERSTRAAT	7th	"	Camp fatigues.	
"	8th	5.30 AM	Exercise. Fatigues. Supplying ammunition to Field Batteries.	
"	9th	"	do.	
"	10th	"	do.	
"	11th	"	do.	
"	12th	"	do.	
"	13th	"	do.	
"	14th	"	do.	
"	15th	"	do.	
"	16th	"	do.	

Army Form C. 2118.

WAR DIARY
INTELLIGENCE SUMMARY of Y/19 T.M.Bty. R.A.

(Erase heading not required.)

Place	Date	Hour	Summary of Events and Information	Remarks and references to Appendices
VIERSTRAAT D/K	Sept. 18th	5.30 A.m.	Supplying Ammn. to Field Batteries.	
"	19th	"	ditto	
"	20th	"	ditto	
"	21st	"	ditto	
"	22nd	"	ditto	
"	23rd	"	ditto	
"	24th	"	ditto	
"	25th	"	ditto	
"	26th	"	ditto	
"	27th	"	ditto	
"	28th	"	ditto	
"	29th	"	ditto	
"	30th	"	Casualties for Month of September; — Nil.	

30/9/17 A.J.Hyett Lieut R.A.
O.C. Y/19 T.M.Bty R.A.

Army Form C. 2118.

WAR DIARY
or
INTELLIGENCE SUMMARY.
(Erase heading not required.)

Instructions regarding War Diaries and Intelligence Summaries are contained in F. S. Regs., Part II. and the Staff Manual respectively. Title pages will be prepared in manuscript.

Place	Date	Hour	Summary of Events and Information	Remarks and references to Appendices
Strazeele	1 Sept	11 a.m.	Moved into new billets in Strazeele area.	
"	2	6 p.m.	} Training	
"	3	6 a.m.	}	
"	4	6 a.m.	}	
"	5	10 a.m.	Inspection by G.O.C. 19th Division at Meats.	
"	6	11 a.m.	Left rest billets and marched to York Road near Vierstraat where we bivouaced. No 36635 L. Murphy awarded military medal	
Vierstraat	7	6.30 a.m.	Camp fatigues	
"	8	7.30 a.m.	Supplying ammunition to field batteries	
"	9	"	"	
"	10	"	"	
"	11	"	"	
"	12	"	"	
"	13	"	"	
"	14	"	"	
"	15	"	"	
"	16	"	"	

Army Form C. 2118.

WAR DIARY
or
INTELLIGENCE SUMMARY.
(Erase heading not required.)

Place	Date	Hour	Summary of Events and Information	Remarks and references to Appendices
Voostraat	17th	5.30am	Supplying Ammunition to field batteries	
"	18	"	"	
"	19	"	"	
"	20	"	"	
"	21	"	"	
"	22	"	"	
"	23	"	"	
"	24	"	"	
"	25	"	"	
"	26	"	"	
"	27	"	"	
"	28	"	"	
"	29	"	"	
"	30	"	"	

Casualties for September — Nil.

Army Form C. 2118.

WAR DIARY
or
INTELLIGENCE SUMMARY.
(Erase heading not required.)

W/19 H.T.M. Bn

Vol 4

Place	Date	Hour	Summary of Events and Information	Remarks and references to Appendices
VIERSTRAAT	Oct: 1		Supplied Ammunition to Field Batteries 19th Division	
"	2		do. —	
"	3		do. —	
"	4		do. —	
"	5		do. —	
"	6		do. —	
"	7		do. —	
"	8		do. —	
"	9		do. —	
"	10		do. —	
"	11		do. —	
"	12		do. —	
"	13		do. —	
"	14		do. —	
"	15		do. —	
"	16		do. —	

Army Form C. 2118.

WAR DIARY
or
INTELLIGENCE SUMMARY. Continued

(Erase heading not required.)

Place	Date	Hour	Summary of Events and Information	Remarks and references to Appendices
VIERSTRAAT	17		Supplied Ammunition Field No 18 Batteries 19 N. Divisions	
"	18		do	
"	19		do	
"	20		do	
"	21		do	
"	22		do	
"	23		do	
"	24		do	
"	25		do	
"	26		do	
"	27		do	
"	28		do	
"	29		Building Arty Group H.Q. at LANKHOF Chateau	
"	30		Building Arty Group H.Q. at LANKHOF Chateau & brought 9. & 5 guns	
"	31		2nd It No Wilkes from O.S.L. 10.2.0. No offest of any kind	
			Casualties during the month Nil.	

O.C. 1/1/15

Army Form C. 2118.

WAR DIARY
or
INTELLIGENCE SUMMARY 3 X.19 T.M. B4

(Erase heading not required.)

Place	Date	Hour	Summary of Events and Information	Remarks and references to Appendices
Fauquembergues	1st	6.30 a.m.	19??	
	2.			
	3.			
	4.		No. 6, 7, 19 Lt. Batteries with Ammunition	
	5.			
	6.			
	7.			
	8.		Bde inspected by 19th C.R.A	
	9.			
	10.	10.30 a.m.		
	11.			
	12.			
	13.			
	14.			
	15.		Nos 6, 7, 19 Field Batteries with Ammunition	
	16.			
	17.			
	18.			
	19.			
	20.			
	21.			
	22.			
	23.			
	24.			
	25.			
Abeele	26.		Marched to Group Head Quarters at Lockly Farm	
	27.		Pitts	
	28.		Came into Action October	
	29.		18.30.	
	30.			G. Ray? Lt. H. R.F.A. 7/16 7.79.B.

WAR DIARY
or
INTELLIGENCE SUMMARY — /Y 19 T.M. Bty R.A

Army Form C. 2118.

(Erase heading not required.)

Place	Date	Hour	Summary of Events and Information	Remarks and references to Appendices
Vierstraat	1st	6.30 p.m	October 1917	× Left, Bde
	2.	"		and 31st Coy
	3.	"		building a
	4.	"		Group H.Q.
	5.	"		at LANKHOF
	6.	"		FARM
	7.	"		
	8.	"		
	9.	"		
	10.	"		
	11.	"		
	12.	10.6 p.m	14/Y/9 Td Batteries with Ammunition	
	13.	6.30 "	Const. Instructed by 14 K. C.R.A	
	14.	"		
	15.	"		
	16.	"		
	17.	"		
	18.	"		
	19.	"		
	20.	"		
	21.	"		
	22.	"	Suffering still suffers with ammunition	
	23.	"		
	24.	"		Lieut R.A
	25.	"		
	26.	"		Lieut RA
	27.	"		/Y/19 T.M. Bty
	28.	"	Carried on for October N/K	
×	29.	"		
×	30.	"		O.C. /Y/19 T.M Bty
×	31.	"		

WAR DIARY
or
INTELLIGENCE SUMMARY. 2/19 T.M.B&

Army Form C. 2118.

(Erase heading not required.)

Place	Date	Hour	Summary of Events and Information	Remarks and references to Appendices
	October 1917			
	1st	6.30am	Supplying Ammunition to field Batteries	
	2nd		"	
	3rd		"	
	4th		"	
	5th		"	
	6th		"	
	7th		"	
	8th		"	
	9th		"	
	10th		"	
	11th		"	
	12th	10 A.M	Went to speak to C.O. at 19th C.R.A.	
	13th	6.30 A.M	Continue supplying Ammunition Field Batteries	
	14th		"	
	15th		"	
	16th		"	
	17th		"	
	18th		Supplying Ammunition to field Batteries	
	19th		"	
	20th		"	
	21st		Battery Group Headquarters at Lauckhofsarm	
	22nd		Cesantie Nr Oclebs	
	23rd			
	24th		1 Gunner wounded	
	25th			

L.R.Mealy Lieut R.H.A

WAR DIARY W/19 H.T.M. Bn.
or
INTELLIGENCE SUMMARY

Army Form C. 2118.

(Erase heading not required.)

Place	Date	Hour	Summary of Events and Information	Remarks and references to Appendices
VIERSTRAAT	1 Nov		Building Arty Group H.Q. at LAMKHOF CHATEAU	
	2		" " " "	
	3		" " " "	
	4		" " " "	
	5		" " " "	
	6		Moved out of Camp to POMPIER CAMP.	
La Clyde	7		Work on construction of horse standings at POMPIER CAMP.	
	8			
	9			
	10			
	11		Moved into billets near BERTHEM.	
BERTHEM	12		Battery parades	
	13		One half battery attached to 19th D.A.C. + one half to D/87 wept lives	
Croix de Poperinghe	14		" "	
	15		" "	
	16		" "	

WAR DIARY or INTELLIGENCE SUMMARY.

Army Form C. 2118. Continued

Place	Date	Hour	Summary of Events and Information	Remarks and references to Appendices
Croix de Poperinghe	17		half Battery attached 19 D.B.S. half Bty to D/87 Bde R.F.A.	
"	18			
"	19			
"	20			
"	21			
"	22			
"	23			
"	24			
"	25			
"	26			
"	27			
"	28			
"	29			
"	30		Casualties during month 1 O.R. wounded	W.J. Barrett Capt R.A. Comdg V/19 H.T.M.B.Ty

Army Form C. 2118.

WAR DIARY
or
INTELLIGENCE SUMMARY

(Erase heading not required.)

of X19 T.M.B.

for November 1917

Instructions regarding War Diaries and Intelligence Summaries are contained in F. S. Regs., Part II. and the Staff Manual respectively. Title Pages will be prepared in manuscript.

Place	Date	Hour	Summary of Events and Information	Remarks and references to Appendices
VIERSTRAAT.	1	6.30 AM	Hut Building T.M. Camp York Road.	
"	2			
"	3			
"	4			
"	5			
"	6		Moved to Pompier Camp. (KEMMEL)	
POMPIER CAMP	7			
"	8		Work on Horse Standings	
"	9			
"	10			
"	11			
"	12		Moved to rest Billets near Berthen	
BERTHEN	13		Battery Parade.	
CROIX DE POPERINGHE	14		Moved to 87 A. Bde Waggon lines at Croix de Poperinghe	
"	15			
"	16			
"	17			
"	18		Attached A/87 Bde waggon lines for duty.	
"	19			
"	20			
"	21			
"	22			

Army Form C. 2118.

WAR DIARY
or
INTELLIGENCE SUMMARY

of X.19. T.M.B.y for November 1917

(Erase heading not required.)

Place	Date	Hour	Summary of Events and Information	Remarks and references to Appendices
CROIX DE POPERINGHE	23		Work on A/88 Blue wagon line.	
"	24			
"	25			
"	26			
"	27			
"	28			
"	29			
"	30		Casualties for November. NIL.	

Bamborough Lt
J.R.A.

WAR DIARY / INTELLIGENCE SUMMARY

Army Form C. 2118.

of 1/1ˢᵗ Heavy Trench Mortar Battery

Place	Date	Hour	Summary of Events and Information	Remarks and references to Appendices
Westhend	1ˢᵗ	8.00a	November 1917. Brigade group Head Quarters at Westhof Chateau & took in Ammunition & new Camp at the Chateau	
"	2			
"	3			
"	4			
"	5			
La Clytte	6	9.30am	Moved out of Camp into Proper Camp at the Second La Clytte Road	
"	7	5.30am		
"	8		Work on Horse lines &c at Proper Camp	
"	9			
"	10			
"	11	9.30am	Head from Proper Camp to Billets near Berthen	
Berthen	12	9.00am	Fatigues Cleaning Billets etc.	
"	13	9.00am	Moved self & Billet to B/19 Brigade Wagon lines near Boy de Nekkey	
Boy de	14			
Nekkey	15		Attached to B/19 Brigade Wagon lines	
"	16			

Army Form C. 2118.

of Y/19 Trench Mortar Battery

WAR DIARY
INTELLIGENCE SUMMARY.
(Erase heading not required.)

Place	Date	Hour	Summary of Events and Information	Remarks and references to Appendices
Going to Flight	17	6 a.m.	November 1917	
"	18	"		
"	19	"		
"	20	"	Attached to B/82 Brigade R.F.A.	
"	21	"		
"	22	"		
"	23	"		
"	24	"		
"	25	7 a.m.		
"	26	6.30 a.m.		
"	27	"	Building battery position for 2/80 Brigade R.F.A.	
"	28	"		
"	29	"		
"	30	"	Consolidation for both B/ brackets N.b.	
"	31	"		

Army Form C. 2118.

WAR DIARY Z/19 T.M.Bg. R.A.

INTELLIGENCE SUMMARY.

(Erase heading not required.)

Instructions regarding War Diaries and Intelligence Summaries are contained in F. S. Regs., Part II. and the Staff Manual respectively. Title pages will be prepared in manuscript.

Place	Date	Hour	Summary of Events and Information	Remarks and references to Appendices
Oversbrack	1 Nov/17	6.30 AM	Building Group Head quarters at back of Chateau & work on construction of new Camp at St Laurent.	
"	2"	"		
"	3"	"		
"	4"	"		
"	5"	"		
"	6"	9.30 AM	Moved out of camp into Pompier Camp on the Kemmel – La Clytte Road.	
La Clytte	7"	8.30 PM		
"	8"	"	Work on construction of horse standings &c at Pompier Camp.	
"	9"	"		
"	10"	"		
"	11"	9.30 AM	Moved out of Pompier Camp into billet at — Berthen	
Berthen	12"	5.30 AM	Fatigues, cleaning billet area.	
"	13"	9.30 AM	Moved out of billet to C/87 Brigade Wagon Lines at M.32.f.5.3. near Croix de Poperinghe	
Croix de Poperinghe	14"	6.30 AM		
"	15"	"	Attached to C/87 Brigade Wagon Lines	
"	16"	"		
"	17"	"		
"	18"	"		
"	19"	"		
"	20"	"		

Army Form C. 2118.

WAR DIARY Z/19 T.M. By. R.A.
or
INTELLIGENCE SUMMARY.
(Erase heading not required.)

Place	Date	Hour	Summary of Events and Information	Remarks and references to Appendices
Croix de Poperinghe	21st Nov 17	6:30 am	Attached to 87th Bryde Wagon Line.	
	22" "	"		
	23" "	"		
	24" "	"		
	25" "	"		
	26" "	"		
	27" "	"		
	28" "	"		
	29" "	"		
	30" "	"		

"Casualties for November — Nil.

M. Kerr, Lieut. RFA
2/Lieut RFA Trench Mortar Battery
Commanding Z/19 Trench Mortar Battery

Army Form C. 2118.

19 DT May / 17
19 Vol 6

WAR DIARY
or
INTELLIGENCE SUMMARY.
(Erase heading not required.)

Instructions regarding War Diaries and Intelligence Summaries are contained in F. S. Regs., Part II. and the Staff Manual respectively. Title pages will be prepared in manuscript.

Place	Date	Hour	Summary of Events and Information	Remarks and references to Appendices
Briox de Poperinghe	Dec 1		Rt. Section attached 87th FA Bde Lt. Section attached DAC — Work on Standings and Parks	
	2		— do —	
	3		— do —	
	4		— do —	
	5		— do —	
	6		— do —	
	7		— do —	
	8		— do —	
	9		— do —	
	10		— do —	
	11		— do —	
	12		— do —	
	13		— do —	
	14		Lt Section rejoined Rt. Section at Blaum camp near Briox de Poperinghe — bt attached DAC	
	15 & 30		} Work for 19th D.A.C. — do —	

Army Form C. 2118.

WAR DIARY
or
INTELLIGENCE SUMMARY.
(Erase heading not required.)

Instructions regarding War Diaries and Intelligence Summaries are contained in F. S. Regs., Part II. and the Staff Manual respectively. Title pages will be prepared in manuscript.

Place	Date	Hour	Summary of Events and Information	Remarks and references to Appendices
Blaris Camp	3	7.20	Entrained at Bailleul (West)	

Army Form C. 2118.

WAR DIARY
or
INTELLIGENCE SUMMARY

of X/19 T.M. B'y for December 1917

(Erase heading not required.)

Place	Date	Hour	Summary of Events and Information	Remarks and references to Appendices
CROIX DE POPERINGHE	1			
	2	9 a.m.	Work on A/58 Bde Waggon Line	
	3			
	4	10.0 a.m.	Inspected by C.R.A. 19th Division	
	5	9 a.m.		
	6		Work on A/58 Bde Waggon Line	
	7			
	8			
	9			
	10			
	11			
	12			
ST. JANS CAPPEL	13		Moved to billets at 41 Faros Dupful	
	14	9 a.m.	Work on A/58 Bde Waggon Line	
	15			
	16		Moved to billets in St Jans Cappel	
	17	7 a.m.		
	18		G.O.R. Work on B/87 Bde gun pits	
	19		Recommencing Personnel — Battery Parades	
	20			

2449 Wt. W14957/Mg0 750,000 1/16 J.B.C. & A. Forms/C.2118/12.

WAR DIARY or INTELLIGENCE SUMMARY

Army Form C. 2118.

of X/19 T.M. Bty for December 1917.

Place	Date	Hour	Summary of Events and Information	Remarks and references to Appendices
ST. JANS CAPPEL	21	7am	6.U.R. Watt in B/71 Ode Gun Pits (detached)	
"	22	"	Remaining personnel — Battery Parades	
"	23	"		
"	24	"		
"	25	"		
"	26	"	Battery Parades	
"	27	"	Entrained.	
"	28	"	Moves to Bapaume — thence to ROCQUIGNY.B.Camp.	
"	29	"		
"	30	"		
"	31	7.26am		

Casualties for December. Nil.

B. Houghnavant/L. R.F.A.
O/C X/19 T.M. Bty

WAR DIARY
or
INTELLIGENCE SUMMARY

Army Form C. 2118.

Place	Date	Hour	Summary of Events and Information	Remarks and references to Appendices
Ridge Obsevatory	1	6.30	December 1917. Building Battery Position for 8/12" in vicinity of Observatory	
"	2	"	ditto	
"	3	"	ditto	
"	4	"	Hy.By 1/2 battery arrived & began work at Observatory	
Arab Pyr.	5	"	All Battery having finished at Ridge Bty moved to new Battery Position	
"	6	"	ditto	
"	7	"	ditto	
"	8	"	ditto	
"	9	"	Remainder of Battery arrived from Rew?	
"	10	"	Received Orders at Gaza	
"	11	"	ditto	
"	12	"	ditto	
"	13	"	ditto	
"	14	"	moved from Gaza to Jolly — H.Q. & b Sub arrived	
Jolly Howash	15	"	to Jolly Hor C/28 Lt 90cms. Coy. R.E.	
"	16	"	have from Jolly Hts to Lt 90 cms. Coy. R.E.	

Army Form C. 2118.

WAR DIARY
or
INTELLIGENCE SUMMARY.

(Erase heading not required.)

Place	Date	Hour	Summary of Events and Information	Remarks and references to Appendices
Antreux	Dec 10 1917		December 1917.	
"	11		Shekleton & Gen Cleaning	
"	12		ditto	
"	13		ditto	
"	21		ditto	
"	22		ditto	
"	23		ditto	
"	24		ditto	
"	25		Church Parade. ditto	
"	26		ditto	
"	27		ditto	
"	28		ditto	
"	29		ditto	
"	30		ditto	
"	31		heavy body for Bapaume	

Army Form C. 2118.

WAR DIARY
or
INTELLIGENCE SUMMARY.

No. Z/19 J 96 B4 B.A.

(Erase heading not required.)

Place	Date	Hour	Summary of Events and Information	Remarks and references to Appendices
Brien Deponist	30/4		Attached to 1/64 Brigade Wagon Line for Duty	
			Inspection by R.P.A. 19th Division	
			Attached to 1/64 Brigade Wagon Line for Duty	
			Shunt to Billets Division It am kaput	
			Attached to 1/64 Brigade Wagon line for Duty	
Mons loaff			Moved to Billets in old time layed	
			Battery Parade	
			Swallowed for December bill Major 2/17 for	
			Arrive KAPAUNE - ROUGOIGNY Commanding	
			thence Z/19 J M B	

WAR DIARY
or
INTELLIGENCE SUMMARY.
(Erase heading not required.)

Army Form C. 2118.

19 D TM Bty
951 7

"WW"1719
HEAVY TRENCH
MORTAR BATTERY.

Place	Date	Hour	Summary of Events and Information	Remarks and references to Appendices
	Jan. 1918			
Roquiny Camp	1		Detrained at BAPAUME; marched to Roquiny Camp	
	2			
	3		Marched to Camp in HAVRINCOURT WOOD	
Havrincourt Wood	4		Battery Parade	
"	5		"	
"	6		"	
"	7		Right Section went into the Line	
"	8			
"	9			Digging gun positions
"	10			
"	11			
"	12			
"	13			
"	14		Left Section relieve Right Section	
"	15			
"	16			

Army Form C. 2118.

WAR DIARY
or
INTELLIGENCE SUMMARY.
(Erase heading not required.)

"W"/19 HEAVY TRENCH MORTAR BATTERY.

Place	Date	Hour	Summary of Events and Information	Remarks and references to Appendices
HARINCOURT WOOD	Jan. 1918 17			
"	18			
"	19			
"	20			
"	21			
"	22		Right Section relieves Left Section	
"	23		⎫	
"	24		⎬ Digging Gun positions	
"	25		⎪	
"	26		⎭	
"	27			
"	28			
"	29		Left Section relieves right Section	
"	30			
"	31		Casualties during month:– T.O.R. slightly wounded	

A.W. Odd
2/Lt RFA

Army Form C. 2118.

WAR DIARY
or
INTELLIGENCE SUMMARY
(Erase heading not required.)

Instructions regarding War Diaries and Intelligence Summaries are contained in F. S. Regs., Part II. and the Staff Manual respectively. Title Pages will be prepared in manuscript.

Place	Date	Hour	Summary of Events and Information	Remarks and references to Appendices
	January 1916			
			Entrained at Bordon	
			Arrived at Havre & marched to Rest Camp	
		10am	Battery paraded	
			Marched out of Camp to New Camp or entraining at Havre	

Digging gun emplacements & laying of Fire Plan.
Cancelled for today.
2/Lt R.A. Phillips N.A.
W.H.A. Ptt
J. Nat Of.

Army Form C. 2118.

WAR DIARY
or
INTELLIGENCE SUMMARY

Y.19 T.M. B+y

(Erase heading not required.)

Instructions regarding War Diaries and Intelligence Summaries are contained in F. S. Regs., Part II. and the Staff Manual respectively. Title pages will be prepared in manuscript.

Place	Date	Hour	Summary of Events and Information	Remarks and references to Appendices
	3/12 – 7/12 17/12		Month of January	
Roquigny	1-1-18		Entrained at Bailleul Nord	
	2		Arrived at Bapaume & marched to Roquigny Camp	
	3		Battery Parade	
	4	10 AM	Handed in B Camp to and camp at in stores went O.7.7.9L	
Hurtrecourt	4			
	5			
	6			
	7			
	8			
	9		Bagging themselves changing clothes & taking up gun	
	10		positions.	
	11		Gun mountings.	
	12			
	13			
	14			
	15			

Army Form C. 2118.

WAR DIARY
or
INTELLIGENCE SUMMARY.
(Erase heading not required.)

Place	Date	Hour	Summary of Events and Information	Remarks and references to Appendices
Hounslow	16			
	17			
	18			
	19			
	20			
	21			
	22			
	23			
	24			
	25		Boxing day. Inspected & telegraph to Command	
	26			
	27			
	28			
	29		Casualties for January Nil	
	30			
	31			

Army Form C. 2118.

Z/19 Howitzer Battery.

WAR DIARY
or
INTELLIGENCE SUMMARY.

(Erase heading not required.)

Instructions regarding War Diaries and Intelligence Summaries are contained in F. S. Regs., Part II. and the Staff Manual respectively. Title pages will be prepared in manuscript.

Place	Date	Hour	Summary of Events and Information	Remarks and references to Appendices
St Tarsapal	31/12/17 1/1/18		Entrained at Bailleul.	
Rocquigny	1/1/18		Arrived Bapaume marched to Rocquigny Camp.	
	2/1/18		Battery Parades.	
	3/1/18	10 A.M.	Marched out of Camp into new Camp in Havrincourt Wood.	
Havrincourt Wood	4/1/18		} Digging for emplacements & taking up position near Havrincourt.	
	5			
	6			
	7			
	8			
	9			
	10			
	11			
	12			
	13			
	14			
	15			
	16			
	17			
	18			
	19			
	20			
	21			
	22			
	23			

Army Form C. 2118.

WAR DIARY

of Z/19 Trench Mortar Battery

INTELLIGENCE SUMMARY.

(Erase heading not required.)

Place	Date	Hour	Summary of Events and Information	Remarks and references to Appendices
Marricourt Wood	24/1/18		Digging pits, emplacements, watching of guns & ammunition.	
	25			
	26			
	27			
	28			
	29			
	30		Casualties for January 1918 Nil.	

J.H. Heazy Lewis Lieut. R.H.A.
Commanding Z/19 Trench Mortar Battery

WAR DIARY
or
INTELLIGENCE SUMMARY

(Erase heading not required.)

Army Form C. 2118.

19 D TM Bty
L.F.L.S

Place	Date	Hour	Summary of Events and Information	Remarks and references to Appendices
HAVRINCOURT WOOD	February 1st-7th		Completion of digging work in Gunpits and making of Ammunition Recesses	
"	7th		Right Section relieved Left Section	
"	8th-15th		Resetting of Pits and completion of beds. Two 6 Inch Newton guns put into Action and connecting trench dug levelled and covered to connect pits to Fork Avenue	
"	15th		Relieved in Line by X.63 T.M.Bty. Personnel in line marched back to HAVRINCOURT WOOD.	
MONTIGNY	16th		Moved in motor lorries to MONTIGNY 14 Kilometres N.E. by E. of AMIENS	
"	17th		Details for reorganization arranged.	
"	18th		19/19 H T M Bty disbanded and personnel formed into X/19 6" Newton TMBty	
"	19th to 28th		Reclothing and training	Numbers to R.F.A. to RysMBys

Army Form C. 2118.

WAR DIARY
or
INTELLIGENCE SUMMARY.
(Erase heading not required.)

Place	Date	Hour	Summary of Events and Information	Remarks and references to Appendices
MONTIGNY	19th to 28th		Redrilling and training personnel of the late 20/19 A.T.M. Bty in the use of the 6" Newton Trench Mortar. Aviation W.R.F.A X/19 T.M. Bty.	in the

Army Form C. 2118.

WAR DIARY
INTELLIGENCE SUMMARY X 19 Y.M. Battery
(Erase heading not required.)

FEBRUARY / 1918

Instructions regarding War Diaries and Intelligence Summaries are contained in F. S. Regs., Part II. and the Staff Manual respectively. Title Pages will be prepared in manuscript.

Place	Date	Hour	Summary of Events and Information	Remarks and references to Appendices
HAVRINCOURT WOOD	1		1 N.L.O. & 2 men in trues with "Z" Battery. Remainder of Battery - Battery Parade.	
"	2			
"	3			
"	4			
"	5			
"	6			
"	7			
"	8			
"	9		2 N.L.O. - 3 men in the lines with Y Battery. Remainder of Battery. Battery Parade.	
"	10			
"	11			
"	12			
"	13			
"	14			
"	15			
"	16			
"	17		Moved from HAVRINCOURT WOOD to rest billets in MONTIGNY	
MONTIGNY	18	10am	Battery Parade. Reorganization of Medium T M Batteries. "A" personnel transferred to "Y" Bty. Casualties for February:- One. N. Gunner wounded. Bombardier F Rook 1x/19	

2449 Wt. W14957/M90 750,000 1/16 J.B.C. & A. Forms/C.2118/22.

WAR DIARY
or
INTELLIGENCE SUMMARY.

FEBRUARY / 1918 of X/19 T.M.B.

Army Form C. 2118.

Place	Date	Hour	Summary of Events and Information	Remarks and references to Appendices
HAVRINCOURT WOOD	1st Feb	6.30am	In Regt billets — Battery Parades.	
"	2	"		
"	3	"	Capt. Lamb awarded Belgian Croix de Guerre.	
"	4	"		
"	5	"		
"	6	9.0"	Battery proceeded to the line for 9 days under X Bty Officer	
"	7			
"	8		Work — Construction of Emplacements & manning guns in Action.	
"	9			
"	10			
"	11			
"	12			
"	13			
"	14		Relieved by 63rd Division. T.M. Personnel.	
"	15		Moved from HAVRINCOURT WOOD to rest billets in MONTIGNY	
"	16			

WAR DIARY
or
INTELLIGENCE SUMMARY.

Y/19 T.M.B.

FEBRUARY/1918

Army Form C. 2118.

Place	Date	Hour	Summary of Events and Information	Remarks and references to Appendices
MONTIGNY	17	9.0 a.m	Battery Parades	
"	18		Reorganization of Medium T.M. Batteries	F.A. Personnel of "X" & "Y" Jones
"	19	6.30 a.m	" " "	1 N.C.O. 2 men to 3rd Army T.M. School
"	20	"		
"	21	"		
"	22	"		
"	23	"		
"	24	"	Battery Parade.	
"	25	"		
"	26	"		
"	27	"		
"	28	"	Casualties for February. Nil.	1 R.A.A. Y/19 T.M.B. Donaghmore Lt

Army Form C. 2118.

WAR DIARY
INTELLIGENCE SUMMARY

Z 19 T. M. Battery

(Erase heading not required.)

FEBRUARY 1915

Place	Date	Hour	Summary of Events and Information	Remarks and references to Appendices
HAVRINCOURT WOOD	2		Construction of Emplacements & manning guns in action	
"	3			
"	4			
"	5			
"	6	6.30am	Relieved by Y 19 T.M.B	
"	7			
"	8			
"	9			
"	10		L' Rest Billets - Battery Parades	
"	11			
"	12			
"	13			
"	14			
"	15			
"	16			
MONTIGNY	17		Moved from HAVRINCOURT WOOD to rest billets - MONTIGNY	
"	18	9.0am	Battery Parades	
"			Reorganization of Medium T.M Batteries. Z.A. personnel transferred to Y/19 T.M.B. Remainder for Heavies - Not on approved [?] for approval 22/2/19

2449 Wt. W14957/M90 750,000 1/16 J.B.C. & A. Forms/C.2118/12.

Army Form C. 2118.

WAR DIARY
or
~~INTELLIGENCE SUMMARY.~~
(Erase heading not required.)

X/19 T.M. Battery

Place	Date	Hour	Summary of Events and Information	Remarks and references to Appendices
MONTIGNY	Mar 1st & 2nd		At rest.	
"	3rd		Moved to SALAMANCA CAMP on HAPLINCOURT — BARASTRE Road.	
SALAMANCA CAMP	4th		Relieved 47th Div T.Ms in HERMIES — HAVRINCOURT — TRESCAULT — METZ positions.	
"	5th		H.Q. Camp moved to HAVRINCOURT WOOD.	
HAVRINCOURT WOOD	6th to 20th		Worked on defensive positions & all mortars took no action.	
"	21st		Stand to all day but no action.	
"	22nd	2 pm	Fired 6 rounds at enemy from gun at J.30.a.90.50	
		2.30 pm	Handed HERMIES mortars over to 17th Div T.M's.	
		4 pm	Fired 36 rounds from mortar at K.27.d.85.25. M.G. Observation owing to mist. Rounds fired at report of 0 infantry.	
"	23rd	10 am	Withdrew 2 mortars from TRESCAULT by order of 63rd D.A.	
		3 "	" 2 mortars " HAVRINCOURT " " "	

Army Form C. 2118.

WAR DIARY
or
INTELLIGENCE SUMMARY. Continued

(Erase heading not required.)

Place	Date	Hour	Summary of Events and Information	Remarks and references to Appendices
HAVRINCOURT WOOD	23rd	6am	Moved Camp to NEVILLE	
		10.30am	" " BARASTRE + stood to all night with 88th Brigade RFA.	
	24th	6am	Moved to MIRAUMONT under orders 63rd D.A.	
	25th	9am	Moved to MAILLY MAILLET + thence to LEAVILLERS	
	26th		At LEAVILLERS — attached to 63rd DAC for rations	
	27th	3pm	Moved to HALLOY	
	28th		at HALLOY	
	29th			
	30th	8.30am	Moved to AUBROMETZ	
	31st	11am	Moved to PETIT. HOUVIN + remained there all day loading vehicles of 19th D.A. on to train	
			Casualties 5 O.R. wounded	

W Marsh Capt RFA
x/149 TMB?

19th Divisional Artillery.

X/19 TRENCH MORTAR BATTERY

APRIL 1918.

Army Form C. 2118.

X/198 T.M. Batty

WAR DIARY
or
INTELLIGENCE SUMMARY.

(Erase heading not required.)

Place	Date	Hour	Summary of Events and Information	Remarks and references to Appendices
PETIT HOUVIN	April 1	6.30 am	Entrained at PETIT HOUVIN; detrained at GODWAERSVELDE and marched to GRAND SEC BOIS	
GRAND SEC BOIS	2		Moved Camp at WULVERGHEM and took over from 2nd Australian T.M.B's on the MESSINES Sector.	
WULVERGHEM	3		Work on gun positions in the Line.	
"	4			
"	5			
"	6			
"	7			
"	8			
"	9			
"	10		Enemy attacked advances as far as MESSINES. Our two officers in charge of mortars in action and their detachments are all missing & are presumed to be either killed or prisoners of war. Remainder of battery proceed from Wagon Line Reserve to all day in full battery area & reverted to 88th F.A.B	

Army Form C. 2118.

WAR DIARY
or
INTELLIGENCE SUMMARY. (Continued)
(Erase heading not required.)

Place	Date	Hour	Summary of Events and Information	Remarks and references to Appendices
WULVERGHEM	April 11		Moved to BULLER CAMP at BRULOOZE CORNER.	
BULLER CAMP	12		Work on dumps at BRULOOZE SIDING and LOCRE	
-	13		Moved to TRALEE LINES, LOCRE. Work on DUMP at LOCRE	
LOCRE	14		Work on dumps at LOCRE	
-	15		Moved into camp on the KEMMEL – LA CLYTE Road	
-			Work on LA CLYTE Dumps	
LA CLYTE	16		Moved to LA CLYTE. Work on LA CLYTE Dumps	
OUDERDOM	17		Moved to OUDERDOM, Work on dumps at OUDERDOM	
-	18		Work on dumps at OUDERDOM	
-	19			
-	20		Moved to HEKSKEN CORNER on RENINGHELST – ABEELE ROAD	
HEKSKEN	21		Work on HEKSKEN Dump.	
-	22			
-	23		Work on HEKSKEN Dump.	
-	24			
-	25			

Army Form C. 2118.

WAR DIARY
or
INTELLIGENCE SUMMARY. Continued

(Erase heading not required.)

Place	Date	Hour	Summary of Events and Information	Remarks and references to Appendices
	1918 April			
HEKSKEN	26		Moved to HILHOEK, N. of ABEELE, POPERINGHE Road.	Work
HILHOEK	27		on dump at HILHOEK	
	28		Work in dump at HILHOEK	
HILHOEK	29		Moved to RAECQUINGHEM, near ST.OMER	
RAECQUINGHEM	30		BATTERY PARADED.	
			Casualties during APRIL :-	
			2 officers - Missing.	
			17 ORs - Missing	
			7 ORs - Wounded.	
			J.J. Doull	
			2nd Lieut R.F.A.	
			X/19th Trench Mortar Battery	

19th Divisional Artillery.

Y/19 TRENCH MORTAR BATTERY

APRIL 1918.

WAR DIARY or INTELLIGENCE SUMMARY

Army Form C. 2118.

X/19 Trench Mortar Battery

APRIL / 1918

Place	Date	Hour	Summary of Events and Information	Remarks and references to Appendices
THEVENT	1	9.30 a.m.	Entrained at Thevent. Detrained at Caestre, proceeded by March route to GRAND SEC BOIS.	
GRAND SEC BOIS	2	9.0 "	Moved to Camp at Wulverghem.	
	3			
WULVERGHEM	4		Battery Parades.	
	5			
	6			
	7			
"	8		Took over from X/9 T.M.B. on OOSTAVERNE Sector, moved camp to GRAND BOIS. Work on gun positions.	
GRAND BOIS	9			
	10	2 p.m.	After heavy bombardment the enemy attacked. No.1 Gun was put out of action by direct hit, two later blown up by detachment. No.2 Gun was brought into action. Ammunition expended at the advancing enemy with good effect. This gun was also destroyed to prevent falling into the enemy's hands. The detachment for No.3 Gun were unable to reach the Emplacement owing to M.G. & Rifle fire, the officer in charge being wounded in the attempt. Owing to heavy and accurate fire from hostile guns at Nos. 4, 5, & 6 Guns were able to retreat, these too close to bring these guns into action, without being observed by detachment. No. 7 Gun was destroyed. 5 Light Clynometers were lost.	

2449 Wt. W14957/M90 750,000 1/16 J.B.C. & A. Forms/C.2118/12.

Army Form C. 2118.

WAR DIARY
or
INTELLIGENCE SUMMARY

(Erase heading not required.)

1/19 French Mortar Battery

APRIL 1918

Place	Date	Hour	Summary of Events and Information	Remarks and references to Appendices
GRAND BOIS	10	7 p.m.	Moved to Bullers Camp near BRULOOZE.	
BULLER CAMP	11		Work on ammunition dumps at BRULOOZE Siding & LOCRE.	
"	12		Moved to JRALEE Lines — LOCRE. Work on Dumps at Brulooze Locre &ctal.	
"	13	9 a.m.	ditto do. do.	
LOCRE	14	"	Moved to Camp on LA CLYTE — KEMMEL Road. Work on Dump at LACLYTE.	
"	15	"	Moved to LA'CLYTE	ditto
LA/CLYTE	16	"	Moved to OUDERDOM. Work on Dump at Ouderdom.	
"	17			
OUDERDOM	18		Work on dump at OUDERDOM	
"	19		Moved to HEKSKEN CORNER on the RENINGHELST — ABEELE Road.	
"	20	9.0 a.m.	Moved to HEKSKEN near OUDERDOM.	
HEKSKEN	21		Work on dump at HEKSKEN	
"	22			
"	23			
"	24			
"	25			
"	26	11 a.m.	Moved to Camp at HILHOEK on ABEELE — POPERINGHE Road.	
HILHOEK	27		Work on dump at HILHOEK	
"	28			CASUALTIES:-
"	29			1 Officer }
"	29	9.15 a.m.	Moved to RACQUINGHEM.	1 O.R. } wounded.
"	30			

J. Vaughan
for O.C. 1/19 Tr. M.B.

WAR DIARY of INTELLIGENCE SUMMARY

Army Form C. 2118.

Y/19 Trench Mortar Battery

Place	Date	Hour	Summary of Events and Information	Remarks and references to Appendices
MONTIGNY	1st Aug/18		At rest	
"	2 "		"	
"	3 "		Moved to Salamanca Camp on Bapaume - Maplincourt Road	
Salamanca Camp	4 "		Relieved 47th Div. T.M.Bs. in METZ – TRESCOURT – HAVRINCOURT – HERMIES defensive positions.	
"	5 "		Headquarters Camp moved to HAVRINCOURT WOOD	
HAVRINCOURT WOOD	20 "		Work on defensive positions & all mortars put in action.	
"	21 "		Stand to all day but no action	
"	22 "	10.30 pm	Fired 50 Rounds at enemy from No 2 Gun at K.28.a.15.80. No observation owing to mist. Fired at request of Infantry.	
			No 4 Gun at K.22.c.55.25 but charge destroyed, as owing to withdrawal in the night 21/22nd this position was about 300x in front of our line. The gun could not be fired as our infantry still held the line this position covered.	
		12 Noon	Fired further 50 Rounds from No 2 Gun at K28a 15.80 at request of infantry. Too much mist for observation	
	23 "		Evacuated HAVRINCOURT – METZ by order of C.R.A. 63rd Div. No 2 Gun withdrawn from HAVRINCOURT at 3 A.M. Beds destroyed. Three guns withdrawn from METZ at 11 A.M. Beds destroyed. Moved to NEUVILLE.	

WAR DIARY

Y/19 Trench Mortar Battery

Army Form C. 2118.

(Erase heading not required.)

Place	Date	Hour	Summary of Events and Information	Remarks and references to Appendices
NEUVILLE	23 Aug/18	10.30am	Moved to BARASTRE, & stood to all night with 88th Brigade!	
BARASTRE	24 "	6 am	Moved to MIRAUMONT under orders C.R.A 63rd Div.	
MIRAUMONT	25 "	9 am	Moved to MAIZY/MAIZZET & thence to IZEL/VIZZERS.	
IZEL/VIZZERS	26 "		At IZEL/VIZZERS. Attached 63rd D.A.C for rations	
"	27 "	3 pm	Moved to HAZZOY.	
HAZZOY	28/29 "		At HAZZOY.	
"	30 "	8.30 am	Moved to AUBROMETZ.	
AUBROMETZ	31 "	10/15	Moved to PREVENT. Loaded vehicles of 19th DIV. ARTY. on to trains	
			Casualties. 3 furnes killed at METZ	
			2 " Wounded.	

M.K Heazy Capt. R.F.A
Commanding Y/19 Trench Mortar Battery

X/19 T.M Battery WAR DIARY or INTELLIGENCE SUMMARY

Army Form C. 2118.

X/19
TRENCH MORTAR
BATTERY

Instructions regarding War Diaries and Intelligence Summaries are contained in F.S. Regs., Part II. and the Staff Manual respectively. Title pages will be prepared in manuscript.

Place	Date	Hour	Summary of Events and Information	Remarks and references to Appendices
DOMINGHEM	12 1918	9.30 am	Fatigues to 83rd Brigade R.F.A.	
	13.14.15.16		In training	
	17	6 am	In training	
ROUEN	18	7.30 pm	Entrained at VIREY-LA-VILLE and marched to camp at VROIL	
AMBRIEF	19		Relieved to 83rd Brigade R.F.A.	
	20		Training & refitment of guns & Trench Mortars	
	27		Training & refitment of guns & Trench Mortars	
BISSUEL	28		Moved to camp at BISSUEL	
NANTEUIL	29		Moved to camp in the trench at NANTEUIL	
DAMERY	30		Moved to camp in the trench at DAMERY	
	31		At DAMERY	

No Boche Army. A/c Bdr R.F.A. awarded the M.M.M.G. / 142 SA. 27th May, 1918.

Casualties for week of May Nil

J.C. Ansley Captain R.F.A.
For Commanding X/19 Bn Batty.

Army Form C. 2118.

WAR DIARY
or
INTELLIGENCE SUMMARY   V 19 Trench Mortar Battery R.A.
(Erase heading not required.)

MAY, 1916

Instructions regarding War Diaries and Intelligence Summaries are contained in F.S. Regs., Part II. and the Staff Manual respectively. Title Pages will be prepared in manuscript.

Place	Date	Hour	Summary of Events and Information	Remarks and references to Appendices
RACQUINGHEM	May 1 to May 13	4.30 am	Fatigues for 66th F.A. Brigade	
"	May 14		Preparing for entraining	
ARQUES	" 18	8.0 am	Arrived at ARQUES	
DAMPIERRE	" 19	4.30 pm	Detrained at VITRY-LA-VILLE and marched to Sandy at DAMPIERRE	
"	" 21		Fatigues for 66th F.A. Brigade	
"	" 25		Training reinforcements & "Stokes" Trench Mortar	
BISSUEL	" 26		Marched to Camp at BISSUEL	
NANTEUIL	" 29		" " " in vicinity of NANTEUIL	
DAMERY	" 30		" " " " DAMERY	
"	" 31		At DAMERY	
	May 29		2nd Lt. G.W. Ayrmash, R.F.A. awarded Military Medal	
			Casualties for May — Nil	

Lt Col ? J? Infantry
A.A. & Q.M.G. 19 F.M. Battery R.A.

Army Form C. 2118.

WAR DIARY
or
INTELLIGENCE SUMMARY.

(Erase heading not required.) X/19 Trench Mortar Battery.

Place	Date	Hour	Summary of Events and Information	Remarks and references to Appendices
VAUCHELLES	June 1st		At Vauchelles has Davery	965/2
"	2nd		"	
"	3rd		6 O.R's attached to D.a.c. 1 O.R. attached 88 F.a.b.	
"			and 1 man attached 88 F.a.B.	
"	4th Pm		moved to Vaudancourt	
VAUDANCOURT	5th		At Vaudancourt	
"	6th		"	
"	7th		"	
"	8th		2nd Lieut Roots attached 171 S.a.C.	
"	9th		At Vaudancourt	
"	10th		"	
"	11th		"	
"	12th		"	
"	13th		"	

Army Form C. 2118.

WAR DIARY
or
INTELLIGENCE SUMMARY.

(Erase heading not required.)

2/1? R.B (Continued)

Place	Date	Hour	Summary of Events and Information	Remarks and references to Appendices
VAUDANCOURT	June 16		At Vaudancourt	
"	17		"	
"	18		"	
"	19		"	
"	20	8.30a	Moved to camp in vicinity of VERTUS	
VERTUS	21	10a	Bannes 15th reported for Eq. and 1 Off. for 82 R?B	
BANNES	22		At Bannes	
"	23		"	
"	24		"	
"	25		Mess and tea reported for 17 N.A.C	
"	26		Gallery Parade	
"	27		"	
"	28		"	
"	29		and preparing to entraining	
"	30		Casualties to June - Nil	

Casualties to June - Nil
L.R.Watts Lieut R.G.A
Commdg 2/17 R.G. Battery

Army Form C. 2118.

WAR DIARY
or
INTELLIGENCE SUMMARY

(Erase heading not required.)

of 1 9/19 Trench Mortar Battery R.A.

JUNE 1918

Place	Date	Hour	Summary of Events and Information	Remarks and references to Appendices
DAMERY	June 1		At Damery. 56059 Cpl A.J. Smith B.T.M. & 84510 Gr R. Mortimer R.F.A. awarded Military Medal.	
"	" 2		At Damery.	
"	" 3		1 N.C.O. + 5 men to No 3 Section 19th D.A.C. for fatigues	
"	" 4	8.0 am	Moved to VAUDANCOURT	
VAUDANCOURT	" 5		At " 85185 Bdr Burdon W.P.F.A. awarded D.C.M.	
"	" 6		"	
"	" 7		1 N.C.O. and 6 men to No 1 Section, 19th D.A.C. for fatigues	
"	" 8		" 9 " " " D.A.C.	
"	" 9		At Vaudancourt	
"	" 10		"	
"	" 11		"	
"	" 12		"	
"	" 13		"	
"	" 14		"	
"	" 15		"	
"	" 16		"	
"	" 17		"	
"	" 18		"	
"	" 19		"	

Army Form C. 2118.

WAR DIARY
or
INTELLIGENCE SUMMARY of Y/19 Trench Mortar Battery R.A.

(Erase heading not required.)

Instructions regarding War Diaries and Intelligence Summaries are contained in F. S. Regs., Part II. and the Staff Manual respectively. Title Pages will be prepared in manuscript.

Place	Date	Hour	Summary of Events and Information	Remarks and references to Appendices
VAUDANCOURT	June 20	8.30am	Moved from Vaudancourt to camp in vicinity of VERTUS	
VERTUS	" 21	10.0 "	" " " Vertus to BANNES	
BANNES	" 22		Officers reported from 19th D.A.C.	
	" 23		At Bannes. 342316 Spl W Shadock P.y.A. awarded M.S.M.	
	" 24		" "	
	" 25		Fatigue Parties reported from R.A. &	
	" 26		Battery Parades	
	" 27		" "	
	" 28		" "	
	" 29		Preparations for entraining at Mailly le Camp.	
	30		Casualties for June - NIL	

J. Ampleronew
Commanding Y/19 T.M. Battery R.A.

X/19
TRENCH MORTAR BATTERY.

Army Form C. 2118.

WAR DIARY
or
INTELLIGENCE SUMMARY.
(Erase heading not required.)

of X/19 Trench Mortar Battery

July 1918

Vol 13

Place	Date	Hour	Summary of Events and Information	Remarks and references to Appendices
BANNES	1st	3am	Marched to SOMMESOUS	
"	"	7am	Entrained at SOMMESOUS	
ANVIN	2nd	6pm	Detrained at ANVIN and marched to FORESTEL	
FORESTEL	3rd		Cleaning Guns, Stores, Equipment etc	
"	4th		Interior Training	
"	5th		"	
"	6th		"	
"	7th		"	
"	8th		"	
"	9th		"	
"	10th		"	
"	11th		"	
"	12th		"	
PEBVIN	13th		Guns moved by Motor Lorry to PEBVIN-PALFART	
PALFART	14th		Cleaning of Equipment	
"	15th		"	

Army Form C. 2118.

WAR DIARY
or
INTELLIGENCE SUMMARY.
(Erase heading not required.)

X/10 TRENCH MORTAR BATTERY

July 1918. Activities

Place	Date	Hour	Summary of Events and Information	Remarks and references to Appendices
REBREUVE	16"		Intensive Training	
DALRAST	17"		"	
	18"		"	
	19"		"	
	20"		"	
	21"	Just	Moved to Billets at GROEUPPE	
GROEUPPE	22"		Intensive Training	
	23"		"	
	24"		"	
	25"		"	
	26"		"	
	27"		"	Casualties for July — Nil.
	28"		"	
	29"		"	
	30"		"	W Tonks
	31"		"	Captain PPCLI Commanding X/10 T.M. Battery

WAR DIARY
INTELLIGENCE SUMMARY

of 2/19 Y.M. Battery

Army Form C. 2118.

(Erase heading not required.)

JULY 1915

Place	Date	Hour	Summary of Events and Information	Remarks and references to Appendices
MAILLY-LE-CAMP	1	3.30pm	Entrained at Mailly-le-Camp	
HESDIN	2	11.0 pm	Detrained at HESDIN and marched to Pouvreuville	
GRAND-MANILLET	3	9.30 am	Marched to billets at Grand-Manillet	
"	4	"	Cleaning & equipment	
"	5	5.30 am	"	
"	6	"	"	
"	7	"	Intensive training	
"	8	"	"	
"	9	"	"	
"	10	"	"	
"	11	"	"	
"	12	"	"	
FEBVIN-PALFART	13	7.15 am	Moved by Motor lorry to Febvin Palfart	
"	14	5.30 am	Cleaning & equipment	
"	15	"	"	
"	16	"	Intensive training	
"	17	"	"	

WAR DIARY
INTELLIGENCE SUMMARY

of B/192 T.M Battery

JULY 1918

Army Form C. 2118.

Place	Date	Hour	Summary of Events and Information	Remarks and references to Appendices
FEBVIN-PALFART	16	5.30 a.m	Intensive training	
"	19	"	"	
"	20	"	"	
"	21	9.45 a.m	Moved to Billets at GROEUPPE	
GROEUPPE	22	5.30 a.m	Intensive training	
"	23	"	"	
"	24	"	"	
"	25	"	"	
"	27	"	"	
"	28	"	"	
"	29	"	"	
"	30	"	"	
"	31	"	Casualties — NIL	

D. Hutchinson
Lieut R.F.A.
Comdg B/192 T.M. Battery

Army Form C. 2118.

WAR DIARY
or
INTELLIGENCE SUMMARY.

(Erase heading not required.)

X/19 TRENCH MORTAR BATTERY.

X/19 Trench Mortar Battery

O.M. Lief

Place	Date	Hour	Summary of Events and Information	Remarks and references to Appendices
GROEUPRE	1st		Interior Training	
	2nd		"	
	3rd		"	
	4th		"	
	5th		"	
	6th	2.30am	Moved by Motor Lorry to CHOCQUES and relieved X/3 Trench Mortar Battery in the line (HINGES Sector)	
CHOCQUES	7th		Training defensive position	
	8th		"	
	9th		"	
	10th		"	
	11th		"	
	12th		"	
	13th		"	
	14th		"	
	15th		"	

WAR DIARY
or
INTELLIGENCE SUMMARY.

Army Form C. 2118.

X/19 TRENCH MORTAR BATTERY.

Continued

Place	Date	Hour	Summary of Events and Information	Remarks and references to Appendices
CHOQUES	16		Training defensive position	
"	17		"	
"	18		"	
"	19		"	
"	20		"	
"	21		"	
"	22		"	
"	23		"	
"	24		"	
"	25		Digging new position at HINGETTE and reinforcing position	
"	26		"	
"	27		"	
"	28		"	
"	29		"	
"	30		"	
"	31		Moved out of Coln. Withdrawn to new position. Twenty Yack 6 Casualties. 10 August. Killed, 2nd Lieut Jno SHROPEY P.O.R., 2 O.R. Sick. Job. Corpn. 2/Lieut R H Collin wounded (Gas)	

WAR DIARY
INTELLIGENCE SUMMARY of 2/19 Trench Mortar Battery R.A.

AUGUST, 1916

Army Form C. 2118.

Place	Date	Hour	Summary of Events and Information	Remarks and references to Appendices
GROEUPPE	Aug 1	8:30 am	Intensive training	
"	" 2	"		
"	" 3	"		
"	" 4	"		
"	" 5	"		
"	" 6	7:30 am	Moved by Motor lorry to CHOCQUES	
"	" 7	4:0 pm	Relieved 3rd Div. 2 M Batteries in defensive positions	
CHOCQUES	" 8			
"	" 9			
"	" 10			
"	" 11			
"	" 12			
"	" 13			
"	" 14		Manning defensive positions in HINGES LeFt	
"	" 15			
"	" 16			
"	" 17			
"	" 18			
"	" 19			
"	" 20			
"	" 21			
"	" 22			

Army Form C. 2118.

WAR DIARY
INTELLIGENCE SUMMARY of 1 5/9 Trench Mortar Battery R.A

(Erase heading not required.)

AUGUST, 1916

Instructions regarding War Diaries and Intelligence Summaries are contained in F.S. Regs., Part II. and the Staff Manual respectively. Title Pages will be prepared in manuscript.

Place	Date	Hour	Summary of Events and Information	Remarks and references to Appendices
CHOCQUES	Aug 23		Manning defensive positions	
"	24			
"	25			
"	26			
"	27		Digging new positions at LES HARISOIRS	
"	28			
"	29		Owing to withdrawal of enemy Mortars out of action Mortars	
"	30		withdrawn from positions & brought back to Billets at CHOCQUES	
"	31		Casualties for August - NIL	

D. Cavanagh Lieut R.A.
Commander 1 5/9 T.M Battery R.A.

Army Form C. 2118.

WAR DIARY
INTELLIGENCE SUMMARY

of Y/19 Trench Mortar Battery R.A.

SEPTEMBER 1918

Y/19 TRENCH MORTAR BATTERY, R.A.

Place	Date	Hour	Summary of Events and Information	Remarks and references to Appendices
CHOCQUES	Sept 1 to 9		Removing Mortars from defensive positions to Waggon lines	
"	9		Personnel attached to D.A.C. and Field Batteries carrying ammunition	
"	10		Parties reported	
"	11		2 Mobile Mortars put in action on Right sector. Wire cutting	
"	12	10. a.m	Waggon lines moved to BETHUNE	
BETHUNE	13		At Waggon lines	
"	14		Wire cutting	
"	15	3.45 p.m 5 p.m		
"	16	6 a.m	Taking ammunition at old defensive positions	
"	17	"		
"	18	"		
"	19			
"	20		2 Mobile Mortars put in action on Left sector	
"	21 22		Constructing ammunition recesses	

Army Form C. 2118.

WAR DIARY
or
INTELLIGENCE SUMMARY

Y/19 TRENCH MORTAR BATTERY, R.A.

of Y/19 Trench Mortar Battery R.A.

SEPTEMBER 1916

(Erase heading not required.)

Instructions regarding War Diaries and Intelligence Summaries are contained in F. S. Regs., Part II. and the Staff Manual respectively. Title Pages will be prepared in manuscript.

Place	Date	Hour	Summary of Events and Information	Remarks and references to Appendices
BETHUNE	6/9/23	1/5:30 3:0	Wire cutting	
"	24	10:30 12/6:15		
"	25		Contacting ammunition recess	
"	26		Concentrations as ordered in 19 D.A. Order 230	
"	27			
"	28			
"	29		Casualties for September — NIL	
"	30			

J M Crummey
Lieut R.F.A.
Commanding Y/19 T.M. Batty R.A.

Army Form C. 2118.

WAR DIARY
or
INTELLIGENCE SUMMARY.
(Erase heading not required.)

X/19 TRENCH MORTAR BATTERY.

No. ....
Date ....

Place	Date	Hour	Summary of Events and Information	Remarks and references to Appendices
CHOCQUES	1st	—	Bivouac & Trench Mortar from detention position to Bethune at Chocques	
"	2nd	—	Personnel of Battery attached to B 88. Bde and 4th D.a.a. Bde for fatigues	
"	3rd	"	"	
"	4th	"	"	
"	5th	"	"	
"	6th	"	"	
"	7th	"	"	
"	8th	"	"	
"	9th	"	"	
"	10th	10am	Personnel of Battery return from B 88. Bde and 4th D.a.a Bde	
"	11th		Bivouac at Bethune	
"	12th			
BETHUNE	13th	3.20 & 3.30 am	were aiding with 6th & 7th W. Yorks	
"	14th		Carrying ammunition - preparing Gun positions and dug-out Battery 6th W. Yorks ammunition	

WAR DIARY
or
INTELLIGENCE SUMMARY.

Army Form C. 2118.

Sheet 2.

Place	Date	Hour	Summary of Events and Information	Remarks and references to Appendices
BETHUNE	15th	-	Carry up Ammunition - Preparing Gun Positions and dugouts	Saltsand
"	16th		6" H. Ammunition	
"	17th		"	
"	18th		"	
"	19th	9h 55a	Registration and wire cutting	
"	20th		Barrage Fire in front of SHEPPERDS REDOUBT & Ammenuli with infantry operation	
"	21st		Digging dugouts to Gun Detachments	
"	22nd		Registration on dugouts	
"	23rd		"	
"	24th		Digging dugouts to Gun Detachments	
"	25th	P.F.how	Fired on dugouts and front in SHEPPERDS REDOUBT Ammunition with infantry operation	
"	26th		Digging dugouts to Gun Detachments	
"	27th		"	

Army Form C. 2118.

WAR DIARY
or
INTELLIGENCE SUMMARY.
(Erase heading not required.)

Sheet 3.

Place	Date	Hour	Summary of Events and Information	Remarks and references to Appendices
BETHUNE	28	—	Two 6" Howitz French moved from Bray to left sector	
"	29		Reconnaissance	
"	30		Fired on posts in MAUDIN TRENCH in connection with infantry operations	
			" " "	
			Casualties during September 1915	
			Killed in action	
			Wounded "	
			" "	
			2 officers (Pomeroy & Dudley)	
			2 ORks	

J.M.W.
Captain R.F.A.
Commanding 2/1/9 I.L. Battery

Army Form C. 2118.

Y/19 TRENCH MORTAR BATTERY, R.A.

Battery R.A.

WAR DIARY
or
INTELLIGENCE=SUMMARY of Y/19 T.M. Battery R.A.
(Erase heading not required.)

October 1916

Place	Date	Hour	Summary of Events and Information	Remarks and references to Appendices
BÉTHUNE	Oct 1	07:30	Wire cutting in front of MOLLY TRENCH	
"	2	07:41	do Woon line	
"	3,4			
"	5	04:00	Moved by Motor Lorry to CHATEAU de LOISNÉ	
LOISNÉ	6		Wire cutting	
"	7		Reconnoitring positions for Public Mortars	
"	8,9			
"	10		Cleaning Guns and Dugout	
"	11		Mortars withdrawn from positions owing to withdrawal of enemy	
"	12			
"	13,14		Cleaning Guns and to agons	
"	15		Handing out to DTMO, 7th Division	
"	16			
"	17	07:00	Moved to CAOEUGRES	
		23:30	Moved to bamb.... arrived at hambrai	13:30 hours arrived at BAPAUME 23:30 hours
CAMBRAI	18	05:00		
"	19		Cleaning Guns	
"	20		Cleaning Guns	

Army Form C. 2118.

WAR DIARY
or
INTELLIGENCE SUMMARY Y/19 Trench Mortar Battery R.A.
(Erase heading not required.)   October 1918

Place	Date	Hour	Summary of Events and Information	Remarks and references to Appendices
CAMBRAI	Oct 21	11.15	Marched to AVESNES-LES-AUBERT.	
AVESNES-LES-AUBERT	22			
"	23			
"	24		Personnel working on Corps Dumps.	
"	25			
"	26			
"	27			
"	28		Personnel withdrawn from Dumps and attached to 22nd Bde R.F.A. for training.	
"	29		Personnel attached to 22nd Bde R.F.A.	
"	30			
"	31		Practice Field Day with 56th Infantry Brigade.	

Casualties for October — NIL.

J.R. Cumming Capt. R.F.A.
Cmdg Y/19 Trench Mortar Bty
R.A.

X/19
TRENCH MORTAR
Army Form C. 2118.

WAR DIARY of X/19 Trench Mortar Battery
or
INTELLIGENCE SUMMARY.
October 1918
(Erase heading not required.)

Place	Date	Hour	Summary of Events and Information	Remarks and references to Appendices
Arthur	1st		Preparing dug-outs for Gun Detachments	
"	2nd		"	
"	3rd		19 men attached to Rt group holding line	
"	4th		1 N.C.O. and 14 men attached to 2nd group for relieving C.H.A.	
"	5th	19.00	Moved to Billets near Chéru	
Loison	6		Fatigues for D.A. ammunition and ammunition collecting	
"	7		to	
"	8		to	
"	9		2 Mobile guns out of action brought back to Billets	
"	10		Guns and Waggon Cleaning. Wires collecting for R.E's	
"	11		2 Mobile guns on actor	
"	12		Registration on La Faux Ferme	
"	13		Owing to enemy retirement guns out of action Detachment returned to Billets	
"	14		Guns & Waggon Cleaning and Fatigues	
"	15		Handing over to 9th D.T.M.B.	
"	16		do	

Army Form C. 2118.

WAR DIARY
or
INTELLIGENCE SUMMARY. October 1918 Continued

(Erase heading not required.)

Instructions regarding War Diaries and Intelligence Summaries are contained in F. S. Regs., Part II. and the Staff Manual respectively. Title pages will be prepared in manuscript.

Place	Date	Hour	Summary of Events and Information	Remarks and references to Appendices
Lozinne	17	10.00	Marched to Bethune. Entrained at 15.00 hours. Arrived Bojeaume 23.30 hours	
Bojeaume	18	22.00	Marched to Billets at Cambrai	
Cambrai	19		Gun cleaning and fatigues	
"	20		Personnel working on Corps Dumps	
"	21	10.15	Moved to Billets at Awoingt les Cullent	
Awoingt	22		Personnel working on Dumps	
"	23		do	
"	24		do	
"	25		do	
"	26		do	
"	27		16 other ranks attached to 84th Bde RFA for Horse lines (withdrawn from troops)	
"	28		Dump work	
"	29			
"	30		All men withdrawn from dumps. Personnel not to return to BGRA	
"	31		Field day	

L'Orub. 2/Lieut RFA
Conroy X/19. T.M.B.Bty.

www.ingramcontent.com/pod-product-compliance
Lightning Source LLC
Chambersburg PA
CBHW081426300426
44108CB00016BA/2312